# An equal chance

# An equal chance

Equalities and inequalities of educational opportunity

**Derek Birley**
Director, Northern Ireland Polytechnic

and

**Anne Dufton**
Dean of the Faculty of Social Sciences, Northern Ireland Polytechnic

London   Routledge & Kegan Paul

First published 1971
by Routledge and Kegan Paul Ltd.
Broadway House,
68–74 Carter Lane,
London, EC4V 5EL.
Printed in Great Britain at the
St Ann's Press, Park Road, Altrincham,
Set in 10 on 11pt. Times Roman.
© Derek Birley and Anne Dufton, 1971

ISBN 0 7100 6968 5

# Contents

Note on references
*Specific references are given only when the year of publication is indicated in the text. Other sources will be found in the list of books for further reading.*

# List of figures

# Introduction

'All animals are equal, but some animals are more equal than others.' George Orwell's sad and cynical masterpiece suggests a deliberate manipulation of the slogans of democracy by self-seeking traitors to the revolutionary ideal. We do not have to suspect hypocrisy in the leaders of our own society to be concerned that democratic practice falls some way short of its theories. Our kind of democracy has in-built uncertainties that make it hard to establish principles, let alone act on them.

This is not an egalitarian manifesto claiming that people are, or should be, equal in merit or ability, or even in wealth and power. It is a book about the education system, the frontier on which the crucial battle of democracy—that for equality of opportunity—is continuously fought. Our concern is that children are equal in educational opportunity, but some are more equal than others; in other words, that in spite of almost universal agreement about the aim of giving every child an equal chance we fall very far short of achieving it. We shall consider how the situation arises, the forms inequality takes, and some of the techniques both old and new for detecting and reducing it.

To ask for an equal chance for every child is something quite different from seeking the same provision for all. An unreflecting uniformity of treatment may not only ignore precious individual differences and stifle initiative amongst the able but also contribute to the problems of the disadvantaged, who may be ill equipped to take advantage of what is offered. At the same time, to believe that as long as places in all types of school are free we have achieved equality of opportunity, or even to imagine that all we need is more of the same, ignores the tremendous weight of environmental handicap that puts some children so far behind others before they even start school, that they may never catch up.

As understanding of this problem has grown, the education service has felt the need to step across its traditional boundaries to give children an equal chance at school. Much of the book will concern practical issues arising from this. How far should teachers become social workers? How can workers in education co-operate with those in other services concerned with children? How should the various specialist services be organized? What of the links between home and school, and school and community? What is the future role of the Education Welfare Officer? Do we make the best use of our resources? Besides helping, perhaps, to contribute to better understanding of these and similar questions, it will also describe the wide range of activities, statutory and voluntary, designed to help children in need. This in itself should serve a useful purpose, for very little seems to have been published that will help students, teachers, social workers and administrators to understand the bewildering array of services and specialisms.

But, although the book should be of value to those who simply want to learn something about a fascinating but maddeningly complicated aspect of education and the social services, it is concerned with principle as well as practice. There is a tendency to discuss such things as home-school links and the professional status of social workers as though they were ends in themselves, when the overriding need is for hard thinking about objectives, for a coherent philosophy, if improved techniques and better organization are to achieve anything of real significance.

Change is part of all our lives today, and much of what the book discusses is, and will continue to be, subject to rapid and far-reaching change. For instance, responsibility for the education of children formerly thought intellectually incapable of schooling has already been transferred from health to education authorities. In the social services the aftermath of the Seebohm Report and the re-structuring of the health services have a high priority in national thinking. The reform of local government, long promised, may now at last be about to happen. Consequently there would be little purpose in producing a mere description of what happens now.

Furthermore in times of rapid change it is doubly necessary to remind ourselves of underlying purposes, to question or reaffirm the fundamentals. Rationalization and reorganization are easy watchwords, slogans that may seem to meet a long-felt need but in fact fall short of what is required. Structural changes in all the social services may be long overdue, but no one should imagine that they will in themselves solve the problems we face. They can be positively harmful if they turn out to be a substitute, rather than a framework, for philosophical advance.

We believe that certain basic principles will continue to be of first importance whatever superficial changes are made in the organization of services or procedures. This book aims to present a picture of the evolving scene, to consider essence rather than accident, and to look towards the future. We hope that whatever small contribution it may make will extend beyond immediate and temporary issues to be of lasting service to those who share our concern that all children should have an equal chance.

# Educational opportunity and democracy

## one

What we call democracy is our own peculiar brand. It finds room for a monarchy and it emphasizes personal liberty as much as equality. In the welfare state we walk a tightrope between concern for the underprivileged and the wish to retain constructive initiative: we want to remove the hazards of the jungle from life without destroying its essential freedom. Then again we have no written constitution and the governments that safeguard and reinterpret our unwritten code regularly alternate between different political parties.

As a result, no one can state with complete assurance, or state for long, what the objectives of our society are or what its values should be. Common objectives exist, largely unstated, because the majority seem to share, without in any way defining them, broadly the same values. Differences arise the moment definition becomes necessary in order to translate values into action. It is much easier to agree in a general way that a free and democratic society is the ideal than on what its essential ingredients are.

The uncertainty of society as a whole is reflected in the education system. Most people would agree that the system should give every child an equal chance. There would be much less agreement about how far it actually achieves this, and violent argument about what equality of opportunity entails in practice. These differences of interpretation stem, at least in part, from disagreement about why we should provide opportunity. Some claim, with justice, that the strength of a small country like ours depends on making the best use of its brains. Others contend that this ignores the reason for our, or any, society existing at all and point to the overriding need to promote the well-being of every citizen as his individual right.

Quite apart from these matters of opinion, however, there are differences arising from the sheer difficulty of understanding what

1

is involved. In education equality of opportunity is a fundamental issue, but there is no more complex or sophisticated question than deciding what the words actually mean. Tackling this analysis in logical or philosophical terms is something like peeling an onion: the removal of layer after layer seems to take you very little nearer the heart of the matter and you may end up with nothing but tears in the eyes and a heap of disconnected fragments. It seems better, therefore, to begin at the point where theory meets practice, which is where the problems, the sources of disagreement, show themselves.

This is more than just a promising theoretical approach: it is a practical necessity. For however difficult the concept of equal opportunity may be, the schools and the local education authorities are daily confronted with the need to interpret and implement it. The degree of skill and concern they show in carrying out their task varies enormously, so if we are not to substitute windy generalization for onion-peeling analysis we must seek a tangible lowest common denominator. This in practice centres on the duty of local education authorities to detect and reduce where possible the handicaps—intellectual, emotional, physical and social—that prevent children from taking advantage of the education that is offered in the schools.

To some this may seem far too lowly an ambition. For one thing, it is a negative goal. But if we are to consider educational opportunity as a live issue instead of an exercise in semantics we are more likely to make progress by removing ills than by trying to agree on positive objectives.

Brian Rodgers (1969) in suggesting as the most fundamental element in social policy 'society's desire to rid itself of social disequilibria' puts it like this:

> We have only to look at the problems that are involved in any attempt to understand and define justice, equality or even liberty, and to compare their elusiveness with the practical realities of injustice, inequality and lack of liberty—all of which constitute disequilibria in society, and present goals and targets that can be reached in legislative terms. Legislation can be enacted to meet the needs of children 'deprived of normal home care' without making any attempt to define a normal home.

## Changing attitudes to education

If we try to establish positive goals we run into immediate difficulties. All important social issues depend on value judgments.

No one can be dogmatic in a democratic society about what education is for in the first place. An educator who wishes to influence the course of events has to recognize that his personal attitudes and the discoveries of research must come to terms with the principles accepted by a consensus of the people—politicians, teachers and administrators—who run the service. And by the time he has done so he may find that opinion has changed. The basis of the consensus, sometimes explicit, sometimes only dimly discernible, has varied widely over the years. A glance at Stuart Maclure's fascinating source-book *Educational Documents* (1965) shows a startling range of assumptions, each presumably representing the advanced thinking of those who cared most about education in their day.

In the early nineteenth century, for instance, the stratification of society could be accepted without question, together with its implications for educational provision. Thus, a Parliamentary Committee in 1816 enquired into the Education of the Lower Orders in the Metropolis and 'observed with much satisfaction the highly beneficial effects produced upon all those parts of the Population which, assisted in whole or in part by various Charitable Institutions, have enjoyed the benefits of Education'. A report of 1818 referred to the problems of the education of dissenters but left no doubt that the ideal outcome of education was a god-fearing, church-supporting community. Private enterprise was to be preferred to state intervention, and even where the support was to be by Parliament—or more correctly by levies on local land-owners— the Church was to control:

> To place the choice of the school master in the parish
> vestry, subject to the approbation of the parson, and the
> visitation of the diocesan; but to provide that the children of
> sectarians shall not be compelled to learn any catechism or
> attend any Church other than those of their parents, seems to
> your Committee the safest path by which the Legislature
> can hope to obtain the desirable objects of security to the
> Establishment on the one hand and justice to the Dissenters
> on the other.

In 1839 Lord John Russell conveying 'Her Majesty's Commands' to the Lord President of the Council about 'the deep want of instruction . . . still observable among the poorer classes . . .' deplored the fact that the gaols were full of poor fellows knowing nothing of the 'fundamental truths of natural and revealed religion'. The assumption was that a main function of providing education was the preservation of order—'by combining moral training with general instruction, the young may be saved from the temptation

to crime, and the whole community receive indisputable benefit'—
an interesting parallel with the general attitude towards the youth
service in the 1940s and 1950s. In the following year the Committee
of Council on Education's instructions to Inspectors spelled it out
more clearly: intellectual instruction was to be 'subordinate to the
regulation of the thoughts and habits of the children by the
doctrines and precepts of revealed religion'.

By 1870 there was a perceptible change. Although the School
Boards were only to fill gaps and the Church was still assumed to
be the prime mover in education, nevertheless in W. E. Forster's
speech introducing the Elementary Education Bill there was an
implicit assumption that combating ignorance is an aim in itself.
The introduction of compulsory education from five to twelve itself
represented a changed attitude, and the legislation authorizing
school boards to issue free tickets to parents unable to pay for
education 'without the stigma of pauperism' went even further in
this direction.

The 1904 Elementary Code, following the 1902 Act, provided a
new statement of purpose, at once more personal and more
humanistic: 'to form and strengthen the character and to develop
the intelligence . . . assisting both boys and girls, according to
their different needs, to fit themselves . . . for the work of life'.
The movement towards a concept of individual opportunity
accelerated in 1907 with the provision of free places in secondary
schools up to twenty-five per cent of the total, and the notion of a
scholarship ladder that could be climbed.

By 1918, H. A. L. Fisher, introducing his Education Bill,
expressed even more radically changed attitudes. The movements
of opinion that led the Government to propose educational changes
included recognition of inequality of provision, contrasting with
the 'increased feeling of social solidarity . . . created by the War'.
Industrial workers 'are entitled to be considered primarily as
citizens' and the philosophy behind the Bill is that 'education is
one of the good things of life which should be more widely
shared . . .'

The aspirations of the 1944 Act are well known: secondary
education for all, the education of children according to their age,
ability and aptitude, and a re-casting of the education service to
try to give effect, as in 1918, to the new notions of social justice
created by the War. The aim of the reforms was described in the
1943 White Paper as 'to assure for children a happier childhood
and a better start in life'.

The intention of this brief survey of changing attitudes is not to
raise eyebrows at previous generations, still less to suggest that
nowadays we know all the answers: the pattern is not a simple

one of progress from darkness into light. On the contrary the message of these changes of outlook is that the problem cannot be solved in terms of pattern-seeking. There are no absolute standards to form the basis of a pattern.

There is of course a clearly discernible change over the decades in assumed educational purposes: from religious to humanistic, from the preservation of order to the development of the individual. But no one today need quarrel with the aspirations of reformers since fairly early in the present century, and there has been for some time a general consensus of opinion that 'equality of educational opportunity' is the ideal. Yet we are still very far short of achieving it. One reason is our lack of success in analysing what it really means at a particular moment in time. We may achieve more if we accept as a first stage the negative aim of removing inequalities.

## Enemies of progress

Even the analysis, detection and correction of the negative is not as easy as it sounds. It is certainly a lofty enough aspiration for most people working in the education service and perhaps a good deal higher than we are likely to achieve in our time.

For one thing we have given too little thought to seeking out the causes of inequality. We have been too often content with assumptions and generalizations: we have not accepted the need to reinterpret in the light of changing circumstances our notions of what the enemies of progress are.

For example, it has been almost a platitude for many years that poverty and 'a poor home' do not necessarily go together. Parsons, teachers, all kinds of social workers and thousands of ordinary people have known this as an accepted fact. Yet the basis of much educational legislation right up to 1944 was the assumption that lack of money was the chief enemy. Scholarships to grammar schools and later free secondary education for all were equated with adequacy of educational opportunity. And when doubts were cast on how really fair the 'objective' testing of ability was as a method of selection, the solution of the comprehensive secondary school was proposed.

It is possible to develop very sophisticated arguments in favour of different methods of organizing secondary education. The choice has wide implications, both educational and social; but from the strict view-point of equality of opportunity there are many more important considerations. To the child from an inadequate home free access to a similar or even the same school as his fellows from better homes does not give him an equal chance; and when the chance comes at the age of eleven or twelve it may be too late to make any difference.

This might not be so if poverty were the true handicap, but it is not enough to equate under-privilege with lack of money. Growing awareness of the inter-play of psychological and physical factors in human life makes it hazardous to nominate any simple causes of disadvantage. But it seems clear that inadequate parental support—a very complex thing—is nearer the heart of the matter than poverty. And there is increasing evidence that this kind of handicap may, in practice, be almost impossible to redress after the early primary years (some think, before the child even starts school). Hence the emphasis in the Plowden Report (1967) on nursery education for the disadvantaged, on positive discrimination rather than mere equality of provision, on compensation through school for poor home environment in the early stages of a child's life.

The next chapter will go further into the causes of handicap. At this stage we are concerned not so much with the diagnosis itself as with the implications of regularly attempting it afresh. Secondary education has occupied the centre of the stage for a long time: first, scholarships to secondary schools, then free secondary education, and finally the comprehensive school, have seemed the essence of equal educational opportunity. But acceptance of inadequate and ineffective parenthood as a prime cause of handicap suggests that, to be effective, compensatory measures have to be taken much earlier than the secondary stage. It also suggests that simply providing institutions is not enough but that the education service must concern itself with detecting and meeting individual and family needs.

This is an example of how further analysis can affect the application in practice of an apparently well-understood aim like 'equality of educational opportunity'. It explains too the education service's growing concern about the world outside the walls of the school, the world in which children and their families live. And it brings us face to face with a moral dilemma.

**Intervention**

In seeking to detect and reduce factors that come between children and their education, local education authorities accept a duty to intervene when necessary in people's lives. This is a problem shared by all the social services. How far is society justified in intervening in the lives of its members? Apart from the basic question of individual liberty there is a built-in implication in any situation involving intervention that there is a superior and an inferior, a potential violation of human dignity.

The question is whether this can be tolerated for the sake of possible improvements to the human condition. If we accept that in a democracy values must be relative, this is not a question that can be settled in general terms: it must depend on the circumstances. One factor is the degree of hardship or handicap involved. In an emergency most people would agree that intervention is justified: you do not leave a man lying on his face in a ditch in case he may be troubled by your infringement of his liberty. But this kind of intervention is only valuable as a palliative, a crisis measure, and we must look to preventive action if we are to achieve any lasting good. In these longer-term measures there is more opportunity for helping the underprivileged, but there are also many more hazards.

Kellmer Pringle (1968) points out the changing emphasis in the 'caring professions' (medicine, teaching and social work), where there has been a transition from crisis intervention to preventive work:

> Oversimplifying, it could be said that medicine initially aimed at curing the sick, education at eradicating ignorance and social work at rescuing social failure. Thus all these professions were largely oriented towards diseases or deficiencies. Now a change is taking place and its direction is parallel in the three professional fields: particular symptoms (in medicine), needs (in social work), or skills and subjects (in education) are no longer seen as main targets of professional attention: rather, positive good health, the education of the whole child and strengthening of the individual in relation to society have become the main aims.

The problems in all three professions are considerable. Perhaps the re-emphasis is more acceptable in medicine—for example, in terms of immunization and ante-natal care—and this may be connected with the fact that in medicine the patient has an unambiguous right to refuse treatment. In education, as in social work, there is an uneasy balance between individual right and community need.

Of course there is a sense in which education has always intervened in this way. As we have seen, the purposes of education have always in the past been held to include moral and religious instruction; and individual teachers can scarcely avoid influencing their pupils whether they are teaching them social studies or algebra. The new departure is in the schools' taking their concern for the 'whole child' to the logical point of following children into their homes.

The question now becomes not just whether to intervene, but whether intervention should ever include going over the parent's head for the sake of the child. When does the state, represented by the school, or the court, or a social worker, have the right to step in and say that parents have abdicated their responsibility towards their children? Does the family have a right to budget in a way which places greater emphasis on cigarettes and drink, dog racing and bingo, than on fresh vegetables, adequate clothing and culturally enriching activities? Or do we regard this family as inadequate? If so, what is the norm against which we measure adequacy? Who are we to do the measuring?

Situations in which there is specific neglect—crisis cases—may make it easier to answer these questions in their own limited contexts. But even here there is scope for some confused thinking. The Seebohm Report (1968) categorically states, 'clearly the primary responsibility for children does and should rest with parents', but the whole of its Chapter VIII is concerned with increasing the efficiency of the educational and welfare services in diagnosing and dealing with need, on the assumption that some parents cannot themselves meet these needs.

This implies that society has a duty to the child that may override the rights of parents. Perhaps the most important factor to be weighed in judging the ethics of intervention is that, as well as parents, there are the children themselves to be considered. This is of course especially relevant to the education service. In the end the case for intervention through education rests on the rights of children to a chance in life not blasted from the start by poor environment. Are we prepared to run the risk that children from inadequate homes may grow up to be themselves inadequate parents?

Thus the Plowden report is less ambiguous than Seebohm: it urges positive discrimination in certain schools, greater efforts to compensate for poor home background by superior schooling. On the other side of the Atlantic we have the blunt assertion of Jensen (1967):

> We are gradually having to face the fact that, in order to
> break the cycle of poverty and cultural deprivation, the
> public school will have to assume, for culturally disadvantaged
> children, more of the responsibilities of good child rearing—
> responsibilities universally regarded among the middle class as
> belonging wholly to the child's own parents. The brutal
> fact is that for culturally disadvantaged children these
> responsibilities are not being met, for whatever reason.

But can we be absolute about this? Jensen says:

Whether or not the public school system should intervene where educationally important environmental lack exists is, of course, strictly speaking, not a psychological or scientific question, but one of social policy.

To call the acceptance of the need for intervention a matter of social policy is fair enough but not, in the end, helpful to the teacher or social worker in the hair-line decisions required by immediate problems that confront them daily. The distinction is likely to be one of degree. These decisions will in practice have to be based on the extent of need in particular circumstances rather than on a general remit from 'social policy'.

Austin (1967) is highly critical of this approach:

> Help is usually a one-sided process with one class 'giving' and the other (primarily minority groups) 'getting', which normally means a transfer from one set of problems or deprivations to another set . . . they are benevolent attempts to impose a particular value system upon a particular group of people.

He seeks to by-pass the dilemma by proposing involvement of the community in the process of intervention:

> . . . there seems to be little concern whether the culturally deprived enjoy some aspects of deprivation or whether they wish to be rehabilitated. And even if they so choose, how often are they asked to take part in the determination of policies and direction of such rehabilitation? To the extent that their views, arrived at in an informal way, are not elicited and considered then to that extent programmes for the deprived are undemocratic.

He has a point: however, the appealing simplicity of his statement masks a serious difficulty for those seeking to involve the disadvantaged in decisions affecting their future. Very often the core problem for teachers and social workers lies in sectors of society that are inarticulate or apathetic or both. Those who are least involved and perhaps least interested in the democratic process are often the people most in need of the social services, and we do not usually know what the attitudes of this group of people are. Of course we must be careful not to impose solutions on their problems that appear right to the professionals or to those with responsibility for government. We cannot assume that because people are apathetic they are happy. On the other hand, we cannot assume that because people are inarticulate they are necessarily against the Establishment. We can only remind ourselves that it does matter what they think.

There may well be other grounds for anxiety about whether the education service should intervene to help the disadvantaged. Some people may simply object to spending their money, paid in rates and taxes, on other people's children, particularly if they are said to need costly extra attention. Apart from the moral arguments in favour of spending the money, there are also arguments based on prudence. Democracy depends in the end on the education of the citizen: it is just as good as the voters who shape it. This is the point at which the child's right coincides with the state's need.

But is this necessarily what happens in practice? Is intervention the way to achieve a sound, self-governing society? Might it not instead sap moral fibre and undermine the sense of responsibility fundamental to democracy? Anyone with experience of social work will be able to produce examples of families who craftily manipulate the welfare state, and it has to be admitted that this represents a real danger. Yet perhaps in the end it strengthens the case for intervention through education. Education's concern is with the child, and if its parents are so feckless and cynical as to regard welfare as a game to be played, then the sooner good influences get to work on the child the better.

For example, looked at in this way, the case for setting up nursery classes rests on the needs of the child, not on helping mothers to go out to work or have more leisure. Child-minding facilities may be necessary for some families, but that has nothing to do with nursery education. This, properly used, is a way of trying to prevent some children from being so far behind in learning (in, say, the ability to communicate with adults or to play with other children) before they get to the infant school that they may never be able to keep up with the rest of the class.

## Prevention not cure

Knowledge does not necessarily confer wisdom, and, in spite of what popular manuals of psychology may say, education does not automatically give power. Nevertheless it is the best long-range weapon with which mankind can battle against its environment. In helping the next generation to arm itself against future handicaps it may be of more lasting value in improving standards than direct social action to deal with crisis situations.

As understanding of educational problems grows, we become increasingly aware that the root causes of handicap are often to be found in the very early stages of children's lives. It is increasingly accepted, too, that the child needs to be considered in the context of his family. It follows that work aimed at eradicating social problems, including inequality of opportunity, needs to be aimed at parents as well as children.

The undoubted good sense of this approach may, however, unwittingly obscure the importance of the educational process itself as potentially the most effective and least obnoxious of all the techniques of intervention available to a democratic society to help those of its members who are in difficulty. In the chapters that follow we shall emphasize the contribution to be made by many social agencies (and indeed call for this to be improved and increased), but we shall suggest that, although the causes of unequal opportunity often lie outside education, the education service has the main responsibility for trying to put matters right and is, surprisingly often, in the best position to do so.

This responsibility—to discover and as far as possible remove handicaps that come between children and their education—may range far beyond the classroom and involve educationalists in a variety of collective enterprises. Yet the teachers, who are in direct contact with the children, must remain central to this process if it is to be successful. To play their part they must be given resources: for example, primary school teachers, on whom much of the burden has to fall, cannot hope to pay attention to individual needs if the size of their classes compels a mass approach. But they also need insight. They have to see the connection between social deprivation and learning problems if they are to be convinced of the need to make the journey into what is for many foreign territory.

# Aspects of inequality

## two

How does inequality of opportunity show itself in practice? Even in education it has innumerable, inter-related facets. In describing them we must be selective and brief, so that we shall oversimplify and perhaps distort. This does not pretend to be a comprehensive treatment of all the issues, but rather a survey of some of the many sides of the problem. First, some of the reasons why certain children are at a disadvantage.

## Causes

### Poverty

We suggested in the first chapter a certain obsolescence in the notion of poverty as the main source of inequality. Yet it can be an important element, and it is perhaps more widespread even today than we sometimes like to think. There are those who suggest that in a welfare state anybody living below the accepted sub-sistence level is doing so from choice, because he spends his benefits on drink or the dogs rather than food and clothing for his family. The investigations of the Poverty Action Groups set up in various parts of the country do not support this view.

A recent survey in two districts of Liverpool suggested that nearly a third of the total sample of 208 family units was 'in poverty'.* Forty per cent of the 'in poverty' heads of family were female as opposed to only 11 per cent in the 'non-poverty' group.

---

\* For the purposes of the survey families were regarded as 'in poverty' if their weekly take-home pay, including family allowances, was equal to or less than the amount they would have received if they had been dependent upon supplementary benefit or pensions scale, plus the £2 that the Ministry of Social Security allowed before reducing the level of benefits.

Families 'in poverty' were not particularly large in comparison with the 'non-poverty' group, but 50 per cent of the wives in the 'non-poverty' group worked full time or part time as opposed to 12 per cent 'in poverty'. Of those 'in poverty' the survey suggests as the most common causes: (*i*) old age, (*ii*) unemployment, (*iii*) sickness and disablement, (*iv*) widows, (*v*) other fatherless families, (*vi*) low wage earners.

In their conclusions the authors state:

> The main cause of poverty—income inadequate to need— must not be lost sight of in a mass of peripheral benefits. The main need is still for adequate wages and higher family allowances . . . so that people may have the resources with which to benefit from the opportunities open to them in society—otherwise the vicious circle of poverty breeding poverty continues, with welfare benefits only alleviating rather than curing. (Peter Moss, 1969).

A survey conducted for the County Borough of Preston in 1965 suggested that for 42 per cent of the 431 families assisted by social workers in the previous year 'inadequate income' was a main problem (*Preston Family Welfare Survey*, 1965).

## Physical factors

*Houses* The connection between poor housing and inequality is well established. J. W. B. Douglas in *The Home and the School* (1964) points out the superior performances in tests of children living on council estates to those living in other rented accommodation. He states:

> When housing conditions are unsatisfactory, children make relatively low scores in the tests. This is so in each social class, but whereas the middle class children, as they mature, reduce this handicap, the manual working class children from unsatisfactory homes fall even further behind; for them overcrowding and other deficiencies at home have a progressive and depressing influence on their test performance.

*General Environment* Physical influences include, apart from the circumstances of individual families, the general effect of the physical environment. Everyone is aware that demolition areas (which may be like bombed sites), back alleys and warehouses can have a bad influence. Another less considered influence is the unutterable drabness of some of our new housing estates where serried ranks of box-like houses stand in the shadow of multi-storey glass and cement tower blocks. There may have been more potential stimulus for a child in the slum environment from which he came.

Flat-dwelling has its own hazards. An advertisement in *Medical News* August 1968, begins: 'She can't change her environment . . . but you can change her mood with SERENID-D;' and over the statement that 'neurotic illness has been shown to occur with greater frequency in women flat dwellers' is a picture of a strained-looking young mother standing in the shadow of a tall block. These anxieties transmitted to children, together with the natural isolation and safety problems of living in flats, may lead to inability to mix easily, or even play, with other children when schooling begins.

Much attention has been given, following the Plowden report (1967), to the influence of poor environment, and there has been a tendency to equate the problem with slum-dwelling. It would be foolish to underestimate the bad influence of slums, but it is worth noting that overcrowding is only one of eight criteria suggested by Plowden to help 'identify those places where educational handicaps are re-inforced, by social handicaps' (the educational priority areas) and that the Report considers this factor 'a less sure guide than some others because it may miss the educational needs of some housing estates and other areas which can also be severe'.

*Schools*   It is a simple matter of observation that some schools have markedly better premises than others. Nor is there any need to argue the point that this affects opportunity. A good physical environment at school can raise morale, thus stimulating good work, and can also be more practical, useful and adaptable as an educational tool. To some extent the incidence of good buildings is a matter of chance. Largely, however, post-war building policy has had to be directed towards 'roofs over heads'. Most of the provision has been for new sectors of population such as new housing estates, which means that better schools only tend to come along with better housing. The inner areas of cities have been neglected partly because schools, though old, already exist there, partly because populations have tended to decline in these areas and partly because even when other circumstances have allowed new buildings no land may be available.

School organization can affect the chances of individual children. Wiseman in the National Foundation's *Map of Educational Research* (Thouless, 1969) cites five recent studies that provide evidence that summer-born children are at some degree of disadvantage, and suggests that the likely cause 'is closely bound up with streaming, mediated by term of entry to infant school, and thus carrying through to the secondary stage'. This same operating mechanism can presumably have the same adverse long-term consequences for any child who starts school at a disadvantage.

*Personal factors*

*Teachers* Wiseman's summary of research findings on streaming suggests, however, that the influence of people may be even more decisive than that of the physical environment:

> The overall conclusion to be drawn from research is now becoming clear, that in any school the particular method of organisation is, per se, unimportant: what matters are the attitudes and the educational philosophy which lie behind the structure. Less disadvantage is likely to accrue from the efforts of 'non-streaming teachers' in streamed schools than from 'streaming teachers' in a non-streamed organisation. The phenomenon of expectancy and the self-fulfilling prophecy is becoming more generally recognised, as is the pervasiveness of its field of application. (Thouless, 1969)

The importance of teachers' attitudes is emphasized by one of the findings in a survey by Goodacre (1968), which reported that in a group of infant schools the 'teachers tended to think of pupils from lower working class areas not only as *socially* homogeneous groups but also as being *intellectually* homogeneous'.

There is no need to emphasize the influence of the quality of the individual teacher on standards of teaching: this is a matter of common observation. Differences in the standards of school staffing are also observable:

(i) Secondary schools enjoy markedly superior staffing ratios, and teachers with higher qualifications have tended to be drawn into work with older children by the national pattern of salary scales. Yet it is at the primary level that inequalities can best be put right.

(ii) In shortage conditions teachers can freely choose in which authorities to serve and many prefer the pleasanter parts of the country: this leaves the difficult areas with less than their share of the best.

(iii) The Plowden report (1967) says of the difficult areas: 'We are not surprised to hear of the rapid turnover of staff, of vacancies sometimes unfilled or filled with a succession of temporary and supply teachers of one kind or another,' and later: 'Heads rely on the faithful, devoted and hard-working regulars'. Very little research has been done in fact on the incidence of staff changes in down-town schools and Plowden here has to rely on impression. Experience suggests, however, that too rapid a turnover can be harmful to a school and that there is more likely to be a rapid turnover of this kind if enterprising teachers find themselves in restrictive physical conditions. Sometimes, though, too little turnover may be a disadvantage; it may mean the overworking and gradual spiritual exhaustion of the faithful and devoted; it may sometimes mean, unhappily, that less gifted teachers, who through chance or lack of opportunity find themselves in down-town schools, may stay there far too long.

*Parents* Few will disagree with Plowden that parents are even more influential than teachers: 'The parents have usually had their children in their care for their whole lives, whereas most of the class teachers about whom information was collected had been with the children only for the best part of one school year. It must, therefore, be expected that differences between parents can explain more of the variations in children than differences between schools.'

These differences take many forms.

(i) Both Douglas and Plowden refer to the effects of parental occupation and the size of families (both of which have an influence on family finances): we know that children from more prosperous homes tend to have better vocabularies and to be in other ways more able to benefit from school, and that the use made of health and welfare services is less amongst manual workers than others.

(ii) Recent research has focused on the question of parental attitudes. Plowden says that over two-fifths of the manual workers covered by their survey left the choice of their children's school entirely to their wives, compared with less than one quarter of non-manual workers. 'Almost half the manual workers, as compared with less than one quarter of non-manual workers had not been to their children's present school at all: less than one quarter had talked to the Head.' And again: 'Considerably lower proportions of parents from manual worker homes bought, for use at home, copies of some of the books children were using at school; two thirds of unskilled workers had five books or fewer in the home, apart from children's books and magazines, as contrasted with one twentieth of professional workers.'

(iii) For these same children there may also be language deprivation. Communication with adults may be limited, sometimes largely restricted to commands and chastisement: communication with other children is also within a limited vocabulary range. (One result of this is that an insensitive teacher may be unaware that he is communicating with only a small number of children in his class and the others may begin to opt out.)

(iv) Emotional deprivation can take many forms. It may include not only the child rejected by its parents and thrown out on the streets each evening but the child rejected by its parents and sent to an exclusive boarding school from the age of six. For the first child, however, the handicap may be only one amongst several, both at home and at school. Furthermore the National Child Development Study found in its investigation of emotional disturbance amongst seven-year-old children that the lower the parents' occupational status, the smaller the proportion of stable children (Pringle, Butler, Davie, 1966).

*Total environment*

Each of these aspects of inequality in environment and in the standard of adult care for children is serious in itself. What makes the inequalities even more telling is the interaction between them.

(i) The disadvantages of home background may be reinforced by the attitudes of the school. Consciously or unconsciously teachers may encourage some children more than others: consciously because they 'know' that home support is more likely to be given to certain children who are therefore more likely to take full advantage of a grammar school place or stay on for G.C.E. examinations; unconsciously because a lower stream is automatically expected to work at a lower level and because it is easier for most teachers to get on well with a nicely spoken, well turned out child than an unkempt, rather smelly and less articulate one.

(ii) The inter-action can apply to whole areas as well as to individuals. Plowden says:

> Not surprisingly, many teachers are unwilling to work in
> a neighbourhood where the schools are old, where housing
> of the sort they want is unobtainable and where education
> does not attain the standards they expect of their children.
> From some neighbourhoods, urban and rural, there has been
> a continuing outflow of the more successful young people.
> The loss of their enterprise and skill makes things worse for
> those left behind; then the vicious circle may turn from
> generation to generation and schools play a central part in the
> process both causing and suffering cumulative deprivation.

(iii) The result, particularly in large industrial cities, is concentrations of children whose total environment is a severe handicap. There is evidence that such environmental conditions cause depression of intellectual functioning. Bloom (1964) suggests that 'a conservative estimate of the effect of extreme environments on intelligence is about 20 I.Q. points'. An improved environment (by giving pre-school experiences, for instance) can improve performance in intelligence tests and school work. The deficiency of these children from environmental causes is cumulative: the gap between disadvantaged and other children increases both in I.Q. and in achievement as they grow older. Children who begin school with language deprivation and poor motivation tend to fall further and further behind. These are often the children who later drop out.

(iv) Poor attendance is at once a possible indicator of a poor environment and a cause of still further declining standards of work. This is referred to in Schools Council Working Paper No. 27 (*Cross'd with adversity,* 1970) summarizing a survey of opinion amongst heads of secondary schools:

> Truancy, slightly more common among boys than girls, was stressed in nearly a quarter of the responses; incidentally, parents often admit that children are beyond their control. Absenteeism with parental knowledge occurs slightly more frequently, in some thirty per cent of the responses. Older pupils, generally girls, are kept at home as 'maids of all work', to look after younger children while mothers are working, pregnant, or just overburdened. The heavy domestic responsibility which some girls must bear is central to the problem. . . .

## Children in trouble

In spite of the growing evidence of the way they inter-act these handicapping conditions are too often considered in isolation, whereas each of them is only one element in a complete set of circumstances surrounding a particular child. And each child is an individual human being, like those we now describe. Each account refers to a real child, one who is actually attending school at the present time, and each one is factual (except for a few alterations of detail to prevent any possibility of identification).

**Sandra** is one of ten children, whose ages range from two to twenty-four. Her father is dead, but there is a reasonable family income from the older children. The family live in a four-bed-roomed corporation flat. Compared with many, their material circumstances are quite good. Sandra, who is twelve, is of average ability but she has fallen far behind in her work through poor attendance. Her mother finds it hard to cope with such a large family, both physically and from the point of view of setting standards. Sandra is kept at home, ostensibly for a variety of reasons, but basically as company for her mother and as a useful pair of hands in coping with the younger children. The home environment is one in which everyone has to fend for himself: one brother has already been in approved school and Borstal and another takes drugs.

**Peter,** who is eight, has four brothers and a sister: he is emotionally disturbed, flying into violent tantrums both at home and at school. His attendance is spasmodic. His mother, who is

West Indian, was deserted two years ago by her husband: she is kind and does her best for the family but finds it hard going. The family income is £12 15s. 0d. a week, including the pension of a bedridden grandmother. The grandmother occupies the only living room of the three habitable rooms the family share in part of a very old house in a depressed area. She complains incessantly about the children, who find it more congenial to be on the streets.

**Michael,** aged thirteen, was found wandering in the street on a school day by an education welfare officer. He shares a flat with his father: his mother is dead and his three brothers and sisters are in the care of the local authority. Michael's father has a good income, but his occupation as a market porter keeps him out for long and unusual hours. He does not know how to control, still less help, Michael, though he realizes that he and the boy both sadly lack his wife's care. The last time Michael went back to school after a day's absence he was beaten, so he now hates his teachers.

**Dawn,** who is just over fourteen, has a younger sister, who she knows is illegitimate. Dawn's own father divorced her mother two years ago and the two girls share two rooms with their mother and a co-habitant. Dawn has for some time been infatuated with this man, and this has led to estrangement from her mother, whose jealousy caused her to reject the girl. Dawn's emotional problems result in violent arguments in the home: instead of attending school she often wanders the streets or visits the department stores in town; when she does attend she is often sullen, withdrawn, and uncommunicative.

**Freddie,** aged twelve, is one of six children. He recently went to grammar school but was ill and away for a term. When he got back he found himself far behind in his work. He kept getting poor scores in tests and for homework and then he was punished. It was worse in certain subjects than others, so he began to stay away on certain days. This made matters worse and he began regular truancy.

**Betty** is eleven, and her mother is only 28. There are five other children, all illegitimate, and their fathers are unknown. Her mother is of low intelligence. She is a very poor manager in the home, and already Betty is more capable, which has caused considerable tension in the home. Betty tends to please herself whether she attends school or not, and her behaviour in school and out is very poor.

**John** is only four and he attends a nursery school. He set fire to a waste paper basket and twice tried to set his home on fire. He is illegitimate and his mother was divorced because of his arrival. She has re-married but her husband is frequently drunk. John has already seen many quarrels and has seen his mother being beaten.

**Ronald,** aged thirteen, is the eldest of seven children. He has been caught stealing on three occasions. His home is clean and tidy and there is a good income; but Ronald's father divorced his mother four years ago and she now lives with a seafaring man. He cares for the children but is very strict. When he goes to sea, Ronald has a free hand, so that when the real man of the house returns he feels the boy is cheeky and bossy and puts him in his place. Then the stealing occurs.

**Stanley,** aged nine, is regularly absent from his school, which is one for educationally sub-normal children. He is one of eight children, some older, some younger. One is in care of the local authority: seven are living with their parents in part of a large house formerly sub-let, which has fallen into ruins because of the landlord's bankruptcy. All the other tenants have left, and Stanley's family have only two habitable rooms, one of which is the communal bedroom. They have no gas or electricity. Stanley's father cannot work because of brain damage after an accident: he cannot remember things, and sits about listlessly for most of the time. Recently, however, after an argument with Stanley's mother he tried to strangle her. Stanley and most of his brothers and sisters witnessed this. There is a closure order on the house.

It may be interesting to the reader to work out what the prime handicap is for each of those children, and how it may have led to another, and that in turn to another; or, if there is no single basic cause, how the combination of circumstances may have produced an inter-action, each aspect influencing and being influenced by the other. The effect of this inter-action has to be kept in mind whenever we discuss single causes of disadvantage (as for convenience we often must). It also has its bearing on the adequacy of schools and the social services as instruments for putting things right.

## Standards of care

For many years authorities have provided specialist services to remedy some of the more obvious handicaps that come between children and their education. Nowadays these can range from the traditional school health service, educational welfare officers and child guidance and psychiatric services, to teachers specially skilled in teaching educationally backward children, counsellors and similar pastoral posts in the schools.

There is inequality in the scale and nature of the provision made by different authorities and, even in the best, staff shortages and lack of effective co-ordinating machinery have tended to diminish the value of the available resources. On Health Services, Plowden points out that too many children—in some areas as many as fourteen per cent—arrive at school in need of treatment. The Report refers to the long waiting lists for attention in child guidance clinics so that the very backward children, who may also be in need of psychiatric support to help deal with maladjustment and unsettled behaviour, tend to be neglected. It points to the Education Welfare Officers, hampered by a lack of agreement about their functions, which tend to be split between routine census work and responsibility for social welfare. Above all it calls for co-ordination and points out that this is not 'simply an administrative or procedural problem; it demands a re-appraisal of family needs and of the skills required to help those in difficulty'.

Plowden indicates another source of inequality, the variable links between the schools and the social services: the problem of the teacher's own knowledge and capacity to identify social problems; the ability and willingness of schools and other services to keep each other adequately informed; and the broader problem of the teacher's understanding and willingness to make contact with what goes on in the home.

The report strongly emphasizes the value of nursery education to help overcome the disadvantages of children from deprived or inadequate home backgrounds: yet existing provision is scanty and there are marked regional variations. Many maintained nursery places are given to children under some kind of social handicap, but priority has also had to be given to admitting teachers' children. There is little evidence, until very recently, of any concerted effort to provide nursery education to reduce educational handicap.

Even where a nursery school is provided in an area of great social need, and where the criteria for admission unambiguously relate to deprivation, the experiences and the character of the experiences provided may be less helpful to the children than they could be. The schools tend to provide experiences suited to the needs of middle class children. Children from middle income homes have regular contact with adults but may lack contact with other children; the nursery school emphasizes play. At home there is rich verbal experience and at school the emphasis is on seeing and doing. At home there may be physical restriction by over-protection and the school emphasizes adventure. At home messy activities may be discouraged but they are pursued vigorously at school. In this and other ways, nursery schools may in fact be providing experiences that are entirely characteristic of many working class home environments, whereas an underprivileged child might benefit more from closer contact with adults and from more exploration of the use of language.

A.E.C.—C

Thus enrichment programmes for underprivileged children may concentrate on trips to the country, soft toys and similar benefits enjoyed by middle class children, whereas it may well be that the best stimulus to underprivileged children would be to try to give them the kind of language skills they need to help them learn. The kind of speech used in working class groups tends to exclude those elements of language such as exposition, instruction or analysis that are essentials to learning. Most nursery schools at present are not used as diagnostic or remedial units for the disadvantaged.

Recent emphasis on the significance of pre-school experience should not be allowed to obscure the fact that the variable standards and attitudes of the schools themselves are a continuing influence for good or ill. The natural orientation of the school tends to be away from the underprivileged. Carl Marburger in 'Considerations for Educational Planning' (1967) says:

> The typical school cannot compensate for the various lacks in the lives of children with limited background. The typical school does not provide those reinforcements to school learning which, in a suitable middle income area and family, are provided for each child by his home and out of school life.
> Many of these reinforcements are intangible. They include an acceptable self-image; knowledge of essentials such as nutrition and health; an implicit sense of identification with a stable family in a stable neighbourhood, security and freedom from want, materially and mentally; the self-confidence and motivation to achieve, which rub off on the child who is surrounded by things and involved in experiences which are accepted both at home and in school, either as samples of success or significant achievements.

Sir Alec Clegg and Barbara Megson in *Children in Distress* (1969) point to startling differences in the attitudes of the schools themselves as a major cause of perpetuating and intensifying inequalities. They first consider schools which offer little compensation:

> An insensitive school is amongst other things one in which those who are undistinguished intellectually count for little, those who are weak are not helped over their weaknesses, and those who make trouble are kept down by superior force and little is done to find out the root cause of their troublesomeness. . .
> In such schools, it may still be regretted that it is no longer possible to 'expel' a child with whom the school has failed.

Social difficulties are regarded as an imposition rather than a challenge. 'You can see how the place has gone down since the moderns came in.' And little attempt is made to spare the child who receives free meals, or whose school journey is paid for, the embarrassment of being made conspicuous by his poverty.

They suggest that authoritarianism is one of the signs. 'If a school, taking a lead from the head, parades its authority, the weaker pupils are likely to suffer.' It may be based on physical punishment, but it may, particularly where the head is a woman, be based on a kind of organized nagging. 'Many rules are a bad sign,' but more important still are the 'attitudes and values by which a school is run'. And 'the emphasis on prizes, mark lists, published examination results and streaming seldom help the weaker children in the school community. These devices are all effective ways of saying to the majority of the school, "You are inferior".' In these schools the ablest are given the most choices of subject and the best teachers. Such schools go in for old-fashioned teaching methods and their premises may be physically neglected.

In contrast, 'A really good school will be both friendly and well-cared for, and particularly if it is a junior or infant school it will be bright with an ever-changing display of children's work . . . In a school with real concern for its pupils, teachers work easily with children, quiet talking in class is normal, and pupils move easily into, out of, and about the school.' 'A sensitive school will always try to reward effort rather than acclaim achievements which are due to natural endowment, and it will make strenuous efforts to discover ways in which the weak can excel and to help them overcome their weaknesses.' There will be an easy but courteous attitude, and the basis of sound discipline will be shared responsibility. 'Relationships with the parents are cordial and secure, but natural and uncontrived.' Informal methods of teaching, it is suggested, get better results for all, but particularly for the underprivileged: they help to compensate for deficiencies in adult-child relationships in the home.

All this is, of course, a matter of opinion, for in the nature of things proof is impossible. But it is opinion based on long practical experience, and one widely shared by those who have studied the question carefully. Unfortunately this careful study has been by no means widespread. Neither teacher training nor the governmental framework provided by education authorities gives any substantial weight to consideration of objectives on the part of schools. Certain objectives such as examinations are built-in to the system, but their influence has tended to be restrictive and narrowing. The system tends to be self-perpetuating and self-strengthening, leaning in the direction of the values of the dominant sector of society. This makes it harder for underprivileged children to contend with the education system on equal terms with their more favoured contemporaries.

Traditionally the approach of the school is a matter for the Head and his staff. Education authorities mainly try to influence them through advisers and inspectors who are former teachers themselves. The community itself (or certain sectors of it) may exert pressures, but this is obviously random in its impact. Parents are the most potent influence, but those of underprivileged children tend to be inarticulate or indifferent or positively unhelpful. Middle income parents tend to be the most active and influential and although there may be specific matters of disagreement between them and the teachers, in general the influential assumptions of home and school appear to reinforce each other in creating an environment in which it is significantly easier for the haves to make progress than for the have-nots.

**Attitudes**

Here we tread very treacherous ground. Our schools and the bureaucratic operations behind them may be intrinsically inadequate to give suitable treatment to working class families and their children, but this is not to say the values they represent are wrong, nor that we do not find deep-rooted prejudices and inadequacies amongst the less privileged members of society.

It is difficult to get beyond environmental influences to discover what people's aspirations are, but as far as we can tell, the attitude of many working class people is not always one of enthusiasm for education. Certainly they often reveal a lack of interest in the education service as it is now. Michael Young in *Innovation and Research in Education* (1965) suggests three reasons. First, that middle class values are apt to make working class people feel inferior so that they react against them. Second, that schools seem not to recognize working class values (particularly perhaps in neglecting the characteristic working class group orientation in favour of an individualistic competitive code). Third, the working class attitude to work tends to overvalue manual labour and thus to underestimate the need for qualifications in order to acquire 'better jobs'.

But discovering people's true attitudes is never easy and when the people concerned are largely inarticulate, it is all but impossible. This above all is an area in which assumption can be disastrous. The research of Cloward and Ohlin (1961), for example, has cast grave doubts on the assumption that the aspirations of working class people are different from those of the rest of society. Their argument runs as follows:

> The disparity between what lower class youths are led to want and what is actually available to them is a source of a major problem of adjustment. Adolescents who form delinquent sub-cultures, we suggest, have internalized an emphasis upon conventional goals. Faced with limitations upon legitimate avenues of access to these goals, and unable to revise their aspirations downward, they experience intense frustrations; the exploration of non-conformist alternatives may be the result.

Any generalizations must, therefore, be treated with extreme circumspection. One or two tentative points may perhaps usefully be made, however.

On the whole, schools transmit and reinforce the values of society. Teachers and administrators are generally recruited from or aligned with the middle classes, and although they differ widely as individuals most of them share certain values such as a regard for authority, order, and discipline; concern for knowledge and educational advancement; neatness, politeness, and correct speech, and respect for property. The school curriculum may reinforce these values. However, exposing the child to values does not mean that he absorbs them, for he is also exposed to the values of his own sub-culture, and the two may be in conflict.

Many schools have not clearly thought through their role as a moral influence and tend to vacillate. Some may accept that all societies and circumstances change so that 'doing right' is not adherence to fixed standards, but action based upon reflection. These schools do not teach values as such, but help their pupils to discover them through reasoning and confrontation with practical issues. Others adopt a more traditional approach, aiming at absolute and immutable standards and seeing the duty of the school as inculcation of these standards, preferably with a minimum of questioning.

Clegg and Megson contrast the effects of these two types of school and recommend the first. But no one should question the sincerity of the second; nor is anyone in a position to prove that the values they advocate are opposed to the interests of the working class. The situation is scarcely a manifestation of the class struggle. Most teachers are concerned initially with preserving adult values compared with those of children rather than upholding the social system generally.

Schools and teachers do best when they are true to their own ideals. There are few sadder spectacles than grown-ups trying to ingratiate themselves with the young (who are rarely impressed by the attempt), and self-conscious schemes to reach out to working class children as if they were creatures from outer space are not what is wanted. However, teachers can achieve nothing if they do not communicate with their pupils, and for this they may have to make an effort of imagination and self-analysis.

The same effort may be required in relation to the curriculum. The emphasis of the Newsom report (1963) on widening the horizons of the secondary school, bringing in the outside world to the classroom to provide experiences more likely to evoke a response from children who have no academic interests, is a useful starting point. But *Cross'd with adversity,* listing many of the approaches being tried in the aftermath of Newsom, illustrates not only the possibilities but the dangers. On the one hand understanding of the need to communicate has grown: on the other there is sometimes a suggestion that the devices used may be seen merely as artifices of an appropriate standard for the less able, and not as ways of extending and stimulating those whose environments have held them back.

In a moment of insight *Cross'd with adversity* (1970) calls for 'intuitive, imaginative and resourceful' teachers who can make sense of the complex situation of each individual pupil and help him to go forward. The need to consider every pupil as an individual is not only a moral necessity, but a way out of the dilemma faced by every teacher who wants to maintain standards but who has to come to terms with different sub-cultures from his own. It may be permissible to accept lower standards for some children provided this does not mean too low a ceiling on their aspirations. If we are to work towards true equality of opportunity we must believe that there is a key to every child if it can only be found. The concern of teachers, and of the education service as a whole, must be, not with children generally, but with every individual child.

# Special educational services three

In moving from the causes of handicap to methods of dealing with them we shall repeatedly make the point that the child's teacher, particularly in the primary school, is a key figure. The previous chapter has emphasized environmental influences on children. This is because we are more likely to be able to do something about these influences than about deep-seated personal deficiencies, and because this book is concerned with equality of opportunity not equality of performance. But it is important to recognize that many children suffer from innate or self-inflicted handicaps. For them a crucial issue is whether or not they are taught by someone who is aware of their affliction and sensitive to the implications.

This sensitivity does not merely mean sympathy, though that can be important. Its most significant quality is judgment, the decision as to how far a child's performance is the result of external and how far of personal factors. This is the basic process carried out by teachers every day of their lives, either consciously or unconsciously, and it is a dominant influence on their pupils' levels of aspiration, which in turn strongly affect how they respond to challenge and to opportunity.

As well as this direct classroom influence there is another important sense in which teachers are, or could be, central figures in detecting and treating environmental handicaps. Apart from parents, the class teacher is normally in the best position to see a child as a rounded human being: the teacher has a more continuous contact with him than anyone outside his own family. For all sorts of reasons the parent may be unable to recognize symptoms of stress or handicap, and the teacher is often best placed to do so. In large measure the success of any efforts a local education authority may make to detect and reduce disadvantage depends on the sensitivity and skill of class teachers in this role and on the ease with which they are enabled to perform it by the administrative arrangements and physical circumstances in which they have to work.

We must be clear about what is expected of the teacher. It is increasingly fashionable to talk as if all teachers should be fully trained social workers as well as pedagogues. This is unrealistic, even if it were desirable. What is reasonable and practical is that the teacher should know enough and care enough to do two things : first, to be aware of when, where, and how to refer a problem to someone else; and second, to be able to respond through his own teaching methods to the child's needs when they are identified. This chapter and Chapter 4 will deal with the first of these points, Chapter 5 with the second.

We consider first the traditional services offered by local education authorities. These services have their roots in history: they arose separately to meet needs as they were perceived. They have done valiant work, which has been largely unrecognized; and they have done it within the straitjacket of their separate frames of reference. The link they form with the schools and in particular with class teachers is a vital one. They have tried to tackle the task of translating the school's recognition of handicap into remedial action, and also of providing their own detection system and passing on their findings to the schools, though their work, and their effectiveness, have been impaired because their objectives have never been clearly defined and because they have been too often left to work in isolation and in obscurity.

In discussing these traditional services we shall try to distinguish four areas of concern. First, attendance and welfare problems which are the responsibility of education departments through their school attendance or education welfare sections. Second, handicaps with a strictly or largely medical basis, normally dealt with through school health services. Third, behaviour problems that may appear to have their origin in psychological disorders, usually the responsibility of child guidance services administered by school health departments either alone or jointly with education departments. And fourth, learning difficulties, usually the concern of school psychological services, frequently administered by education departments probably with joint use of staff with child guidance services.

Obviously there is overlap between the work of these services: indeed that is one reason for the increasing emphasis on co-operative working between them and on new forms of organization. The division of these responsibilities in this book is one of convenience, and one that recognizes existing realities. We begin with the Education Welfare Officer because from the point of view of regular and continuing links with schools he is nearest the point of contact, the teacher. He is also very often the central figure in the complex network of relationships that can develop.

## Education welfare

The Education Welfare Officer is the most common modern name for the School Attendance Officer. This was a post that came into being after the Education Act of 1870, when School Boards were empowered to appoint officers to enforce their bye-laws on the attendance of children at school.

Since 1870 parents have been legally obliged to ensure that their children at certain ages received education. The Education Act of 1921 gave the School Boards' successors, the Local Education Authorities, power to enforce bye-laws requiring parents to ensure that their children were educated unless there was some reasonable excuse. The 1944 Education Act imposed two duties on parents: first, to see that their children receive education appropriate to their age, ability and aptitude, and second, if they are registered pupils at a school, to see that they attend regularly. The Local Education Authority has a duty to see that parents comply with these requirements, and in the event of failure the right to take legal action.

In the early days, the School Attendance Officer was frequently known as the 'Board man' and the association in parents' minds with his function as a law enforcement officer often led to his having the popular name of 'School Bobby'. Two changes have already taken place in the functions of School Attendance Officers: first, additional powers given to authorities to assist with clothing and grants in needy cases have in practice been administered by these officers because of the connection between, say, the provision of a pair of boots and a child's ability to attend school; second and more recently, greater understanding of the causes of serious absence from school has led to dissatisfaction with the processes of law as a means of ensuring good attendance. Thus the name of School Attendance Officer has changed in most areas to that of Education Welfare Officer in an attempt to reflect not only the broader range of duties but also the different approach required towards the specific question of school attendance.

Nevertheless, as with many other institutions, the official change of name has often not completely caught on with the general public: even the name the 'Board man' is still in use, often in the very areas where his services are most frequently called upon. This retention of the old name reflects a deeper difficulty in the Education Welfare Officer's own attempts to grapple with the more complex requirements of his role in the modern world. Most people connected with the problems of school attendance recognize that the sanctions of the law which provide for a small fine at the end of a protracted procedure have little relevance to the deep-seated problem of truancy. The grave environmental difficulties incurred by many families, the effect of broken homes, parental indifference or fecklessness, the very traditions of certain neighbourhoods, tend to be much more potent influences on the attendance patterns of children than the superficial and tardy ministrations of the law, so authorities and their officers have gradually tried to turn their attention towards detecting the causes of poor attendance and to applying remedial treatment rather than imposing penalties after the event.

One of the effects of this is that the E.W.O. is increasingly regarded as a liaison officer between the school and the home. Naturally many of his visits are to the homes of families of truants, but in the first place the role he performs, even on these visits, may be changed, and in the second place he is increasingly called upon by schools to visit the homes of children who have behaviour or other problems. The Education Welfare Officer's function in these circumstances is best seen as one of investigation and of exploration. He can convey the effects of the school situation to the home and can give a school information of the utmost value in dealing with children in the classroom: for example, about situations in which the children have to get themselves off to school or in which they must let themselves in at four o'clock because both parents are working.

The possibilities for detecting and preventing neglect of children in this way are considerable, but the change of emphasis has generated a good deal of heat. In particular the prospect of the E.W.O.'s 'assuming a social worker role' has alarmed many people, notably professional social workers themselves. They point (quite properly) to the skill and training required for family case work and (again quite properly) to the lack of training amongst E.W.O.s, and then appear (rather less properly) to question whether the E.W.O. should be allowed to visit homes.

What is often lacking is understanding of the crucial importance of school attendance itself, not only to the potential performance of the individual child, but as an indicator—often the first—that something more serious may be wrong. It would be a great pity if otherwise highly desirable efforts to improve the training and career prospects of Education Welfare Officers were to lose sight of their specific contribution to the fundamental matter of school attendance.

The E.W.O.'s 'new' role is in fact essentially an enlargement of his traditional one: the purpose is to cast more light on the reasons for absence from school. In fact of the ten per cent or so of children who are away from school at any one time, eighty per cent or more are likely to be away because of sickness, short- or long-term. Some two per cent of the school population may be away for other reasons, which may of course include quite legitimate ones. Parental indifference, or active retention of children at home, is the largest category of the illegitimate reasons, and truancy the next. 'School phobia'—fear of going to school—is a rare condition though the term may be wrongly applied to reluctant attenders generally.

The Education Welfare Officer keeps a check on reasons for absence and tries to give special attention to those where there is some avoidable cause. He passes on what he knows about these causes to the school and, if necessary, to the education office or other agencies. Co-operation between home and school is known to be helpful in improving attendance, and the first concern of any links between home and school by the E.W.O. is to achieve this narrow but important objective. If his relationship with the school and the neighbourhood it serves is good, then he can be of considerable help in bringing the two together, in the interests of the children.

This in itself is a difficult job, but it is not family case-work nor is it intended to be. To say that poor attendance is often a symptom of something worse is not to suggest that the E.W.O. should be required to cure or even diagnose this greater evil. In practice the existence of other sensitive and skilled agencies such as child guidance or the children's services are a considerable help to the E.W.O. as an alternative to the process of law, and he is usually only too willing to use them and to deplore that there are not more of them. His problem is in the cases that do not lend themselves to treatment of that kind, where there is a social or behaviour problem that is serious but falling short of an abnormality that can be 'cured'. If the law is no longer thought appropriate, what action can he take? He and the school are usually left to work something out together and it is here where the difficulties of his new role in linking home and school begin.

First, he still represents, in fact, the authority of the Court, and this may be an obstacle to his establishing a useful relationship with parents. Second, his own background and early patterns of working may make it difficult for the E.W.O. to adjust to the requirements of the new situation: although no family casework is involved it may be that some E.W.O.s have insufficient expertise to play a helpful part in this delicate operation.

A third difficulty arises from the very shift of emphasis from court action on the part of authorities. Persuasion can be a powerful weapon, but superficially at any rate it can appear lacking in bite as an approach towards persistent absence. The new methods, furthermore, take time, and time can only be spared for dealing with difficult problems by spending less time on the less difficult. Thus many heads of schools, and Education Welfare Officers themselves, fear a general decline in standards through slackening of efforts towards enforcement of attendance by traditional methods.

Most people tend to look for tangible measures of their own and other people's performance. Traditionally heads and E.W.O.s have concerned themselves with percentage returns of attendance and have prided themselves upon bringing about a gradual improvement. If time spent on rescuing one family from grave difficulties results in a worsening of average attendance levels, the old standards of assessment have to be replaced by more sophisticated performance measures. When, as is increasingly so, E.W.O.s have to work, not independently, but in co-operating teams, the degree of sophistication required increases yet again. For example in Liverpool the Education Committee's Prosecution Sub-Committee, which previously determined whether or not to take Court action, has now very largely delegated its powers to officers working in the field. In practice this means that the area officers of the Education Welfare Service and their child care colleagues must agree before Court action is recommended. In this situation the E.W.O. has to adopt a completely new approach to measuring the success of his own efforts.

The Education Welfare Officer has undoubtedly had to raise his sights and to extend the range of his activities. His job, by any standards, has become a more difficult one. Yet his change in role has not appeared to bring about any significant change in status. One reason for this may be the clinging tradition of association with the sanctions of the law. Another may be the ambiguous role of the E.W.O. in the education service: in most authorities this officer has an important but not necessarily highly skilled function in the census work that provides the L.E.A. with its basic material for identifying and enumerating its school population changes. In any event there are at present limited career prospects for E.W.O.s, with salaries that compare unfavourably even with the not very attractive scales to be found in related social welfare fields.

The Seebohm Report proposed that social work in schools should be the responsibility of a new social service department, E.W.O.s being given the opportunity to transfer to the new service which would be reorganized so as to provide adequate training and an attractive career structure. Others, it was suggested, might prefer to remain in the education department undertaking the more routine administrative work associated with school attendance. Although these proposals drew attention to present shortcomings, the service they would offer falls short of what is needed. General social workers might or might not devote adequate time to the welfare needs of school children but they could only hinder the development of a unified approach towards what is neither an 'educational' problem nor a 'social' one, but an amalgam of the two. The Local Authority Social Services Act 1970, excluding education welfare from the new social service departments it proposed for local authorities, took the more perceptive line of leaving it open to authorities to transfer family casework elements from education welfare to the new departments as and when they wished.

From the point of view of identifying and helping to eliminate inequalities in educational opportunity there must be an approach from within the education service itself. The Education Welfare Officer has a vital part to play in this approach and if the post were to disappear the gap would have to be filled by the education authorities and the schools, not by outside agencies. In this context the authorities have a clear obligation to tackle the problem of the objectives and, thereafter, the training and career structure of Education Welfare Officers. The service today is attracting younger and better-educated men and women, and these recruits are strongly interested in the specifically welfare aspects of the job. Unless the service can provide job satisfaction, training, salary and career prospects to match their aspirations, many of these men and women will continue to leave education welfare for other branches of social service.

Whatever the organization, schools and E.W.O.s must work closely together. By no means all schools appear willing to use the services of the E.W.O. to best advantage. To some extent this may be reflected by the attitudes and outlook of individual E.W.O.s, some of whom may regret the erosion of their traditional function. Sometimes, however, it must be stated that the problem arises from a reluctance on the part of heads and other teachers to accept E.W.O.s as professional colleagues. History has played its part in this, and the training of teachers in the past (even to some extent at present) has not led them to a full appreciation of the inter-relationship of educational and social issues. The result is that there are still schools where Education Welfare Officers can penetrate no further than the secretary's office, and others in which regular but brief and limited meetings with the head take the place of the kind of co-operation between teaching staff and social workers that the situation demands.

It is for this reason that some local education authorities have begun to re-think their traditional organization patterns for the education welfare service. Instead of a simple geographical area organization, L.E.A.s tend nowadays to base the work of their

Education Welfare Officers on schools or groups of schools. With this kind of framework it is obviously much easier to establish the right sort of relationship between the partners in the enterprise. Sir Alec Clegg in *Children in Distress* suggests a possible scheme for the future, with schools considered in a pyramidal pattern in which a large number of primary schools feed into a small number of middle schools serving one large neighbourhood secondary school. In this form of organization, one or more E.W.O.s working with the schools in the pyramid can begin to make a reality of their basic function, bridging the gap between school, home, and local education authority.

But this is to move beyond the boundaries of the traditional services that this chapter describes. We now turn to the second of the four areas of concern, handicaps with a medical basis.

## School Health

The School Medical Service began with the Education (Administrative Provisions) Act of 1907, and the powers and duties of local authorities have since been increased and clarified through the Education Acts of 1921 and 1944 and the School Health Service Regulations of 1953 and 1959. Every L.E.A. has to have a Principal School Medical Officer and an equivalent Dental Officer and supporting staff—medical, dental, nursing and ancillary. Quite often, particularly in smaller authorities, these appointments may be jointly held with appointments in Health Departments.

Their first duty is to provide medical inspection of pupils at appropriate intervals. Since 1959 authorities have been able to examine children on a selective basis rather than by age groups. The intention of this is to concentrate the resources of the authority so that doctors mainly see children referred to them by parents, teachers and others concerned with child welfare. Clearly a thorough selective examination of this kind is potentially more useful in relation to problems of educational handicap: apart from the more purposeful and detailed examination that can take place, the system offers a better chance of enabling parents to be present. At the same time this method places a greater burden on the techniques of detection and referral that are used and there is some danger of children's problems that might have been brought to light by general inspection remaining undetected. For this reason, and also to emphasize the importance of prevention rather than cure, efforts are now being made to improve the examination given to school entrants and to provide the doctors with full information when they make it. Statistical information and individual reports from services concerned with housing, maternity and child welfare, and questionnaires to parents can all be valuable in this.

The scope of medical inspection is very wide, including for instance defective vision and hearing, speech defects, respiratory and heart ailments, and of course general physical condition. Today the great majority of school children are considered to be in good physical health. In 1964 and 1965, the proportions considered to be of unsatisfactory physical condition were the lowest on record— 0.45 per cent and 0.38 per cent (*The Health of the School Child*, 1966). The distinction between children from different districts in terms of physical characteristics has lessened considerably and this reflects the generally improved social and economic conditions of many families and the value of school meals, milk and medical inspections. However, in his report for 1966–8, the Chief Medical Officer of Health of the Department of Education and Science draws attention to the need to safeguard the nutrition of children in families where the income falls below the standard of adequacy as assessed by the Ministry of Social Security. He advocates publicity campaigns encouraging parents to take up free school meals for children who are entitled to them.

Some factors discernible through medical inspection, correctly interpreted and detected in time, may have an important bearing on a child's educational progress. But of even greater importance for our present concern is the duty of the health services in relation to children requiring special education. The 1944 Education Act laid down the duty of

> every local education authority to ascertain what children
> in their area require special educational treatment, and for
> the purpose of fulfilling that duty any officer of a local
> education authority authorised in that behalf by the authority
> may by notice in writing served upon the parent of any
> child who has attained the age of two years require him to
> submit the child for examination by a medical officer of
> the authority for advice as to the nature and extent of
> any such disability (Taylor and Saunders, 1965).

This is the basis of the procedure followed by authorities, so that children found to be in need of special education can then be given the appropriate type of schooling.

The procedure emphasizes the importance of the medical officer in intervention. His role is, however, not without ambiguity. The position relating to physical handicap is relatively straightforward, but the very use of the terminology 'disability of mind' indicates a lack of sophistication in the Act that can and does lead to difficulties. The implication that, for example, educational sub-normality is (a) a medical condition and (b) one that can be 'ascertained' in absolute terms cannot be sustained in practice. In reality it is an assessment (of which children require special educational treatment) that is only meaningful when considered in relation to the range of possible treatments: it is in fact a predominantly educational exercise in which assessing the child's potential is only a part. Furthermore the asssessment itself requires in many cases elaborate and searching testing procedures which it is doubtful that many medical officers are competent to administer and interpret. Yet the only officer given any official status in this matter by the Act is the Medical Officer, a fact that has sometimes led to the assumption that a doctor's examination is enough and that it is conclusive.

By 1961 the Ministry of Education were suggesting to local authorities that all the formal procedures need not be carried out if parents were willing to have their children admitted to a special school. It is arguable that many more would be willing if it were not that the generally accepted requirement for entry is a sort of inverted eleven-plus examination, and worse, one in which the doctor's place in the affair gives it even more undesirable overtones.

Perhaps, also, teachers would more readily refer children with severe learning difficulties to the school doctor if he operated more as an adviser than as an umpire. The Chief Medical Officer's report for 1966–8 shows welcome signs of self-analysis: he criticizes situations in which teachers ask for help and the child concerned does not seem to need special schooling.

> The teacher may then be told only that the child is not educationally subnormal: the child returns to his school and no recommendation is made for special education and no advice is given to the teacher. This sequence of events should not arise if the school doctor concentrates on making a diagnosis of the cause of the child's educational backwardness and an assessment of his needs rather than on the question of whether or not the child should be ascertained as educationally subnormal.

The report goes on: 'These children are the concern not only of the school health service but also of the school psychological service, and it is essential that both services should work in close partnership.'

This partnership exists in most authorities. Sometimes the school doctor carries out initial attainment testing before referring to the psychologist for more sophisticated appraisal. In other areas, children are referred first to the psychologist, who undertakes preliminary testing and will then refer to the school medical officer should 'ascertainment' be necessary.

An even more important partnership, however, is that between doctors (and psychologists) and teachers. This applies whether the child's problem is predominantly intellectual, physical, or social. In this matter theory and practice are often poles apart. Ideally the process will begin with a thorough physical and developmental examination of all school entrants by the school doctor, including a questionnaire to parents. If there is a register in the local authority of children who may be at risk (stemming from the home visits at the time of birth by Maternity and Child Welfare Services), information from this will be available. Then there will be discussion of the findings with heads and class teachers, and these will continue in relation to any children who have difficulties throughout their school lives.

Teachers need this contact: doctors can give information about possible handicaps, can clear up possible misunderstandings about them, and can give valuable clues to the way the child should be handled in school. And doctors need the information that the special position and skill of teachers can give if they are to diagnose correctly and to give their advice in relation to real situations.

The reality falls far short of this ideal. At a practical level there is often failure of communication: as the Chief Medical Officer's report says: 'If the results of specialist investigation were more often communicated to teachers in a form that was of practical assistance to them in teaching the children, the teachers might be more forthcoming with referrals.' To read this report is to be aware also of a deeper need. It is a sensitive account of the contribution a school health service can make to the well-being of school children. However, it not only shows up the shortcomings of the way things work in practice, but also serves as a reminder that doctors can cast light only from one particular angle on what is a many-sided problem. There are more things in heaven and earth than what is included in the professional philosophy of many doctors. Only an approach through the organized partnership of different disciplines is likely to come anywhere near what is needed.

It is to be hoped that this is borne in mind in future changes in the structure of health services. A Government Green Paper published in 1970 proposed the inclusion of the school health service in new area health authorities 'organised according to the main skills required to provide them rather than by any categorisation of primary user'. As we shall see in the next chapter there is much need for rationalization of health services, but to do this on the basis of what is convenient for the professionals seems to owe more to expediency than to ideals. So far as school health is concerned the proposals seem to urge one kind of unification at the possible expense of another, that of the education service. Throughout this book we shall try to pursue the notion of co-operation between specialists in the various departments beyond superficial changes in administrative structures. This will become even more important if these re-groupings make administrative links between education and other services more formal.

No one should doubt the actual and potential importance of doctors in securing an equal chance for children. Properly interpreted (as adviser, not oracle) the role of the school doctor can be vital in detecting educational sub-normality and maladjustment. The inter-relationship of physical and psychological disorders is now recognized and the corollary is close links between the doctors, phychologists and psychiatrists. Environmental influences, particularly those of the family, have an important bearing on the child's ability to take advantage of educational opportunity and the school doctor is clearly well placed, through his links with general practitioners and maternity and child welfare services, to secure early information about families and children who may be 'at risk'. Through his traditional relationship with the public he is also well placed to give general advice to parents with good hope that it will be accepted as objective and free from moral overtones.

These relationships emphasize that apart from his technical expertise the doctor can play an important role in the social services. Two further examples illustrate the point. First, the school doctor might well be involved in planning and giving a Health Education programme as an aspect of preventive medicine and also of general social welfare. Second, the medical inspection of school children, properly used, provides an ideal opportunity for discussion with parents on related social as well as strictly medical matters.

The School Health duties of inspection include those related to cleanliness, particularly verminous infestation. It is a sad fact that as the role of the school nurse is often associated in the minds of the public, and even of teachers, with one particular duty—that of examining heads—she may still be inelegantly known as the nit nurse. It may be that this type of inspection and such activities as routine eye testing are the only occasions on which some schools see their nurse. But in theory if not always in practice, her duties are very much more broadly based. The basic responsibility of the school nurse is that of following up recommendations arising from the school doctor's work. This involves, or should involve, her visiting homes as well as schools; so that she is ideally placed to help with the important job of linking home and school in the interests of children who are in difficulty. She is in effect a health visitor as well as a nurse.

The functions laid down by the Council for the Training of Health Visitors include:

1. The prevention of mental, physical and emotional ill health and its consequence.
2. Early detection of ill health and surveillance of high risk groups.
3. Recognition of need and mobilization of appropriate resources where necessary.
4. Health teaching.
5. Provision of care; this will include support during periods of stress, and advice and guidance in cases of illness as well as in the care and management of children. The health visitor is not however actively engaged in technical nursing procedures.

Compare this with the Notes for Guidance on the function of school nurses in Liverpool:

1. To advise parents on the means of promoting health and welfare of their children.
2. To undertake Health teaching in schools in co-operation with the teaching staff.
3. To provide information about Home Conditions to the School Medical Officer at Medical Inspections and to interpret his findings to parents unable to be present and to emphasise or explain the advice given to parents present as necessary.
4. To help in the selection of cases where Selective Medical Inspections are conducted. Selection is normally done by the Headteacher or Housemaster, School Medical Officer and School Nurse who contributes by her knowledge of the home background and may make a decision following a Home Visit where there is some doubt, or inadequate information, supplied by the parents.
5. To be a principal link not only with the school and home but with all outside agencies dealing with school children. This is reinforced by her need to bridge the numerous gaps during the execution of her statutory responsibility, e.g. voluntary bodies elect to open and close a case as they see fit—but the school health service cannot do this and must ensure continuity of advice and help.
6. To assist in making investigations for the control of communicable disease.
7. To assist in special investigations made by the School Health Service, University and Ministry of Health and Social Security on various aspects of child health.

8. To arrange for pupils to attend school treatment centres and special clinics if required.

9. To visit the schools for health surveys and for periodic inspection of children for personal hygiene. A hygiene survey is usually carried out once a term by Nursing Auxiliaries working under the supervision of a School Nurse. The School Nurse sees and deals with all unsatisfactory cases.

10. School Nurses pay a weekly visit to school or department where the school is large. This visit is paid on the same session each week—it is over-ridden only by a Medical Inspection in one of the School Nurse's other schools and then the Headteacher is offered another appointment in that week. If a School Nurse is sick a clerk informs the Headteacher.

    The object and use of weekly visits:

    (a) The head teacher knows when the nurse can be expected. Much information can wait for this visit.

    (b) An interchange of information between Headteacher, Staff and School Nurse.

    (c) Routine work—Medical Follow-up
        Vision Testing
        Hygiene Follow-up.

    (d) The health education programme is often fitted in this visit.

    (e) Special surveys.

    (f) Immunisation.

    The school nurse is absolutely dependent on the Headteacher's and school teaching staff's co-operation to derive maximum benefit from this visit.

11. School nurses visit all nursery schools and nursery classes and are responsible for pre-school children from 2 years who are registered in Education Committee Nursery places.

12. Special Schools nurses have a much smaller case load, for all their children present a 'problem'. School nurses visit schools for physically handicapped and deaf children daily. Schools for the Educationally Sub-Normal and Maladjusted children are visited two or three times a week. Many of the parents of these children need constant support, help, advice and close supervision from the School Nurses.

The potential value of the school nurse as provider of information to the school doctor and as a link between home and school is obvious. So too is the potential overlap between the work of both doctors and nurses and those of other agencies concerned with home visiting. What, for example, is the relationship between the post of school nurse and that of area health visitor? In some areas the school nurse is also the health visitor for the district with the consequent advantage that her work in the neighbourhood and the schools which serve it gives her knowledge of the children and their families which can be of great assistance to the teacher in interpreting the needs of the child in the classroom setting.

But this presupposes that the school's admission area is the immediate neighbourhood; this may well not be so, particularly in secondary education. Furthermore the arguments for and against this system for nurses are linked with those about whether there should be separate school doctors. If an authority is big enough to employ a corps of doctors exclusively for work related to schools then there are clear advantages of specialism. We must not forget that the child *is* a child in our anxiety to see him as a member of a family; nor that the child at school is a child with special needs.

The problem has to be looked at in the context of possible reorganization of health services generally. The Government's Green Paper of 1970 may help towards a solution, but whatever pattern emerges, the link between a school and a visiting nurse will continue to be an important and sometimes a critical one. Effective communication is not just a simple organizational issue and the need for communication extends beyond the health service staff themselves.

Links with health departments' maternity and child welfare services can give the school nurse knowledge and understanding of how family background and early health influence the child at school, and similar ties with the family doctor service are needed. But teachers and parents have also much to contribute to, and much to gain from, close association with the school nurse. This potential is not always realized, for a variety of reasons, some of which are variants of problems we shall encounter over and over again and none of which is likely to be resolved by administrative reorganization.

The first is a limited, formalized conception of the purpose of the nurse's visits by school or nurse or both. Contact may be limited to the occasions of formal inspections; a room may be set aside for the inspection, the children withdrawn from class and returned to it, after which the nurse leaves. Her contact may be only with the Head and that only briefly and formally. A staff-room discussion over a cup of tea, or even better, individual interchange of information with teachers, would be more likely to establish useful relationships with the school as well as adding to the productive value of the use of the nurse's time as she works her round of the schools.

The second reason is closely related: the issue of confidentiality. For obvious reasons the medical profession must respect personal information acquired in confidence and, understandably, this ethical requirement tends to be interpreted strictly, not only by doctors but also by ancillaries. We shall need to consider the general concept more fully later, particularly as it is interpreted by the emergent professions undertaking social work. At this point we need only make a few brief observations:

(i) Those outside health service circles may sometimes get the impression that confidentiality is used as a pretext for avoiding the tiresome business of consultation or for preserving superior professional status.

(ii) Teachers may point out the one-sided nature of some of the interpretations of confidentiality. Doctors may (quite properly) seek maximum co-operation from schools in providing a good deal of useful information but prefer not to reciprocate; and nurses and other social workers may follow this lead. It seems to the teachers that these experts do not accept that there is a need for teachers to know everything relevant about their pupils if they are to teach them properly.

(iii) Co-operation becomes much more difficult if there is a feeling of limited trust from one side or other. Certainly too rigid a concept of confidentiality makes it much harder to contemplate reduction in the number of agencies dealing with particular families, since this reduction can only happen if agencies in actual contact with families thereafter draw on the resources of the others concerned and keep them fully informed on all relevant matters.

(iv) Perhaps the word 'relevant' is the key. There is normally a middle way between the extremes of revealing all the details and revealing nothing. Information passed on does not always, to be useful, need to be detailed. In practice of course it may already be known, or partly known, to the teachers (they may be the very people to notify the doctor or nurse). And there is no doubt that relevant information about, say, home conditions or an ailment can make all the difference to the way a teacher approaches the job of teaching a particular child.

A third reason for under-use of the potential of the school health service may be under-emphasis by schools and authorities on the preventive aspects of health. Health education, for instance, is surprisingly neglected. Where the school nurse visits schools to talk on health education or personal relationships it is an invaluable opportunity for nurse and teacher to exchange information about children's needs. Even when health education classes take place, however, this opportunity may not be used. One difficulty is that the full and free discussion essential to classes of this kind tends to happen only when the pupils do not identify the nurse with the 'establishment'. And anyone entering a school and deliberately seeking a markedly different relationship with young people from that of the teachers may find it difficult to achieve a completely harmonious relationship with the teachers.

## Psychological services

The Education Acts make no mention of educational psychologists nor of the child guidance and school psychological services in which those employed by local authorities work. These services are established under Section 48 of the 1944 Act, which lays a general duty upon authorities to secure the provision of medical treatment for pupils in maintained schools, and further sections of the Act, which allow extension of these facilities to pupils who receive education elsewhere than at school.

There is thus no specific power under which school psychological services are provided; they are established under the ancillary powers which stem from the Education Act as a whole. This may reflect the still somewhat ambiguous status of psychology as a science. Whatever its causes, one effect has been to produce, so far, an imprecisely defined and under-staffed contribution to educational guidance. Another source of difficulty is the uncertain position of the child psychologist whose work appears to straddle the worlds of education and health. In 1955 the Underwood Committee recommended that there should be a comprehensive child guidance service available for the area of every local education authority based on the inter-related activities of a school psychological service ('primarily non-medical'), oriented towards educational aspects of psychological work which might range from reading difficulties to aptitude testing; a child guidance clinic run by either local education authorities or hospital boards and the school health service (Underwood Report, 1955).

In the pattern envisaged, the school psychological service was intended to deal with children with learning difficulties, and the child guidance clinics those with behaviour problems—in crude terms, the educationally sub-normal and the maladjusted. Can we justify a separate approach to two such closely related problems, the origins of both of which may in any event be closely connected with environmental factors? These doubts were implicitly recognized by the Report's emphasis on co-operation, including the suggestion that the 'educational psychologist in the child guidance service should work part-time in the child guidance clinic and part-time in the school psychological service'. This pattern was recommended to local authorities in Circular 347 of March 1959, but attempts to implement it have been bedevilled by a lack of trained and qualified staff.

The Underwood Committee envisaged a team consisting of psychiatrist, educational psychologist, and psychiatric social worker under the clinical direction of the psychiatrist. The psychiatrist would usually work only part-time in the child guidance clinic and part-time in the hospital service or private practice or both. He would thus be the main link between clinic, hospital, and general practitioners in the area. However the Summerfield Report in 1968 saw no prospect of sufficient psychiatrists and psychiatric social workers being available: returns made to the Department of Education and Science showed a short-fall from the modest target set by the Underwood Report for 1965 by 21% for psychiatrists and no less than 62% for psychiatric social workers.

One or two local authorities are attempting to meet this need by giving appropriate in-service training to senior and experienced school doctors who then become responsible for the medical work in the child guidance clinic. Consultant psychiatric advice is still available for the particularly difficult cases. But even if implemented, the concepts of the Underwood Report would do nothing to resolve the problem of who should best administer the services, and there is at present no clearly established pattern for the organization and administration of the psychological services within education. Sometimes psychologists may be on the staffs of Health and sometimes of Education Departments; they may be shared or belong to a School Health section with allegiance to either Health or Education Committees or to both.

It scarcely seems possible, and may in any event be thought unprofitable, to separate the child guidance and school psychological service elements in work of this kind. A child and his problems need to be considered as a whole and in context. The inter-relationship of environmental, physical, emotional and learning problems is by now well established. Furthermore as a practical issue in the use of resources it is better to deploy the services of psychologists so as to cover both 'child guidance' and 'educational' aspects of the detection and treatment of handicaps; and this is likely to provide a more satisfying role to most psychologists than separation into separate branches.

The Summerfield Report recommended categorically that all educational psychologists should be within the administrative framework of the education department of local authorities. However, the Government's 1970 Green Paper merely promised to 'consider further where responsibility for the child guidance service should be'. The arguments for and against this are in the end less important than the degree of co-operation practised in the field, but there can be little doubt that closer involvement with the work of the schools is essential if psychologists are to make the best contribution they can. The Underwood Report saw the educational psychologist as 'the main link between the schools and the clinic', but the importance of these links tends not to be recognized by those outside the education service.

The role of the child psychiatrist as consultant caseworker for children with emotional or behavioural problems is probably well understood. There is more ambiguity, however about the functions of the other members of the team. The psychiatric social worker usually works from the child guidance clinic, helping the psychologists with preliminary assessments of the social background of children referred for investigation, visiting homes when necessary. Ideally two such visits might be made before the psychologist interviews child or parent, and thereafter, if psychiatric treatment is given, supporting social casework with the family would be undertaken. Some suggest that, to get most value from the psychiatrist's skills, as many as four visits for each psychiatric session are desirable, but this is a much more lavish standard than that usually reached.

Plowden comments:

> . . . while the child guidance clinic was a natural base for these workers between the wars, when this branch of the profession was new and not widely understood, the current demand for their services may not justify their concentration in these clinics. Concentration may not mean isolation but it sometimes does. Increasingly psychiatric social workers are able to carry their influence outside the clinics to other social workers, to health visitors and to teachers. And, of course, many are now employed altogether outside the clinics and outside the educational service too. It may well be that some should work more in direct contact with the schools rather than in child guidance clinics.

The educational psychologist is the lynch-pin of the service. He is concerned with the needs of children whose development is impeded by difficulties of adjustment or constitutional handicaps or both. He aims at prevention through early detection and remedial action, and in this he is of course concerned with the child in the family as well as the school setting.

The Summerfield Report indicated four main areas of operation:

1. *Appraisal and evaluation* which are essential to determine the nature of the problem posed and the decision as to the service best suited to deal with the particular problem.
2. *Investigation* into the nature of the problem and the amassing of all the relevant information.
3. *Action* which includes decisions about treatment and follow-up required, and
4. *Communication.*

It is, of course, in this last area that weaknesses in organization can mean that opportunities are neglected to make effective use of psychologists' skill. None of the first three jobs can be satisfactorily done without adequate communication between all those concerned, the children, their parents, their teachers and the medical and social services. As with school health, however, communication between the educational psychologists and staffs of child guidance clinics has not always been as effective as it might have been. Early detection of difficulties has long been recognized as of primary importance in effective treatment but the essential and continuing liaison with the school which this demands has not always been so readily appreciated or put into practice.

Lack of good communication is doubtless due in part to the national shortage of educational psychologists. Sometimes, however, the failure in communication may be harder to excuse; for example, neglecting to send written reports to a school about children who are receiving treatment at a clinic or who were referred for diagnosis by a school. An inevitable consequence is the inability of a school to co-operate in the treatment of the child. When this happens teachers cannot feel any real sense of involvement. Heads and teachers may even actively resent the activities of the psychologist if this is the prevailing pattern. And rightly or wrongly, many teachers associate this attitude with the kind of medical orientation that may place such emphasis upon confidentiality that it neglects to pass on information essential to avoid a worsening of the condition that led to the referral in the first place.

Another important factor in communication is the system used by authorities for referral of learning problems. When trained staff are in short supply the system must clearly try to avoid unnecessary referral if they are not to be overwhelmed by largely fruitless investigations. Some form of screening may be used, through tests conducted either by teachers in the schools or by specially trained remedial teachers or on a group basis by psychologists. This carries the possible danger of making direct relationships between class teachers and psychologists more difficult. Regular close contact is therefore needed, by visits to schools, in addition to any formal arrangements. This may well, by building up mutual confidence and exchanging information, reduce the need for screening procedures, but in any event it should emphasize the importance of free access from teacher to outside expert without which any system may work to the detriment of some children.

It may be helpful to consider how one authority tried to meet these conditions. The schools were first of all informed of the resources available. Heads were told that, in the end, it did not matter what referral procedure was adopted—through visiting school nurse, E.W.O., psychologist or doctor—so long as it was done early enough. The important thing was that they themselves and, particularly, their class teacher colleagues should feel free to pass on their doubts about children in difficulty. Procedures were suggested, however, as a way of bringing method to bear on the problem: in certain areas where remedial teaching teams had been set up and were visiting schools regularly, this was an obvious channel: elsewhere the school nurse or doctor would be the normal first point of reference. Pupils' record cards were on issue in all schools and certain screening tests were recommended in connection with their use if heads wished to undertake their own: if not, the remedial teams (advised by educational psychologists) would help with group testing.

Later specific attention was given to the time of referral. Infant school heads were invited to send to the office during the summer holidays the record cards of any pupils who might be in need of attention and who were due to transfer to junior schools. These cards were then distributed amongst the remedial teaching teams; at the start of the following term the teams were able to discuss many of these cases with the junior school heads, so that proper arrangements could be made from the outset if the problem appeared to be one where intensive and skilled attention to learning difficulties could help.

Other cards, and subsequent discussion with heads, suggested that there might be more deep-lying problems, involving educational sub-normality or maladjustment. Here the cases were referred at once to the educational psychologist. One result was a much earlier opportunity for the resources of the authority to get to work in the interests of the child.

Methods of referral need to embrace emotional and behavioural problems as well as learning difficulties. In both, the timing is important; indeed crucial. We shall see in the Southampton scheme discussed in Chapter 7 that secondary school teachers found that their plan to reduce delinquency by co-operative methods was hampered by long waiting lists and, by implication, inadequate action from the child guidance services to whom they referred problem children. But by then, quite apart from heavy case-loads, the opportunity for action was limited.

An argument in favour of an organized pattern of screening in the schools is the reluctance of most people to take what seems to be a drastic step with possibly sinister overtones. If we look at some of the problems referred to a particular child guidance clinic the point may be made clearer. All the cases eventually came to light through poor attendance.

(a) **Mary** was nearly six before she attended school, in spite of pressure from the Education Welfare Officer. Once there she behaved oddly, rocking backwards and forwards and hiding things—she found school life difficult and soon stopped attending. The E.W.O. told the school of the unusual home background. At the routine medical inspection a little later the school reported their concern and the doctor brought in the psychologist. It was a broken home, with a dominant grandparent and a completely withdrawn mother, and it appeared there was anxiety lest the child should mix with other children (it was a rough neighbourhood). An invitation to the clinic was declined and a test had to be conducted in the home: the indication was of low intelligence but no obvious innate emotional disturbance.

(b) **Joan** is fourteen: her fairly frequent periods of poor attendance had hitherto been short, but she suddenly stayed away for a fortnight. The E.W.O., who knew the family, referred the matter direct to an education psychologist. Joan refused to be seen by anyone either at a clinic or at home, and whenever the issue was forced ran away, but always to London.

(c) **Michael,** one of seven children, was six when he suddenly began to truant. The Educational Welfare Officer, discovering a history of mental illness in the family (the father is an in-patient in the mental hospital and an elder sister had attempted suicide) referred the boy to the child guidance clinic. The psychiatrist diagnosed school phobia and Michael is now receiving treatment.

(d) **Henry** is an intelligent fifteen-year-old. He had always been withdrawn but usually obedient; then he got at odds with his school and refused to go. After six months of attempts to persuade and threaten, the case was referred to the child guidance service. Henry's quarrel appears to have extended to society as a whole and he intends to drop out of the education system.

(e) **Peter** is fifteen and is a pupil of a special school for the educationally sub-normal. In the last year he has not attended school and the Educational Welfare Officer has not been able to persuade him to do so. The parents have been fined in the magistrate's court, but they say they cannot make him go to school. Peter is happy working with a milk roundsman in his holidays and at weekends: he wants to leave and start work, but under the special school regulations he has to continue until he is sixteen.

It will be obvious that the last three of the five cases were referred far too late for any constructive action. With each of the three older children there had been difficulties, known to the various agencies, for some time. Yet no one had taken action. One reason appears to be that the children concerned had not done anything illegal or strongly anti-social before. Observation suggests that schools are more likely to refer problems of aggressive or obstructive children than of those who are withdrawn. This is natural, but unfortunate. One side effect is that it tends to be at the secondary school stage, when matters come to a head, that help is sought. Another reason is common to teachers and outside specialists—a reluctance to intervene. This problem was explored in the first chapter, and it is not an easy one. Apart from the basic question of individual rights there is the reluctance and sometimes the hostility of parents towards intervention to contend with.

Here we may be closer to the seat of much of the trouble. The attitude of parents, and even of many teachers, towards the remedial and guidance services is one of distaste. The child guidance service is often a last resort, not through neglect, but because of its association with mental disorder. There are no quick ways to alter the attitudes of generations, but informal arrangements and personal contact may help. Links between experts and school, the phraseology of letters to parents, the place where interviews are held—does it have to be a clinic?—all these are relevant.

Apart from deficiencies in referral, however, the cases described underline another point. We tend to regard the specialist services as methods of cure. In fact they can very rarely achieve anything dramatic on their own; sometimes they can make very little headway at all. One implication of this is that the approach to treatment should not be narrow or exclusive: a point to which we shall return. Another implication is that in many instances the services provided can most helpfully be considered as support for the school, not as an alternative. This in turn has implications for the way they are organized. Every school cannot have its own psychologist, but it can have ready access to one: the procedure should not be so restrictive as to make it appear that it is a privilege for the school to take part in it.

## Special education

Many children referred to psychologists, psychiatrists, and doctors are subsequently admitted to special schools. Ten categories of pupils requiring special education are recognized by national regulations, and local education authorities are under a duty to detect the need for and provide it. They are the blind, partially-sighted, deaf, partially-deaf, delicate, educationally sub-normal, epileptic, maladjusted, physically handicapped and those with speech defects. The blind and the deaf have to be educated in special schools, either the authority's own or run by another authority or a voluntary body. The others may be educated in special schools or in ordinary school as the authority thinks best.

The proportion of children helped in this way varies widely between authorities. To some extent this will, naturally, depend on the incidence of the various handicaps in each area, but in practice in the largest group, the educationally sub-normal, and that of the maladjusted, the 'incidence' depends on the effectiveness of the machinery for detection, on such factors, for instance as the number of psychologists employed. These handicaps cannot be assessed objectively. Maladjustment is particularly difficult in this respect, for there is little agreement about what exactly it entails or about how to treat it. Similarly, children ascertained as e.s.n. in some areas would not be so considered in another: sometimes severe cultural deprivation can so affect the child's performance in testing procedures that he appears to be innately backward.

Whether these children go to a special school or not often depends simply on whether the authority has made generous provision. Those authorities with lavish provision are justly proud of their efforts, and of course they represent a concern for the unfortunate that must be the mainspring of attempts to grapple with the problem of inequalities of opportunity. Yet the amount of provision may not be a satisfactory criterion of effectiveness. If a large number of children in e.s.n. schools are of secondary age, and they include a fair proportion who are reasonably intelligent but sadly deprived by their home environment, this may be a sign that the authority's detection system is inadequate, leading to action too late in the day to make the remedial process effective enough to secure the return of those who have been helped in the ordinary school. Those who could, given the right treatment early enough, attend ordinary schools, undoubtedly would benefit from doing so. They are more likely to be extended there, to their own advantage—special schools can sometimes over-protect and under-estimate their pupils' capacities—and of course the relatively wide range of abilities implied by this 'generous' interpretation of educational sub-normality makes it difficult for these schools to know exactly what their objectives should be. Unfortunately also there is social stigma attached to the idea of special schooling. The resistance of many parents to the idea often leads to delays and uncertainties whilst the legal sanctions are applied: during this period children can suffer great harm. Sometimes, too, the stigma felt by the parents is transmitted to the child, which adds to his handicap. A preponderance of children of secondary age in special schools can mean that referrals have tended to happen because the children as they have grown older have become more of a nuisance in their ordinary schools. A high proportion of social problems can make clear objectives for special schools difficult to achieve.

It is true that, relatively speaking, children with handicaps singled out for treatment in special schools can be considered the lucky ones. A good deal of money is spent on them and the schools are generously staffed. But sometimes there may be ways of doing more good to more children in need by spending the same money. Given, for instance, a really good detection system, special remedial action in the primary schools might be more effective. This might for instance include special units within primary schools dedicated to the purpose of fitting as many children as possible for the ordinary school system by the secondary stage. If the severe cases thereafter went to special schools the remainder could often be better helped by the secondary schools, particularly those with specialist teachers for the less able.

Special education in relation to opportunity is a suitable theme for a book in itself. It is mentioned here briefly because, properly deployed, its resources can be a most effective weapon in an authority's armoury. For the severely handicapped it is a way of ensuring the best possible education and the prospect of leading a useful and happy life. For those on the border-line or presenting symptoms masked by other factors, the traditional pattern may not always be so valuable.

These brief comments have mainly applied to the e.s.n. and the maladjusted. The other handicaps tend to be easier to detect and measure, and it is easier to determine the best method of treatment. There are problems; separate special schools for these children may mean a smaller unit with fewer curriculum options, particularly as they grow older. But at least they are quantitatively fewer and most authorities manage to contrive somehow to ensure that those with a measurable handicap get as good an education as they are physically capable of receiving.

# Social work

## four

The suggestion that every teacher should be aware of when, where and how to refer a problem to someone else is more exacting than it sounds, even when applied to the traditional local education authority services. Much bigger difficulties arise when we consider other agencies concerned with social welfare.

The origins of social work lie deep in the past. As in education, its deepest roots are voluntary, beginning with the charitable work of individuals. Group charity was well established by the seventeenth century and flourishing, particularly under the influence of religious revivals, in the eighteenth and nineteenth; it is still a notable feature of our life today. Statutory effort has less of a past: the workhouse created by the Poor Law of 1601 was the main feature of public aid for the destitute for over 250 years.

The contemporary social worker stems from the voluntary rather than the statutory side: for instance, health visitors from ventures initiated by bodies like the Manchester and Salford Sanitary Association and many of their colleagues from the case work methods evolved by the Charity Organization Society set up in London in 1869. The Y.M.C.A. and Y.W.C.A. had launched into youth work even earlier, and by the end of the century university settlements in the East End and other poor areas had given a lead in community development.

The legacy of the past is hard to shake off, and anyone in social work today has to contend with the aftermath of two undesirable features. On the statutory side there is the stigma of the workhouse tradition; on the voluntary the aura of superior beings bestowing favours on the lower orders. The counter-blast to both is the movement towards legislation that gives protection to the underprivileged as of right, beginning with the Liberal reforms of the early years of the present century and culminating in the welfare state. This,

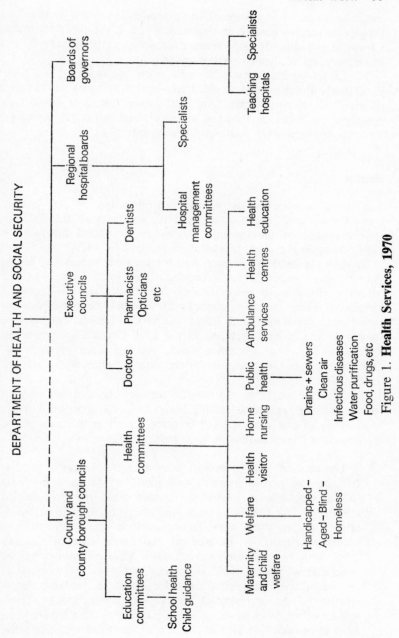

Figure 1. **Health Services, 1970**

too, has its critics, because of the attitudes it is said to breed in those who receive benefits in this way. But it is the powerful mainstream of modern efforts to remove the worst of life's hazards and to create a stable, healthy community.

This brief commentary will begin with the statutory services, particularly those related to children—health, services for children deprived of parental care, and for young offenders—will then comment on relations between statutory and voluntary agencies, and will finally discuss youth and community work.

## Health

The health service is one of the central pillars of the welfare state. Its workings are complex and the interplay of the different elements hard to understand. The much simplified diagram on page 53 shows the stage of evolution reached by 1970.

By then the need for revision had for long been clear and led to Government proposals for reorganization aimed at ending the tripartite division of responsibility for health services between hospital boards, executive councils for doctors, dentists, pharmacists and opticians, and local authority health committees. Inevitably the outline sketched in the 1970 Green Paper, a document intended as a discussion draft, was far from precise: the diagram on page 56, again much simplified, indicates the pattern suggested.

The general problems of health service organization are, of course, outside the scope of this book, but reference has already been made to one proposal (to transfer school health services to the new area health authorities), of great relevance to our theme.

The services will be provided by doctors, especially paediatricians and general practitioners, dentists, nurses and others in the employment of, or in contact with, the area health authority. Their close contact with the schools will be maintained. At the same time, the new arrangements will help to secure continuity in the medical and dental care of children from birth through their school days. This continuity will be beneficial whether a child is in good health or has a physical or mental handicap that calls for constant medical supervision and perhaps special educational arrangements. There will be other benefits, too, notably a closer association between what is provided as part of the school health service and what is provided for the child and his family by general practitioners, other community health workers and hospitals. The risk of duplication of services will also be avoided and there will be opportunities for improved efficiency in the use of medical, dental and nursing staff.

The service will continue to be provided in a manner acceptable to the local education authority and its staff. Medical examinations will as now be fitted in with educational requirements. Similarly, there is no reason why the present good working relationships between the teachers and the doctors, dentists and nurses should not continue (Department of Health and Social Security, 1970).

The document is precise on the benefits to be secured but vague (and unduly complacent) about 'relationships between the teachers and the doctors'. Certainly the new structure will do nothing to strengthen those relationships. Whether it does harm will not depend on generalized expressions of the importance of goodwill but on careful analysis of the requirements for inter-professional co-operation and careful arrangements for bringing it about.

In seeking to separate health from other personal social services, the Green Paper appears to be saying in effect: there are teachers, there are doctors and there are social workers, and each ought to be organized in separate departments with 'suitable administrative arrangements' for linking them. The Paper itself says: 'Any line drawn between the health services and the personal social services can scarcely avoid creating difficulties at particular points.' It seems that these difficulties largely stem from the deliberate choice of grouping by profession rather than function. For example, the dilemma created over the future of child guidance services can apparently only be solved by an arbitrary decision about whether they are mainly 'health' or mainly 'educational'. They are in fact neither: they are services for children, almost all of whom are in attendance at school.

Should we not instead be saying something different? 'There is education, there are other social services and there is a health service. Each has its own objectives, though they overlap in places. Let us organize them so that they can best achieve these objectives. This will mean that each service may need some professional staff trained in the disciplines of the other services, which will make it easier to arrange for co-operation between the services in the areas of overlap.' As it is, quite apart from the problems of school health and child guidance, the proposals seem likely to widen still further the already unfortunate gaps between teachers and doctors and social workers.

Like education, the health service has its own specialist social

Figure 2. **Proposed Health and Social Services Structure, 1970**

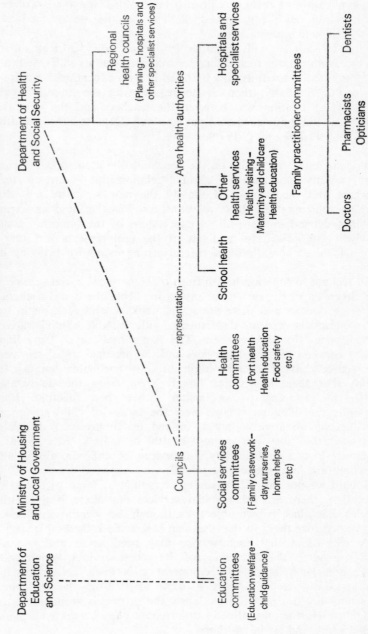

workers. We have referred already to health visitors, and to social workers employed in child guidance services. There are also medical social workers. As almoners based on hospitals, they were until recently still associated with their historical role of helping to sort out the genuinely needy cases from the rest, among the many applications for free treatment. Today they work as members of the medical team either at hospitals or in local authorities, conducting interviews and investigations into social conditions and family backgrounds to give the doctor fuller information relevant to the patient, as well as helping with advice and information about social benefits and arranging home visits as an after-care service. Not all doctors use the services of medical social workers to their full potential, largely because they do not entirely accept the full rigour of the argument that social and emotional factors can influence the course of an illness or a cure. The important point in the context of this book is that the medical social worker is amongst the many people involved in social work with families, one amongst many who employ casework methods.

Family caseworkers are increasingly employed by statutory bodies but most still belong to voluntary agencies, such as the Family Welfare Association and the Family Service Units. The help they offer is many-sided but the essence of it is in helping with family relationships, or personal problems affecting a family, through helping people to understand the source of the trouble and thus the possibilities of making things better. Sometimes problems may be such that they require years of patient support: there may be no solution other than showing people in trouble that someone else cares for them. Apart from the health service, education and children's departments may find such appointments useful, and in some areas there are special welfare departments who make use of this approach. Significantly, however, most training for it still rests with the voluntary bodies: when we consider the future role of voluntary organizations generally it may be that this is the type of service, involving personal relationships, that voluntary bodies are best able to perform.

Contact between health and education services is, however, less likely to be through casework than through certain specific activities. The first relates to intellectual disability. The 1959 Mental Health Act divided functions between local authorities and hospitals and put mental illness as far as possible on a footing with other forms of sickness. The intention was to remove the stigma of 'madness' and distinctions between types of mental disorder. Gradually acceptance of neuroses, depression and similar afflictions as wide-spread, and not a sign of permanent and rather blameworthy abnormality, has to some extent put mental illness in a new light for most people. The process is now being taken a step further for children, and education authorities are taking over responsibility for the education of sub-normal children formerly required to attend Training Centres run by Health Departments. Thus the distinction between mental sub-normality and educational sub-normality will wither away. It will have considerable repercussions for the education service: if the world of special education is to absorb this new responsibility it will need to co-operate even more closely with that of medicine. The existing special schools may, regrettably, lose some headway in public esteem by association with the former Training Centres. In both the education and medical services, the professionals have to pool their ideas and energies not only in the skills of treatment and training but in the major task of changing public attitudes.

This is important throughout the social services, but particularly in those related in any way to mental and psychological conditions. To some, the special school is still 'the daft school', and many unhappy children have resisted going there because that is what they and their parents fear it is, and that is what their friends and neighbours may call it. Until all kinds of guidance are regarded as neutrally as advice over university grants or consulting a National Health Service doctor, the scale of provision and the skill of professional workers will count for a good deal less than they should.

Within the local authority side of the health service there are many points of contact with education. Transfer of these to other authorities will make more difference to the education service in theory than in practice for the potential of these links has been largely unrealized. One of the most important is the duty of local health authorities to make arrangements for the care of expectant and nursing mothers. Clinics are provided for pre- and post-natal care and the routine examination of young children, and maternity and child welfare centres give a preventive and advisory service, offering supervision by doctors, midwives and health visitors. As a part of this general provision for the health and welfare of mothers and young children, some local authorities provide day nurseries for children under five who have special health or social needs; for example if their mother is the breadwinner, or if they come from bad home conditions. Some day nurseries have places for severely handicapped children.

Children in need are thus being identified before they come within the purview of the education service—an obvious opportunity for close co-operation—but the relationship is rarely as good as it should be. So far as nurseries are concerned, education departments have responsibility for nursery schools and classes (for children between two and five years old). The health department's day nurseries may make charges; nursery schools may not: the orientation of the day nursery is towards the needs of the mother; of the nursery schools towards the needs of the child: hours, methods and general outlook tend to differ.

There is thus a history of divided responsibility for closely related services, and furthermore services of inestimable significance in the early detection and treatment of handicap. The proposal in the Green Paper of 1970 to split them three ways, with maternity and child welfare services going to area health authorities, and day nurseries to local authorities' social service departments, will require careful and conscious effort to link the services in such a way as to complement, rather than compete with each other.

The potential importance of the health visitor is much increased by possible administrative changes. The 1946 Act required authorities to provide health visitors for the purpose of giving advice on the care of young children, persons suffering from illness, and expectant and nursing mothers. The 1956 report of the Jameson Committee suggested that the role of these officers could and should be widened considerably, emphasizing the social welfare aspects of their work. These recommendations were accepted and commended to local authorities in 1959, and whilst health visiting of young children remains her primary function, the health visitor is responsible for much general work in the prevention of illness, care of the sick, and after-care work.

We have already noted that in some areas the health visitor also acts as the school nurse, but whether or not this is the pattern, it is clear that the increasing emphasis upon the social and community aspects of her role can make her a valuable member of the team of people concerned with spotting disadvantage in its earliest stages. She has to visit the homes of all mothers with babies, and in the course of her work she is brought face to face with poor home conditions, inadequate physical and emotional care, physical and mental strain in the family. And her information can of course be invaluable to teachers and educational planners. The compilation of an 'at risk' register of children from birth is a job that local health authorities are well placed to perform, with great advantage to their own preventive role in health and to the education service in detecting handicap at the earliest possible stage.

We should not leave the world of health without considering briefly the role, actual and potential, of the general practitioner. The help that can be given to the education service by the hard-worked front line of the health service is yet another variable in our complex of relationships. Part will depend on outlook; part on training and knowledge. Doctors do not always regard an approach through social work as helpful in their own job and are likely to be troubled by the possibility of breach of confidentiality in disclosing personal information to others. They may not be aware of what resources are available. A study by Jeffreys (1965) suggested that general practitioners often did not know of the range of social services that would help their patients. On the other hand, doctors in underprivileged areas may be only too ready to co-operate with any fellow-workers.

An imaginative venture in Liverpool began in a group practice, in an inner ring area mainly of old housing, where the doctors found that patients were approaching them about psycho-social rather than strictly medical problems. They therefore sought help from other workers in the district. First, health visitors from two local authority clinics in the area were invited to discuss families for whom they shared clinical responsibility. This was useful, and gradually more and more people were called in on what became regular case conference sessions: home helps, and other welfare workers, occupational therapists and, notably, the local school doctors. There were also occasional visits from other doctors, medical social workers, probation officers, police juvenile liaison officers, and the manager of the local office of the Department of Health and Social Security.

The doctors naturally grew increasingly aware of the potentialities of social work, and through the good personal relationships with the other professionals were able to come together in the interests of the patient. The social workers responded well to the unusual phenomenon of general practitioners involving them in co-operative action. Through these conferences came a link with a voluntary social work agency who subsequently seconded a family case-worker to work at the surgery and follow up with home visits.

This, of course, is an unusual if not unique venture, but it indicates what can be done. We shall return in a later chapter to the team approach, the problems and the possibilities.

## Children

Transition from emphasis on cure to prevention is characteristic of all the social services, though it is a recent trend. Until the period just after the Second World War, services for the care of children stemmed largely from the Poor Law on the one hand and legal sanctions on the other. Reformatory Schools became Approved Schools under the Children and Young Persons Act, 1933, but it was only during the formative years of the Welfare

State that anything other than holding measures was attempted. Local authority children's services as we know them began as recently as 1948, when the Children Act gave them the duty of caring for children who were deprived of normal home life, and although additional powers, in adoption for example, were later given to them it was not until 1963 that the duty was given to develop preventive work to reduce reception into care or appearances before the courts. We can see in the developing provision a gradual bringing together of the welfare and legal aspects of the problem.

Since the 1948 Act local authorities have been under a duty to receive into care any child in their area who has no parent or guardian, who is abandoned or lost, or whose parents are for any reason unable to provide for his proper accommodation, maintenance and upbringing. They have had the right to acquire parental rights and powers in respect of a child received into care, subject to appeal by the parents or guardian in the Juvenile Court. In addition the court may commit a child to the care of a local authority as a 'fit person', for instance when a child is found guilty of an offence for which an adult could be imprisoned, or when a child is brought before it in need of care and protection or control, or because he has failed to attend school regularly.

Local children's authorities have the task of placing children in approved foster homes where this is practicable, desirable and in the child's best interests. Where fostering is not the answer or is not possible, the authority can place the child in a home maintained by them or an approved voluntary association. Reception centre accommodation must also be provided with facilities for observation of physical and mental condition, with a view to advising on the best kind of subsequent placements.

Even at this stage of development there is clear need for links with the education service. Children in care (other than on remand or in approved schools) are also children in school, so there is need for close co-operation between the children's department and the schools where children are in care or 'at risk'. The child through force of circumstances moved from one foster home to another may well exhibit behaviour problems in the classroom, and, unless the child care officer and the teacher consult, the school may be reinforcing the problems for this child.

But it is with the growing emphasis on preventive work that children's and education services are seeing the need to work most closely together. In 1950, a joint Home Office and Ministry of Education and Ministry of Health Circular drew the attention of all local authorities to the need to use all existing services to prevent the neglect or ill-treatment of children in their own homes.

The circular referred to the powers of the local authority as health authority, education authority, welfare authority, housing authority as well as children's authority, and also the interests of voluntary organizations and the National Assistance Board. Local authorities were asked to ensure that the most effective use was made of existing resources. It was suggested that each authority should designate an officer to be responsible for seeking co-operation among all the statutory and voluntary agencies concerned with the welfare of children in their own homes, and for holding regular meetings of the officers concerned. Consultative Committees were set up in some areas as a result of this, but in most places little was done to achieve working co-operation in the field of a positive kind.

Until the 1963 Children and Young Persons Act local authorities had no statutory powers or duties to undertake work with children in their own homes. Section One of the 1963 Act (based on the recommendations of the Ingleby Committee (1960)) placed a duty on local authorities to:

> make available such advice, guidance and assistance as
> may promote the welfare of children by diminishing the
> need to receive children into or keep them in care . . . or to
> bring children before a juvenile court.

Authorities were also authorized to enlist the aid of voluntary organizations in this work.

As part of the preventive work duty imposed on local authorities by Section One of the Act, the Home Office suggested to Chief Officers of police (in February 1964) that arrangements for consultation between police and local authorities before the institution of proceedings might be extended. In August 1965 the Government published as a basis for discussion a White Paper *The child, the family and the young offender*. This set out provisional proposals for practical reforms to support the family, forestall and reduce delinquency, and to revise the law and practice relating to offenders up to the age of twenty-one.

Yet until the legal and social branches of children's work come even closer together, there is bound to be difficulty in forging close links with education. At best the co-operation has tended to be bifurcated: a link between School Attendance and Welfare branches and Children's Departments, and another and weaker one between School Health and Psychological services and the other aspects of children's officers' work. In 1968 this process of bringing the legal and social together was taken a stage further by the publication of the White Paper *Children in Trouble*, which formed the basis of recent legislation.

The 1969 Act sets out the circumstances in which young people may be dealt with by juvenile courts as in need of care and control: if their development or health is being avoidably impeded, or they are being ill-treated or exposed to moral danger, or are beyond parental control, or are not receiving appropriate full-time education, or are guilty of offences other than homicide. It gives the courts powers to make orders, including those of supervision and of care. No prosecutions are to be brought except for homicide for actions of those under fourteen (younger, if an earlier age is specified under a court order relating to them) and none for actions of those under seventeen except by consent of a juvenile court magistrate. The minimum age for borstal training becomes seventeen instead of fifteen, and approved school, remand home, and probation orders are abolished for the under-seventeens.

The supervision of children under fourteen will in future normally be by the local authority, though probation officers already working with certain families may continue to work with younger children. The supervisors will be able to use a wide range of facilities to be co-ordinated and newly created by children's regional planning committees: they will include 'community homes', statutory or voluntary, to replace children's homes and hostels, approved schools, remand homes and the accommodation for under-seventeens in probation homes, detention centres and borstals. The system of fostering will continue, but in a more flexible way, so that more attention can be given to special cases.

These are imaginative proposals which, if properly implemented, can simplify and co-ordinate some of the arrangements at present uneasily wavering between children's departments, police and probation service, and also give a significant re-orientation to the public attitude to care and protection of the young. The emphasis will in fact be less on 'offences' and 'punishments' and more on care. This clearly will not impress many people who consider that juvenile problems are mainly those of delinquency, but it brings out a point made in the first chapter—that there is a distinction to be drawn between the needs of children, and the behaviour patterns and standards of their parents. The ethos of the new proposals can be clearly related to that behind the argument for intervention through education: children's handicaps detected early enough can be treated (as part of the child's right and in the interests of the state) by removal of bad environmental influences, including that of parents. It also supports the thesis that social advance often includes a process of considering certain actions first as crimes, later as the result of mental or psychological disorders, and ultimately as susceptible to treatment through education. The new law relating to children has moved to some extent away from the first stage, and its orientation is moving from the second into the third: the community homes, for instance, will be run in consultation with education committees.

Of course the categories suggested are not precise, and it would be wrong to try to push the notion to the point of a general theory: the education service itself is concerned with both the first stage (in relation to prosecution for poor school attendance) and the second (in relation to diagnosis of handicap), and there is always likely to be an element of each in any social approach until human beings attain higher standards of self-discipline than at present seems likely. The practical implication of the notion is the emphasis it places on increased co-operation between education and children's services: the community homes concept is one specific instance; another is new arrangements that will be possible for joint consideration of cases of poor school attendance, where in the past the disciplinary side of the law might have been invoked as a matter of course.

This is not the place to compare the many different methods of care used by the children's authorities—children's home, fostering (the modern name for boarding out), reception centres as temporary and diagnostic units, lodgings, residential occupations and so on. Nor are we concerned with the details of adoption. It is important that these techniques of intervention should be known by those in education, however, and the resources should be used. Similarly, delinquency is not our direct concern, but it is essential for people associated with school children to know about the legal machinery applicable to them.

What we should explore a little more are the attitudes and methods of professional officers in children's departments and related work, for it is here that there are more opportunities for constructive co-operation. Preventive work of this type is not the exclusive concern of children's departments, though they have the main responsibility for it since the 1963 Act. It is chiefly exercised through child care officers who are, or should be, trained social caseworkers. The technique, with its emphasis on personal assistance to individuals or families through exploration of the problem in relation to the environmental factors that impinge upon them, is often an invaluable approach. But its development can be regarded as a major source of tension in the various social work agencies.

First, it is at this point that approach through specialization leads to some of the biggest, most explosive confrontations. To bore deep into the heart of a family from one specific starting point may be to encounter similar thrusts from other directions, and the delicacy of the probe may be impaired. Child care officers, medical social workers from hospitals, psychiatric social workers from child guidance clinics and probation officers may all represent attempts by various specialisms to achieve results through casework. Family caseworkers from voluntary organizations such as the Family Welfare Association and Family Service Units may be seeking to do the same thing from the starting point of the well-being of the client.

Second, the caseworker may find that inroads into the family situation are made by representatives of separate departments who are not themselves caseworkers. Here his training and concern for the relationships he may be patiently trying to build may lead him to fear the intrusion of, say, an Education Welfare Officer or a teacher.

Third, the slow therapeutic process of casework may conflict with the sharper, cruder methods of approach, from grants to fines, used to adjust social disequilibria. Some social workers suggest that caseworkers are too concerned with helping people to adapt themselves to their environment, whereas the real need is to change the environment. Often this is unfair—the caseworkers are simply not in a position to alter the environment—but the feeling exists.

The conflict exemplified in this last point exists not only between different disciplines but within them. In children's departments the requirements of the law and the inclinations of trained social workers may pull in opposite directions. The same division exists even within the services aimed at young offenders where the element of crime inevitably slants the service towards correction.

## Young offenders

For the police, emphasis on prevention rather than expensive imprisonment after the offence can be a matter of ordinary prudence. Enlightened police authorities have set up juvenile liaison branches to work with schools and other agencies with considerable success.

One scheme was described as follows:

> Our pilot experiment of juvenile liaison officers was brought into being whereby the co-operation was sought of the various shops, stores, warehouses, etc. in order that all juveniles caught pilfering were notified to the police without discrimination. With the co-operation of parents and the help and advice of teachers and the various social services, it was decided that as soon as the police were aware that a child had committed an offence for the first time, and it was not a serious one, and provided the offender admitted the facts and the owner of the

property or persons offended against did not wish to prosecute, then the specially selected and trained officer would, with the full co-operation of parents, take the child under his aegis. Our specific object was to prevent a recurrence of this bad behaviour.

Its methods were these:

The success of the scheme depends on the whole-hearted co-operation of all who are interested in the direction and welfare of children and it is the duty of each juvenile liaison officer to:

(a) establish and maintain a close liaison with headteachers, ministers of religion, youth club leaders, and any other persons in their respective divisions who are interested or concerned in the welfare of children or young persons

(b) collaborate with the Probation Service without usurping or overlapping any of its functions

(c) keep individual records of juveniles dealt with or who have come to the notice of the police in respect of offences committed by them

(d) maintain a regular contact with juveniles cautioned by the police, and their parents. (*The Police and Children*, 1964.)

In services like these the emphasis is on guidance rather than on court action for young first offenders. The tensions within the probation service are much greater because, although its work is with law-breakers, its basic purpose is preventive and therefore geared to the needs of the individual.

There are 94 probation areas; one is the metropolitan magistrates' courts area of London, and 33 are cities or county boroughs. Nearly all the rest are composed of petty sessional divisions of combined areas, for the most part of administrative counties and in many instances of county boroughs as well. The Home Secretary is responsible for the service.

The changes now taking place in the organization and attitudes of the personal social services and of the penal system will alter the emphasis in the work of the probation officer, an emphasis reflected in its full title. Probation and After-care Service. It will in future be more concerned with adult criminals, but we shall refer here briefly to those aspects of the service most closely related to children and young persons.

Until the 1969 Act courts were empowered, except where the sentence for the offence is fixed by law, to make a probation order in respect of an offender of any age, if, having regard for all the circumstances, the court was of the opinion that this course was expedient. The new legislation makes children's departments responsible for younger offenders, and the role of the probation officer will in future relate mainly to those over fourteen. Although the greatest increase in work will probably be in after-care of those released from prison or detention centres, borstals and so on, there will still be a good deal of preventive work with younger people. With the fourteen- to seventeen-year-olds it is likely to increase, since borstal training will be ended for them and the emphasis will be on supervision or care in one of the facilities provided by the children's regional planning committees.

In the public mind, and in that of many offenders, there is an initial assumption that the probation officer has a quasi-penal function. In fact, the probation officer is under a statutory duty to 'enquire in accordance with any directions of the court, into the circumstances or home surroundings of any person with a view to assisting the court in determining the most suitable methods of dealing with the case' (Home Office, 1964). Except in trivial cases, juvenile courts must be provided with comprehensive reports on all persons under the age of seventeen appearing before the courts, either by the local authority (children's department) or by the probation officer. A probationer may be required to live in a par-ticular place, e.g. with relatives or in lodgings, or in a specified institution if it is decided that training and discipline are required.

The responsibility of probation officers towards their clients is expressed by statute as 'to supervise the probationers and to advise and assist and befriend them' (Home Office, 1964). This is a case-work relationship which seeks to prepare for the time when the probationer will no longer have the support of the officer. How well it can be achieved is problematical: certainly the probation officer is most anxious to shake off any lingering connection in people's minds between his role and that of the police. One result of this is that he may feel impelled to preserve at all costs the confidentiality of his dealings with his clients. Clearly this is of vital importance, but it does make difficulties for lay people, such as teachers, who wish to co-operate. Team-work becomes less of a reality if one partner appears to be holding back.

The probation officer faces serious problems in his attempts at social work. The state's purpose in employing him is primarily to uphold the law. To do this by befriending law-breakers is a very sophisticated concept. The social casework doctrine of acceptance means that he must accept the criminal but not the crime, which sounds hard enough in theory and must be well-nigh impossible in practice. How can a genuine relationship arise from the unpromising beginnings of compulsory confrontation?

To the outsider the probation officer's anxiety to overcome these tremendous obstacles and establish a satisfactory relationship can seem like an unreasonable concern for one black sheep in relation to the rest of the flock. A good example of the tensions suffered by the probation officer is given by Phyllida Parsloe, who points out that the developing role of the probation officer in relation to after-care means that he will be working with men who may well feel that their years in prison are the result of a probation officer's report:

> 'The probation officer cannot have it both ways. He cannot demand a share in the decision making of the courts by pressing for the use of social enquiry reports and then not face his responsibility when challenged by prisoners' (Parsloe, 1967).

## Statutory and voluntary

The dilemma of the probation officer is an acute form of an important general question: how far statutory organizations can both provide services (including laws) and help people to use them properly. The tendency of organizations is to require individuals to fit them, not to adjust in order to meet the needs of individuals. This is largely inevitable with laws, if they are to have any meaning. Other institutions may share the same propensity without the same excuse.

Much of this book is about the need for the education service to reverse this tendency: if education is not concerned for individuals it is worthless, and it must project its concern into satisfactory relationships with individuals outside its institutions as well as those within them. Similarly because of its orientation it may stand a better chance than some services of being accepted by the public in this role. To approach parents because of concern about a child's education is different from approaching them because they have not paid their rent or because they have beaten their neighbour over the head. Yet it may be that all services, including education, need to consider whether some of the functions they are seeking to perform could not be better done by the voluntary agencies.

'Voluntary' does not mean what it did. In years past it meant, very often, the philanthropic application of private fortunes to worthy causes not thought (by anyone, including the philanthropists) to be the state's concern. Today the amount of truly private benefaction is a small and diminishing part of voluntary effort. There may be the same bands of dedicated workers as before, but two things have happened. They are more likely to find that the state is also involved in the problems that concern them; and they are likely to have to ask the state for financial support.

These factors may mean that the growing number of state-employed professionals are less enthusiastic about voluntary effort than some of the volunteers would like. They may say, for instance, that the voluntary services are not really volunteers: they have paid staff who are little different from those in the local authority service, and much of the actual voluntary effort involves sitting on committees rather than actually working.

There is considerable overlap between what is being attempted by the officers of the statutory and of voluntary bodies. The overlap and its attendant tensions are a complication that makes confusion worse confounded in many aspects of social work. Nor is it enough to say (though it is largely true) that the voluntary agencies are able to engage paid workers at considerably less cost than the authorities seem able to do: perhaps they would get even better workers if they could pay more. What is needed is clarification of the objectives of the agencies concerned.

The fundamental question is: what can voluntary bodies do that local authorities cannot? In helping individuals in need, local authority workers must acknowledge the great and persisting problem of how to develop a satisfactory relationship—of confidence and of trust—with the client. However hard they try they cannot always entirely break through the barrier erected by their association with authority. Some official agencies may seem less authoritarian than others to the public, but the difference may be too small to matter.

If this were not so, there would be many fewer advice columns in local and national newspapers and journals. These will range from 'Worried Blue Eyes' in women's magazines to hints about investments. They are, of course, a national institution, and in their extreme form are suspected of being fictitious, the contributions being invented in order to provide an entertaining format for gobbets of information. Many are genuine enough, though, and they should give food for thought to the authorities.

An educational advice column was set up in a national newspaper with a Professor of Education as its consultant, suggesting presumably expertise on matters affecting the education of readers' children. Yet arising from the column, local education authorities throughout the country began to receive letters from the newspaper enquiring about this or that matter raised by readers. Sometimes the point might be a dispute about parental rights or alleged injustice within a particular authority, in which case the newspaper quite legitimately performs one of its classical functions if (with or without professional support) it asks the L.E.A. to explain or seeks to right a wrong. At other times, however, the questions were general ones (for instance about university grant regulations) of a kind that are daily answered by education office staffs. Why could not the enquirer seek his answer by letter direct, in person or by telephone, in order to get the full story?

The accessibility and acceptability of local education offices (and schools) are matters to which we shall return in later chapters. But, however informal and welcoming these institutions might be, there is perhaps something beyond this that would inhibit development of a closer rapport between statutory agency and consumer. On a recent occasion the weekly information column of a local newspaper dealt not only with things like how to sell an aspidistra or a second-hand wig but also a whole range of transactions between citizens and the various authorities. They included faulty heating which thirty-three visits from the Gas Board had allegedly not put right, eligibility for a disability travel pass, maternity grants for New Zealand visitors, G.C.E. classes in Welsh, compulsory purchase orders and long-standing blockage of drains. In this last the letter complained that nothing had been done in over six weeks whilst the authorities replied that four visits had been made to the premises by an inspector and several by a contractor without being able to gain access.

What the rights and wrongs are is irrelevant. The situation represents something more than a failure of communication: it has an element of 'us' and 'them'. People evidently feel the need for someone unconnected with the system itself to help them contend with it. Even councillors, by association, tend to become part of the system and to be associated also with political attitudes. Who then can fulfil this important function?

Might not this be an important future role for the voluntary services? In the past, the apparent need for them has declined with the increase of state provision. If they are seen as specially concerned and equipped to protect the individual against the system, then the need will increase, not diminish, as the state provides more and more. If we accept that in the long term preventive action must in a democracy have its roots in a desire for change in the community itself, then the potential role of the voluntary side becomes very vital indeed.

Emphasis on voluntary effort underlines the importance of safeguarding the freedoms in our kind of democracy. This does not imply that the whole weight of the task should be put on voluntary effort, still less that statutory institutions should not adapt themselves to people's needs, but merely that state intervention should be tempered by those not owing full allegiance to the machine, even though much of this 'voluntary' effort would need in fact to be heavily subsidized. The element of self-help implicit in the objectives of social work at its best would be strongly emphasized by encouraging and planning for voluntary activity on these lines.

In the kind of situation represented by some of the case histories we have quoted—crisis cases—the tradition of many of the voluntary services in family case work already follows this line. In that sense there would be nothing new about this direction. But it would be a new slant deliberately to plan the statutory system to include this provision, not only in individual cases of need, but in terms of community development and organization aimed at helping individuals and neighbourhoods to work out and express their thoughts on the kind of society they want.

## The individual, the group and the community

To propose an important function for voluntary bodies in both casework and community development is to suggest that they be given a key role throughout the social work spectrum. In discussing casework earlier we pointed out the need to seek adjustment not only in individuals but in their environment. Part of that environment is the community of people in which individuals and individual families live, and social workers could arguably do more good by seeking to help influence the larger unit, i.e. the community, than by concentrating on individuals in particular need. Similarly work with groups of people can be valuable.

Perhaps the most relevant example of group work is the Youth Service, which in turn is closely associated on an adult level with what, for want of a better term, we must call Community Service. In view of the essentially preventive orientation of these services it is perhaps not surprising that their aims, activities, and organization are even more difficult to pin down than other branches of social work.

A report by the Youth Service Development Council in 1969 produced this despairing account:

At national level, a Cabinet Minister has a general overall interest in the social services. In the Department, schools are dealt with by one branch, 'formal' further education by a second, and 'informal' further education, including the Youth Service, sport and community provision in the educational sense by a third (FE II). FE II and Schools Branch are in regular touch with the Schools Council. Other Ministries, notably the Home Office and the Department of Health and Social Security, have an interest in community work. Most of the voluntary organisations concerned are members of the Standing Conference of National Voluntary Youth Organisations, an associated group of the National Council of Social Service. Co-operation between these bodies is by consultation, mostly ad hoc, to consider such particular problems as, recently, Immigration and Service by Youth. At local level, various departments of local authorities and a number of voluntary organisations are involved. The L.E.A. has the major interest and its attitude, expressed in its methods of working, influences local relationships. 'Youth' with several meanings is dealt with by different committees in different areas and these have varying executive powers. Sometimes there are youth committees with members from local voluntary organisations. There are local councils of social services, of varying calibre and status. Local education authority staffs are organised differently to deal with youth work, and in particular, the status of the Youth Officer (or equivalent) varies widely. Some authorities deal with youth matters entirely through their further education staff, others handle them separately, though still in association with further education. Local consultations between all concerned with youth matters are rare and, even when they take place, vested interests can lead to long delays or even stalemate.

The Youth Service as a statutory entity began in 1939, when the Board of Education was given responsibility for young people recently having left school. The 1944 Education Act continues the tradition in slightly broader terms relating to leisure time occupation for those over school leaving age. The local education authorities, through further education and youth committees, have a mainly co-ordinating function and the voluntary bodies make much of the direct provision, especially in the form of clubs and club leaders, though with increasing financial assistance from public funds. The amount of money spent both nationally and locally has always been relatively small, and, along with adult education, youth and community services have usually been the first to suffer in any economic crisis.

Since the publication of the Albemarle Report in 1958 and the setting up of a National College for training youth leaders there has been an expansion of youth work, particularly in less formal institutional methods than in the traditional youth club. Albemarle emphasized the need for challenge as well as recreation and also the importance of work with the unattached (the unclubbables). Group work is now increasingly undertaken away from club premises, in the places naturally frequented by young people. By a process of infiltration into their social and occupational groups youth leaders experiment with counselling and group work techniques. For various reasons links between schools and the youth services are in some ways less than they were in the early days of the statutory service: strengthening these links could lead not only to valuable activities and good influences for many more young people in their later years at school, but also turn the energies and undoubted idealism of many young people into voluntary social work, for example, running baby-sitting services or helping nursery schools or day nurseries with out-of-school activities.

The Youth Service Development Council Report (1969) set out to answer the question: 'Has the Youth Service got a future?' It concluded:

> The pace of change has been so great since the Albemarle Committee reported that the Youth Service cannot continue the fiction that the same provision meets the needs of all young people in the 14–20 age range. In fact there is often a greater generation gap between 14 and 18 than between 18 and 28. Our enquiries, supported by statistics shortly to be published by the Government Social Survey, have confirmed the considerable fall-out in membership after the age of 16 or 17, particularly of girls. This surely means that the present Youth Service is irrelevant to their needs, yet we firmly believe that many of these young people can be helped to create their place in society. The problem is to establish the contact.

In calling for 'a new and imaginative approach' the Council suggests less emphasis on clubs and more on meeting the needs of individuals:

> . . . There must be the maximum exchange of expertise between teachers and youth workers in the field. Schools should no longer be built for one purpose but for wider community use. . . .
> We believe that joint appointments covering youth and education can be a major factor in breaking down barriers. . . .
> The pattern of Youth and Community Service for the upper age-range must be governed by a clear recognition of their adult status and level of sophistication . . . young people must be encouraged to play an active part in a society which they themselves will help to mould. There should be no upper age limit since people will use the service as long as they need it. . . .

The new Youth and Community Service will bring exciting possibilities for new partnerships between the Service and industry, trade unions, commercial enterprises, the social services and education. This will mean strengthening old working relations which have sometimes been more apparent than real.

Community service work has followed a similar pattern to that in the youth service. It was initiated by voluntary action, notably the settlements such as Toynbee Hall in East London, in which educated people from the churches, universities and public schools established meeting places in areas of social deprivation, and lived there as part of the community. Later, community centres, at first voluntary and afterwards grant aided by the then Board of Education, were set up particularly in new housing estates. The Physical Training and Recreation Act of 1937 and the 1944 Education Act enabled local education authorities to build centres and employ wardens, usually managed by local volunteers. These voluntary bodies, known as community associations, established themselves in various parts of the country and immediately after the war they flourished and seemed likely to spread. However, there has subsequently been very little advance, and support for this kind of venture has been at the bottom of most education authorities' lists. Recently, as in the youth service, there has been re-emphasis and the prospect of new growth through the concept known as community development.

The emphasis in community development is on helping people to make their needs known, to join together for the common good and to improve their own way of life. In areas of proposed or actual change these aims are particularly relevant. The nature and status of professional work in this approach are difficult points. There has been little relevant training available: in any event the suggestion of superiority inherent in the idea of training may be out of place in this kind of activity. The problem of intervention is at its most acute. If the person concerned (he can hardly be called a leader) is a paid employee of the local authority he may well have conflicts of loyalty since much of the work of community development is inevitably concerned with protecting the people against uncongenial official activity such as planning or with gingering up sluggish social service programmes, such as housing. Hence the argument for a voluntary basis for professional work of this kind.

In communities where a more sophisticated level of activity evolves, community development can turn into community organization work; that is, co-ordinating the efforts of various groups that may be active in an area. This is a rather less sensitive concept, but one that is subject to the affliction known as committee-itis: the same people tend to appear, first in one role then another, but always serving on committees. Nevertheless, in large towns particularly, the Councils of Social Service can perform an invaluable function in creating a good relationship with the various voluntary organizations and bringing them into discussions about co-operation and a collective approach to settling priorities: thereafter they can put across a coherent, reasoned view of community needs to the statutory bodies and work with them to achieve common objectives.

The benefit to schools in this work is of course in the hope of helping communities to develop to their full potential. Such a community is a better environment for a child than the forlorn, lifeless, hostile or sterile neighbourhoods in which many now live. For their part the teachers, perhaps by making the school's resources available for the community, can make a major contribution. So too can their colleagues—doctors, caseworkers, youth leaders, clergy, councillors and so on—who live or work in a neighbourhood together. In so doing they may themselves come closer together and thus become more effective in giving a lead to others.

# The role of the school

## five

'The only professional service which is in contact with all children for at least a ten-year span is the school. Thus it could well serve as the focal point from which caring for children radiates during this period.' Kellmer Pringle, in her address at the Association of Children's Officers' Conference in September 1969, went on to describe the growing concern of all schools with the environment from which their pupils are drawn. The particular contribution of teachers in the past has been based on their continuous knowledge of children over a period, their opportunity to see children in the round. Yet schools change: like the rest of the world they are becoming more complex every year. This chapter will look at some of the changes and their implications for the caring school.

The need to provide the highest quality of education in a wide range of subjects has increasingly led to the appointment of specialists rather than class teachers. Specialists may see more children in the week but for shorter lengths of time. As a result, knowledge of the needs of children with educational or social handicap has itself become a matter for specialization.

This has not happened overnight nor is it a complete transformation, but the present situation is very different from that of thirty or forty years ago, and the rate of change is accelerating. In the past the outlook of a school depended very largely on the attitudes and personality of the head. The head is still the biggest single influence on a school but nowadays the influence may be less direct and is almost certainly less absolute.

Not so very long ago a high proportion of heads of schools were well known, long-standing residents of the areas they served. They were leading members of the local community, socially as well as professionally. Many of them are part of the history of the inner areas of our great cities. Stories are still told of their personal eccentricities and of the pioneering work in fighting for extra help with the tremendous social problems with which they had to contend. Their concern was for the children in their schools and for their families.

Today the picture is different. The decay of the inner areas, the growth of the suburbs, and the arrival of the motor car have meant that few heads of down-town schools now live in the areas served by their schools. There is not necessarily less dedication: it is simply that our whole pattern of living has changed. Dedication has to manifest itself in different ways and it has become harder for an individual head to make an impact on the community through his school.

Other changes have played their part. Reorganization into separate primary and secondary schools broke up one of the most significant influences of the school, for it no longer happens that succeeding generations, cousins, uncles and aunts all attend the same local school from the beginning of their education to the end. Larger units have come into being, both at primary and secondary stage, and this has made it more difficult for heads to run schools, as some once did, as an extension of their own personality. Specialization has become necessary and expected. Rapid turnover of staff and sometimes equally rapid changes in the community through, for instance, re-housing have added to the uncertainties. Consequently informal, personalized, *ad hoc* provision can no longer be so effective. The head's philosophy is still a vital factor, but it has to operate within an increasingly complex structure.

## Pastoral care

In large secondary schools, it is usual for house tutors or year masters to be responsible for the care of the young people in particular sub-divisions of the school. 'Pastoral care' is a term in common use for this oversight, but it has many connotations. It may be restricted to supervision of a child's progress solely during the time he is at school; on the other hand time may be allowed for making home visits or for co-operation with social work agencies or attending court when children get into trouble, and perhaps even for counselling. Schools may have members of staff as counsellors or teacher-social workers with widely varying functions between school and school.

They may be full-time specialists, or teach part-time and practise their specialization for the rest of the week. Composite appointments may be the result of necessity, but they may also reflect a belief that to be effective a counsellor needs to be a full member of the teaching staff with full knowledge of the practical problems of teaching a class. They may be the result of anxiety that appointing a specialist in social welfare might imply that the rest of the staff need not bother.

Whatever the nature of these appointments, this last point is fundamental. There are no experts in human nature, and human nature is at the root of many of the problems. Furthermore, every teacher has to be sensitive to human needs and human potential. Concern for children and their opportunities is not something that can be grafted on to a school through expertise: it is a basic requirement of every teacher.

One of the key points at which schools show their concern for children's individual needs is in the kind of time-table they devise. Partly this is a question of the basis on which it is compiled—curriculum development is intended to force consideration and evaluation of the principles and objectives of what is to be taught. Partly it is a question of the trouble that is taken to give the child a real say in choosing between subjects and courses. This process, on which the child's whole future can quite literally depend, is often pitifully inadequate. It is at this point that we can best begin to think about the need for counsellors.

It is a truism that good teachers have always performed many of the functions of the counsellor. They know all about face-to-face interviews, diagnostic tests and many of the other counselling functions. And sensitivity is a continuing requirement for every member of staff. Yet if in this fundamental question of pupil-choice the situation is so often unsatisfactory, can we be complacent about the standard of general concern? Do we not need a radical break with at least some of the traditions? How many schools offer a range of subjects that is really adequate to all their pupils' needs: and how many allow, still less ensure, serious consideration of other possibilities by children and their parents? In small schools where there is most difficulty in providing a choice-range there is room for skilled investigation of the possibility of exploiting what facilities there are. In larger schools the very range of specialisms, with its staff to match, has its own problems. Choice is harder when there are many alternatives, and specialist teachers may not find it easy to perform what they see as their main tasks as well as advising children from a general point of view: indeed they usually have less opportunity to see children in the round.

There is a case, then, for counsellors on purely educational grounds. In the first instance they could attempt to influence their colleagues and heads in compiling time-tables and curricula in a flexible, imaginative way, as well as helping individual children to cope with the system.

An extension of this role is into vocational guidance: the choice of career is an essential ingredient of the problem of curriculum choice. The local authority's Youth Employment Service can contribute ideas and information about the requirements of jobs and the range of possibilities, but their efforts in matching child with opportunity are more likely to be successful if reinforced by informed assessment of individual potential and individual need. The traditions of many of our schools, even the best of them, have often led to unrealistic attitudes to the importance of earning a living. To resist clamour for vocational training is right: it is not the best way of giving a foundation for later specialization and it is too restricting too early, both vocationally, and educationally. But recognizing the significance of the importance of a career is another matter entirely: it can give a valuable incentive to some of the most reluctant learners.

This underlines the value of vocational counselling within the school. We may also note in passing that the sensitivity of a school to its pupils' needs includes welcoming and co-operating with the Careers Officers of the Youth Employment Service. Much of the discussion about handicap must emphasize the importance of early action. Most of the educational effects of inequality cannot be eradicated by the time the secondary stage is reached. Yet getting the right job is a very practical manifestation of equal opportunity: for many people it is the main consideration. It seems foolish, therefore, to give informed and increasing attention to individual needs in the early stages if at the end everything is left to chance in this crucial matter.

The pure doctrine of personal counselling as it has evolved in America has been characterized by Peter Daws (1967) as including continuity and globality of concern, with active client participation and a preventive orientation: the counsellor is also 'well-placed to help co-ordinate the work of his colleagues by identifying in individual children where the collective school effort is failing, and the forms of such failure'. For various reasons Mr Daws concludes that this is too exacting, too novel and ambitious to be more than a source of inspiration for this country at present. As well as the educational and vocational counselling which we have just discussed, he suggests another more limited but equally useful modification—therapeutic counselling. This, as the name implies, would concern itself only with children in difficulties, the problem that we have called the lowest common denominator. Mr Daws's description of the role not only puts the argument clearly but also adds an important point that serves as a corrective to blanket assumptions about the causes of inequality of opportunity:

Our endeavours to understand childhood development have been disproportionately directed toward the pre-school child, and we consequently remain much less well-informed of the factors critical to the mental health of the school child. If we had learned more about the adjustment difficulties of school children, our educational purposes might already reflect a stronger concern for the pupil's personal development as distinct from his scholastic progress. We still too readily assume that the causes of breakdown during the school years are to be sought in development mishaps in the pre-school years.

This reminder that the school itself is part of the child's environment reinforces the argument for any counsellor needing to influence the whole approach of the school as well as simply dealing with individual cases himself.

There are perhaps three main elements in this. The first is activity in relation to individual children: this may take the form of counselling or remedial teaching with the backward, or special attention to the needs of immigrants. The second is the link between home and school. The third is the link between the school and those outside agencies also concerned with the problem. If the person undertaking this work is a specialist, we have to add a fourth: the link between his work and that of his fellow members of staff. It needs very little imagination to see that any specialist coming into a school will need not only tact and skill but humility if he is to get anywhere at all. It is all too easy to give the impression to other members of staff that a self-styled miracle man has arrived, someone wanting to turn the school upside down and adopt unrealistic policies without doing any of the drudgery attached to handling large or badly behaved classes.

We come back then to the question—given the need for these functions to be performed by a school, who should perform them and how? Some would opt for out-and-out specialism. 'Teacher-social worker' for instance is to some people a way of indicating a helpful attitude on the part of any teacher to his role in contemporary society. To others it appears to mean an expert with certain specific functions.

A course to train 'teacher-social workers' of this kind was set up at Edge Hill College of Education, but the original notion has now been considerably modified, partly because of new thinking about the idea and partly because of the realities of the employment situation. The response of heads of schools and other teachers to the idea is a relevant factor. Some argue: 'The appointment of a teacher with special responsibility for welfare of children will certainly allow other teachers to opt out of this part of their responsibility and this can only be to the detriment of the children'; or: 'Many children would be embarrassed in the knowledge that the school knew about their personal home circumstances'; or: 'The children would soon recognize that appealing to the teacher-social worker would be a desirable alternative to the punishment they really deserve and school discipline would be bound to suffer in consequence.'

A particularly revealing criticism is: 'Such a specialist appointment will encourage some teachers to heave a sigh of relief that they can rid themselves of their caring role and get on with their primary role—teaching.' For a distinction of this kind to be made in these terms is surely a sad reflection on some orthodox teacher training programmes. But it also demonstrates that too rigid a notion of 'training teacher-social workers' can carry in it the seeds of its own destruction. A specialist in social work is no use if he does not increase the amount of concern for children in need felt by his colleagues. The role of every teacher can and should include the three areas of concern we outlined above.

The Edge Hill course now lays less emphasis on the concept of teacher-social worker as a dual role (i.e., a teacher role with specialist welfare responsibilities) than as an example of a teacher type (i.e., as indicating the kind of attitudes and approach essential in all teachers). The overwhelming evidence of the influence of home environment cannot be ignored by any teacher, nor is it sufficient simply to know this as an abstract academic fact. On the contrary, he must know and understand the individual circumstances of each child in his class before he can organize a relevant programme of work. Equally important is the need to remember that the teacher's primary concern is the educational development of the child; he is unlikely to see himself as an auxiliary social worker.

The value, as well as the danger, of the notion of the expert teacher-social worker is in its acceptance of the need for skill. Plowden has pointed out that not all teachers would want to visit homes, not only because (particularly in the primary school) such visits might well have to take place out of school hours, but also because of basic fears and insecurities. Clearly no teacher can be forced to visit a home, and in any event an unwilling and fearful teacher is not the best person to knock on the door of the resentful or apathetic parent. Nor is willingness enough: interviewing parents, whether it is about the length of a boy's hair, progress in school, truancy or behaviour, requires a degree of skill which is not automatically bestowed with a certificate of education.

However, whether a teacher undertakes home visits himself and whether he makes contact with social workers about particular children may well depend upon the ethos of the school. There are some schools, such as the one described in the Appendix, where it has been felt desirable to appoint a teacher with a specialist role: she has a very real responsibility to ensure communication with colleagues on all relevant information about children, and staff can refer children about whom they have particular worries to her. On the other hand, the head of another primary school in Lancashire believes that all his teachers should have the opportunity to visit homes, and in this he has the full support of his staff.

It is not appropriate to argue the merits of either system, for there can be no blueprint which is equally applicable to all schools; nor is it helpful to generalize, for example representing schools as on a continuum, on which those in the most deprived areas have the most social problems, the suburban schools have fewer problems, and so on to superior grammar schools with no problems at all. This can be far from the truth.

## Remedial teaching

Whether or not they make any specific provision for socially disadvantaged children, most schools do their best to help the academically less able. One of the oldest traditions in schools is that of varying class sizes according to the needs of the pupils: increasing the size of some classes has enabled small groups to be taken out for remedial work. This has seemed not only better for the children but fairer for the staff, since it is generally thought to be harder work dealing with less able children than with the brightest. And one of the first of the new specialisms developed in post-war education was that concerned with teaching children who have learning difficulties.

This pattern singles out for special attention those children in urgent need of it, and at the same time improves the lot of teachers who teach in the remaining classes by reducing class sizes and removing the slowest workers. Introduced early enough, it can help many children to remain in ordinary schools who would otherwise need segregated special education. Yet to appoint extra teachers on this scale in all primary schools would be beyond most authorities' immediate reach, even if the quota allowed it. Some selection of schools for the appointments would be inevitable.

As support to internal schemes, an external remedial service designed to help individual children may be the most realistic way of helping the schools to help the children. Sometimes these services have left a good deal to be desired. If they are considered as an adjunct to the school psychological service, a pattern may have been established in which children with learning difficulties attend at a central clinic for an hour or two a week. The disturbance and the amount of travelling involved often makes this of dubious value. The degree of reporting back to schools can also be limited, and this again limits the value of the exercise.

It is perhaps easier to justify this method of working as an arm of a child guidance clinic, dealing with emotional and behavioural problems, so that childen receiving psychiatric treatment can also be given remedial help, but effective communication between school and clinic is essential.

A scheme describing good co-operation between school and a (voluntary) clinic is given in Schools Council Working Paper No. 15:

> The scheme serves, at present, four schools intensively and two further schools marginally. These include four primary schools, one comprehensive Boys' school and an all-age ESN school. A number of other schools in the vicinity of the clinic have expressed their wish to join this service, but at the moment the clinic cannot provide the staff to make such an extension possible.
>
> The professionals most involved in the service are the head of the school and the psychologist of the clinic, but these may involve the help and advice of many other professionals.
>
> These include first of all the professionals nearest to the head and the psychologist: the staff of the school and the clinic staff, i.e., all teachers and ancillary staff, and the psychiatrists, psychiatric social workers and psychotherapists of the clinic. In most cases the social services concerned with the school also play a part, particularly the care committee and the school medical officer. In addition to these, the whole social network may be involved: the health visitor, the probation officer, the child care officer, the N.S.P.C.C. inspector, G.P.s, youth leaders, speech therapists, clergy, in short anyone who might have anything to do with the child and his family.
>
> Meetings between the head and the psychologist are at regular intervals: weekly, fortnightly or monthly. This arrangement is made between the head and the psychologist and depends mainly on the needs of the school. By and large we have found that meetings have to be more frequent in the beginning of the work with a school. The length of the meetings also varies from 2 hours to 4 hours, and a visit

often includes meetings with members of staff of the school
or some social agency. Sometimes the psychologist may also
see a child for testing, and in some of the schools reading
surveys are carried out with children of a particular age
group.

Generally, the child and his problems in school are first
discussed between the head and the psychologist. At the
same time every effort is made to explore the child's family
situation. The head and the teachers supply most of the
information at this point, but the school files and the medical
files are also consulted and contact is made with the school
care committee and the school medical officer if there is
evidence that either of these have any special knowledge of
the case.

At this stage decisions for the first plan of action will be
made; if referral to the clinic is considered desirable and if
it seems possible to obtain the parents' co-operation, the
various ways in which the clinic might be introduced to the
parents will be explored. The head might see the parents and
hand them the clinic's application form; or he might see
them and suggest that they meet a member of the clinic
staff at school, usually the psychologist or the psychiatric
social worker; or he might suggest that the child will first be
seen by the psychologist who will later discuss his findings
in a joint meeting with the parents, the head and the child.
The possibilities are numerous.

If referral to the clinic seems unlikely, the head and the
psychologist generally consider which helping agent of the
social network should be approached. This often includes more
than one person, particularly if the child belongs to a
'problem family'. In this case all workers involved with the
family might be invited to a meeting at the school to discuss
how the social network might be used to best advantage.
Such meetings often include the clinic's PSW or the
psychiatrist.

There is, of course, also the possibility that only the school
can help a particular child, and plans might be made with
the head and the teachers concerned on how best to adapt
the school's opportunities to the particular needs of the child.

At times, it is also a matter of waiting for the moment when
the family will be sufficiently anxious to accept referral to
the clinic, and in these cases the psychologist will inform
the clinic team so that the family can then be seen at short
notice.

In fact, the head and the psychologist, drawing on the school, the clinic and the social network, provide as complete a diagnostic service as the family will accept. The treatment is equally varied and ranges in intensity from psychotherapy in the clinic to ad hoc contact between the family and one of the helping agents. It includes referral to schools for maladjusted children, remedial teaching, home visits, or regular or occasional interviews with the parents at the clinic or at the school.

Usually it is better for the service to be taken entirely to the schools. One variety of this is in the West Riding, which has a plan for a number of centres offering full-time remedial education to classes of fifteen children each. The children attending remain on the books of their primary school, to ensure an effective link and to make a transfer back possible at any time. Short-term enrichment programmes of this kind, offered in the neighbourhood without the stigma of special education, can undoubtedly do much to reduce handicap.

In Liverpool, area teams have been set up with headquarters in one school but serving others in the area. The team leaders work out programmes in association with heads of schools, on the basis of individual or small group tuition, so that the service fits in with the normal pattern of the school's own work. Again this is an attempt to use scarce resources economically, but at the same time naturally, in the school setting and with close contact between class teachers, teams and specialists.

There is another purpose in the Liverpool scheme. The remedial teams work closely with the educational psychologist and with heads of schools to devise screening processes with a view to the early detection of more serious weakness. When a problem is referred to them, the remedial teams try to analyse it and if possible deal with it themselves. If, however, they suspect that reading difficulty may be the result of educational sub-normality or of some serious emotional disturbance, they refer the problem to the psychologist. After further investigation the question of special education may arise, but every attempt is first made to see what early remedial treatment can achieve in association with the school. This early intervention can often save considerably more trouble later, and, of course, the regular contact with schools can do a great deal to sensitize them to the needs of children with difficulties. An important practical point is that the contact between class teachers and outside specialists has two purposes: one is to help individual children and the other is to advise heads and their assistants about methods of teaching backward children generally.

## Immigrant children

It seems appropriate to follow consideration of problems of back-wardness by turning to the needs of immigrant children, if only to make the point that the two things are not identical. That they may be so considered is a reflection not so much of British insularity, perhaps, as of the suddenness with which immigration has become a problem for the schools.

The recent increase in numbers of these children, many of whom have serious linguistic handicaps, has caught the nation unawares. Anyone writing about this subject must have considerable misgivings: apart from the possibility of unintentionally giving offence or arousing controversy, no one knows enough about the problem to write with any confidence of avoiding error. The social and political factors related to immigration have made dispassionate discussion of educational issues almost impossible.

In this context the seductiveness of the arguments for not dealing specifically with immigrant children in a book about inequality of opportunity in education is increased considerably. They are valid arguments, too. For instance, immigrant or not, a child is first of all a child, and is entitled to be so considered. It is possible, also that the label 'immigrant' may be thought sufficient explanation of educational need, a comprehensive term prescribing a certain course of action in every sense. Yet there are many, many varieties of need amongst immigrants as amongst the resident population: any individual may have any or all the types of handicap we have discussed.

But we must go beyond this thinking. The problem does after all represent an extra burden for many schools, already struggling under other difficulties. And a book on educational handicap would be incomplete without at least some reference to the question, for immigrant children may be especially susceptible to a wide variety of handicapping influences. In particular, they often provide clear examples of environmental conditions adversely affecting a child's chances of success at school.

First, many have profound language difficulties. Second, large numbers live in conditions of poverty, insecurity of employment, and, particularly, overcrowding. Third, having had not only a change of school but a complete change of country can be a setback in itself. Finally there are often cultural differences that may prevent an immigrant child from becoming attuned to our schools.

It is a natural tendency amongst many who are kindly disposed towards immigrants to want to minimize the differences, to behave as if they did not exist. But if these differences are ignored handicap may go undetected, and this is not in the best interests of the community or of the people concerned. Early identification is always important where there is a risk of handicap. Keeping separate records, from primary schools to Youth Employment Service, is never popular amongst people of good will, because of the implication of segregation and possible prejudice. But in the context of our enquiry into educational handicap the fact of being an immigrant is highly relevant and should be recorded.

For one thing, it will emphasize to anyone who has to teach such a child that home–school liaison will be even more important than usual. Many parents from overseas are much more enthusiastic about their children's education than their resident opposite numbers. Yet they will tend to know very much less about our system, often to have different cultural standards, and sometimes to speak their native language in the home. Sometimes in fact classes for parents may be almost as important as special attention to the language problems of a child.

Authorities with substantial numbers of immigrants may find it advisable to provide reception centres for children where their capacities and problems can be thoroughly examined, and where they can be sympathetically prepared for school life. The school itself is unlikely to have such resources: the nearest equivalent may seem to be a remedial class, but this is very far from the same thing. As with all children with environmental handicaps it is important (however hard it may be) to try to get beyond the external appearances to the truth beneath. Nervousness, strangeness, language problems may all give a false impression of an immigrant child's abilities and attitudes.

A major question in some areas is whether the reception centre idea should not be prolonged to the extent of providing separate schools or classes for newcomers from overseas. Quite apart from social questions, authorities are likely to consider this only as a last resort: segregation as an educational instrument is decreasing, not increasing, in this country. Housing problems leading to sudden increases in immigrant population in certain areas where older sub-let accommodation can be had, can, however, completely transform a school and perhaps give it too great a burden of children with learning difficulties. Teacher shortages do not help, but, if possible, reception centres and subsequent additional help within the neighbourhood school by specially appointed teachers seem preferable to distribution of children over wider areas by use of special transport. But dispersal may be essential. Sometimes, in fact, the educational problem can only be solved through housing policies.

The implications of these factors for the training of teachers in specialist skills are profound. The teaching of English as a second language to children in the one class from as many as six or seven different linguistic and cultural backgrounds is a specialist skill not normally a part of initial teacher training. Further, the direct-teaching methods needed, whilst familiar to the infant-trained teacher, are almost entirely unknown to her secondary-trained counterpart. For the most part, teachers have had to cope, and to cope under considerable strain.

Authorities have tackled the problem in different ways; in Birmingham for example, specially trained peripatetic teachers take special classes in different schools, provide support and encouragement to the class teachers, and offer in-service training to teachers at an authority centre. The I.L.E.A. also organizes in-service courses for its teachers at a specially equipped centre which is attended by children requiring extra help with language. Other authorities provide crash courses varying in length from a few days to series of meetings throughout the term, as in Preston County Borough. These sessions are invaluable to teachers but of course they are limited by time in the extent to which they can cover all facets of the training required.

In some authorities immigrant teachers have been employed but unless their own language development is of sufficiently high standard, to employ them as teachers of immigrant children may be to confound the confused. However, immigrant teachers can be invaluable in interpreting to their colleagues the cultural factors which cannot be separated from language teaching. Early on, some schools made the mistake of believing that they had only to teach the immigrants English, and all other difficulties would eventually dissolve, but this failed to take into account the fact that language is but an expression of a culture. For a teacher to help a child from Pakistan to speak English, he must know about the cultural heritage of Pakistan, about the social and religious constraints on this child. The importance of this kind of knowledge for teachers of immigrant children is pin-pointed by Horacio Ulibarri in an essay in *Education and Social Crisis* (1967). He points out that teachers generally value achievement, success, competition and even aggression;

> The teachers, therefore, use praise, competitiveness, and
> pressure as some of their motivating practices. Children
> from different cultural backgrounds may not have internalized
> any of these values and may not respond to these types of
> motivation. Hence, if teachers are unaware of cultural
> differences in the motivation of children, motivational
> structures such as drive, reward and punishment, and level
> of aspiration may become very unreal to children with

cultural orientations different from those of middle-class society.

The unsympathetic school, or the sensitive but ill-informed school, may inadvertently cause much distress to the Indian Sikh child, who cannot eat beef, and the Muslim child, who cannot eat pork. (It is surely not necessary to comment on the schools which give a wink and say that they continue to cook the food in beef or pork fat, and as long as the children do not know they are quite happy. Compare this with, say, Spring Grove School in Huddersfield, which provided extra protein vegetables for the children who preferred not to eat meat.) (Burgin and Edson, 1967.)

Similar problems can arise for Muslim girls, who must not show bare arms or legs in front of boys, unless they are to risk their status as individuals in the eyes of the community. Physical education may therefore be difficult and mixed bathing impossible.

The school may argue that the children ought to conform to the British way of doing things, and that in this way they will more easily be accepted as a part of our society. This has a certain appeal, but misses the point of the differences and assumes that 'our ways' are better than 'their ways'. In practice, some immigrant groups do seek to identify with the host community in as many ways as possible (it may largely be rejection on the part of the host community which prevents this) but often this kind of adaptation takes place over two or three generations. On the other hand, the newly arrived immigrant often clings to the culture of his native country and he may regard himself as merely a temporary resident and speak of the time when he will return to his own country. For such groups, imposition of new cultural norms would be undesirable and impractical. It is the succeeding generations which identify with the culture into which they are born. An understanding and sympathetic education system can do much to ease this transition period, which may well prove difficult for the parent generation clinging to old ways and the new generation seeking an independence unknown to their parents.

Immigrant children are in one sense a very separate, special, problem. In another sense, however, an influx of non-English speaking children throws into focus once again the fact that handicaps are rarely isolated manifestations, that language and culture are inextricably related.

## Strengthening the school

All schools need to adapt themselves in the light of our growing knowledge of the causes of disadvantage in children. For some a transformation may be needed. We cannot expect them to make these changes unaided, and for some the implied tension between the demands of specialists and the need to see children as a whole to which we have referred, may seem like a joke in doubtful taste, in view of the realities of the resources they can call upon. Others will undoubtedly regard specialists as inessential and irrelevant as long as primary school classes are as big as they are.

Concern to reduce class sizes and the possible employment of outside specialists are not necessarily aspects of fundamentally differing attitudes. Both are undoubtedly needed; indeed a major effort to reduce primary class sizes is essential. It is no use asking class teachers to become aware of their children's individual needs or to link with outside experts if they are daily confronted with the need to teach groups so large that this sensitivity is impractical. Smaller classes are a prerequisite of advance.

Nevertheless it is not helpful merely to assert that more of everything is needed. Priorities have to be established, and this is not easy, even if there is general agreement about targets. Very few people now dispute the logic of Plowden, that we should place greater emphasis on the needs of primary schools, particularly those with a preponderance of underprivileged children. Yet turning the tide of the flow of resources is overwhelmingly difficult. The greater number of teachers trained for primary schools emerging from the colleges in the late 1960's coincided by happy chance with this acceptance of the Plowden ethos. Unfortunately it also coincided with a period of economic stringency for local education authorities, and in this situation neither the Department of Education and Science nor the Government as a whole could do anything to make authorities employ any extra primary school teachers. The quota of teachers imposed on the authorities fixes an upper, not a lower limit, and it has nothing to say about the relative proportions of primary and secondary teachers to be employed. Thus, although everyone agrees in theory that early effort is best in combating educational and social handicap, the machinery for putting agreement into practice is cumbersome and unreliable.

This is another aspect of the uncertainties and imprecisions inherent in our kind of democracy, to which the opening chapter referred. No one is able to state unequivocally what the priorities should be, and then to ensure they are observed. For instance, the influence of teachers' associations is considerable in making decisions about the priorities of deploying teacher resources. Different associations have somewhat different views, but their main emphasis recently has been on general reduction of class sizes. This from the associations' viewpoint is of course a legitimate objective and most people would agree that an overall reduction in primary school class size would enable much greater assistance to be given to the disadvantaged children within those classes. Yet as a general principle it cannot easily be reconciled with the Plowden concept of educational priority areas, nor with the concentration of specialist teacher resources on small groups of less able pupils, both of which try to single out the greatest needs and give them extra help as a first priority.

Again, when it comes to specialization, although local education authorities control the purse strings, their relationship with the schools is usually such that heads are given reasonable—often total—freedom to deploy the above-scale salary allowances that are usually paid for specialist work. This means that the policy of the head is often the most influential factor in deciding what kind of specialist teachers are appointed.

Obviously this is a major reason for the great variety of provision, and it can to some extent be justified by pointing to the great variety of need in individual schools. But this is to leave too much to chance. Local education authorities can influence the situation. They can of course take direct action to ensure that certain appointments are made. And if the freedom of heads to allocate their resources is to be preserved they can still exert strong indirect influence, for example by their policy in seconding teachers for extra training, by running in-service courses of their own, and by influencing heads through advisers, conferences, and so on. They have very little influence on the pattern of full-time initial teacher training. So far as specialist appointments are concerned, this is largely a question of the training institutions attempting to assess demand in advance and then trying to meet it. It is hardly surprising that most of them change so little: no college wants to run the risk of producing specialists who are unable to use their expertise later. Yet this can happen. This is partly because L.E.A.s are often themselves uncertain of their needs, partly because our system of government and finance for education makes it very hard to plan ahead.

The first requirement, then, is for something extremely difficult to bring about—long-term planning of specialist teaching needs by the authorities. The second is for something equally difficult— better planning of the output of the training institutions. This is very largely outside the control of the L.E.A.s.

Expenditure on teacher training by local education authorities has since 1944 been pooled, perhaps an inevitable device, since not all local education authorities provide colleges but all need to employ their products. But this has meant that the individual authority's influence on what goes on in a college has been less than if it had a direct financial commitment. (Now that the colleges have been given considerably more independence, in line with their increasing orientation towards the universities, the local education authority's influence will be even less.) Some colleges of education are provided by the churches and they work directly with the Department of Education and Science. The universities, in their Departments of Education, provide courses of training, and the authorities have no control over these; nor, in fact, does the Department of Education and Science. The shaping of the direction of teacher training is by the staffs of the institutions and by the University-dominated Institutes of Education.

One result is that in courses with social work, counselling, or similar emphasis there is an unhelpful variety of practice. Keele, Reading, Exeter and Leeds University Institutes of Education offer courses. So does the Manchester University Department of Education. A few colleges of education are experimenting with varying degrees of specialism: notably the revised full-time course at Edge Hill College. The Tavistock Institute of Human Relations has a course of its own based on case-work seminars. Youth Leadership training is an optional element in some dozen colleges of education, including Edge Hill, which also has as a subsidiary course an introduction to educational development, and one on the teaching of immigrant children. There is a similar picture in relation to specialization in backwardness, and the various forms of educational handicap associated with special education.

Training problems do not end there. If teachers are to co-operate with all the statutory agencies we have mentioned, as well as the multiplicity of voluntary bodies, their training must take this into account. Adequate training for teachers specializing in social work needs to be inter-professional. Further, if we accept that all teachers must be attuned to the importance of environmental influences in their children there is a clear case for all initial teacher training to have an inter-professional flavour. (There is, of course, a strong argument on other grounds for replacing the present monotechnic structure of colleges of education by some form of liberal arts college and/or multi-professional training organization. Eighteen is very young for someone to choose a profession like teaching, and thereafter spend three years training exclusively for it.) Meanwhile, as normally happens in this country, a few pioneers are arguing for the idea and experimenting with less revolutionary approaches.

A handful of people concerned with training teachers, youth and community workers, and social workers have been exploring in recent years the possibilities of training members of these three professions within the one institution. The idea was to bring the three groups of students together at certain points of their course where there is an overlap of interests, and at the same time to give them an opportunity for some practical experience in a profession other than their own. After the initial idea was mooted a working party was established to keep the idea alive, to sponsor conferences and encourage the setting up of local inter-professional groups. At an Interprofessional Conference held in Reading in September 1969, teacher trainers and social workers met together to discuss courses of interprofessional training as the basis of a possible research project. At this meeting, many people felt that whilst teacher training courses had much to learn from social work training methods, and social work training could learn from teacher training, it was not practical or perhaps even necessary to provide integrated initial courses of training. However, there was strong support for the idea of bringing social workers and teachers together at an in-service level, when both groups would have had practical day to day experience on which to draw. Courses like this would go a considerable distance towards improving communications between these professions, and it would be improved communication based upon a real understanding of each other's roles.

In the long term, improvement in the schools' handling of their responsibilities towards the disadvantaged must depend to a large extent on improvements in the pattern of training. The local education authorities ought logically to play a greater part in setting this pattern (and, in the process, clarifying their own objectives). Indeed the local authorities as a whole, not just education authorities, should be involved, since the pattern of training for other specialists outside teaching is even more chaotic. Here is a field in which the Department of Education and Science could forget for a while its preoccupation with control and take the initiative in bringing together all the interested parties to hammer out a policy for the future.

How realistic this proposal may be hinges on the question of the Department's relationship with the other partners in the service. There is no direct financial link between the Department of Education and Science and local education committees, which is a grave handicap in the way of national influence over local educational policies. The link between the D.E.S. and the University Departments of Education is even more tenuous, for basically the University Grants Commission decides how much within the overall national provision each university gets, and the universities decide how to allocate it. Even within the college of education sector, control is limited. As many of the colleges of education are voluntary, run by the churches, this again places the emphasis on persuasion rather than direction from the top. On the other hand, the Department is in a strong position in relation to maintained colleges of education, since it administers the national pool on behalf of local education authorities. On these it has made its influence felt, for example in planning the total output of the colleges and the balance between primary and secondary training. Unfortunately manpower planning is one of the hardest tasks in a democracy, and there have been wild fluctuations in the quality of the exercise, not all of them of course the fault of the Department. In any event, what is needed is more than quantitative control, and national policy has to influence the whole of teacher training, not just the colleges of education.

Achieving this would create the distinct possibility of impinging on the traditional freedom of universities, and therefore the chances of substantial change are not great. Still there is room for initiative. All the checks and balances tend to cause inertia which means that there is a power vacuum. It has been wisely said that the vehicle which moves best through a vacuum is a bandwaggon; and there are many less desirable bandwaggons than this.

## Parents and parent-substitutes

The school's role in relation to disadvantaged children logically centres on extra help in the classroom for them, and a generally more sensitive approach to their education. Yet although school can have a profound influence, it normally extends only to some five or five and a half hours a day on five days a week, for less than forty weeks a year.

This book has a good deal to say about the importance of relations between home and school. At this point we need to look briefly at circumstances when the day school may be fighting a a losing battle for a child's future, when the parents contribute little or nothing, or are a negative influence. Broken homes, or those unbroken but under strain; shockingly overcrowded homes; homes full of cruelty or massive indifference; corrupt or criminal parents—these factors may be too much for a school to try to counteract.

Of all the difficulties of intervention, perhaps the greatest is when we reach the point where the only thing for it is to remove the child from his home. Sometimes the law may take the step, and the child will come under the care of the local authority. Sometimes a boarding school may be the answer.

A serious problem about boarding education for the disadvantaged is that, in cases where it may be most needed, the parents may be least willing to agree. Resentment at intrusion, the fact that a child may be handy around the house, or a fecklessness that seems incapable of even accepting reduction in the number of problems, can all prevent a child having the opportunity for a fresh start. Then again it usually cannot be contemplated for very young children, though in some ways they might benefit most from the opportunity. For these children, hostel accommodation reasonably near their homes may be an answer: younger children in difficulties, for whom boarding education is too severe a change, might still attend their local day school and visit home occasionally but have the protection of a secure residential environment at critical times in their lives. In other cases a short period of close observation might be valuable; sometimes potential maladjustment might be checked by closer supervision or more attention than the home can give. Some parents would, of course, resist this as they resist boarding education and any other form of help, but many might be glad to use the facility, and others might more easily be persuaded to this rather than permanent commitment to a distant boarding school.

Boarding accommodation has the serious disadvantage of being highly expensive, so it can probably only be considered in the most urgent cases. It is only then, however, that intervention to this extent can be justified. The important thing is to use the resource, if it exists, to the full. Shorter-term provision early on will not only enable more children to benefit in this way, but also be likely to do more good.

One important problem that besets many attempts to help the handicapped is that schools, including boarding schools, have holidays. These long intervals can sometimes undo much of the good during the previous term; this is another case for hostels. But the holidays need to be filled in other ways too. Sometimes the disadvantaged might benefit more from extra tuition during holidays than from the break itself. Ventures such as the Northope Hall scheme near Leeds can do a great deal: this provides a short-stay holiday home for children at risk socially, and helps to keep them out of trouble by giving them something to look forward to other than their own unsatisfactory home environment. Sir Alec Clegg, impressed by the French Colonies de Vacances (community holidays with a strong cultural flavour), successfully introduced a variant in the West Riding. This had the extra advantage of involving the youth service in running the scheme: fifty eight-to-ten-year-olds were looked after by twenty-five teenage girls.

## Youth service

This particular venture, interesting and valuable in itself, points to another series of possibilities for supporting the main-stream activities of schools. Presenting the challenge of social service to young people can give purpose and direction to youth work quite apart from the direct benefit. Links between secondary schools and youth clubs and nursery schools or playgroups can be a great advantage to both. The youth service is in need of orientations such as this, that can give it purpose and life: with such reinterpretations it can be of direct value to the schools.

In the early post-war days the aspirations of the youth service seemed to rise little higher than keeping young people off the streets, and the schools seemed convenient places in which to do it. The premises were used for activities that seemed to concentrate mainly on dancing. To many heads of schools this became something of a nuisance: apart from possible damage and the problems of dual use of premises, there seemed to some a threat to day school discipline through the totally different evening activities and attitudes of school-age youth club members. For the young people, especially the unclubbable for whom the Albemarle Report expressed concern, the tie-up with school was a deterrent to participation. Thus the youth service and the schools tended to drift apart.

The youth service, in some areas at least, has more serious purposes than clubs and play. The Young People's Consultation Centre in Hampstead is an example: it is, as the name implies, a freely accessible place where young people can get confidential advice from skilled professional workers: The Open Door provides a similar service in Birmingham. Liverpool is experimenting with unattached 'leaders' who mingle with young people in their ordinary activities. The common thread is that of counselling. It seems possible that work of this kind could link once again, to their mutual benefit schools and youth service. A scheme of this kind run by a secondary school could be an experiment in counselling for those not yet convinced that the concept should be introduced into the affairs of the school itself.

## Nursery education

It may be generally agreed, however, that the most valuable outside support that could be given to the schools is a substantial increase in nursery education facilities, particularly in underprivileged areas. The earlier good educational influences can be brought to bear on children from broken, neglectful or generally chaotic homes, the better. If educational need is made the first criterion for admission, and the activities the schools pursue reflect the purpose of the provision, a great deal can be done to ensure that some of the children with the greatest environmental handicaps are brought much nearer to starting their infant schooling on equal terms with their more fortunate fellows.

In the nature of things evidence of the beneficial influence of nursery education is hard to come by. The research by Douglas and Ross (1964) reaches this rather bleak conclusion:

> The educational findings of this study may be summarised as follows: at eight years, children who have attended Local Education Authority Nursery Schools or Classes make slightly higher scores in tests of ability and school performance than children who went straight into infant schools at five. This is not owing to better skill in reading—indeed the boys from the nursery school group read rather less well at eight than would be expected from their performance in the picture intelligence test given at that age, and the girls read no better than expected. Nor is it explained by the family background of these children as described by crude measures such as social class, standard of maternal care, family size or standard of housing. Between 8 and 11 the nursery school children lose their initial advantage in measured ability, and by 15 they all do slightly less well than expected—in no year, however, are the differences statistically significant.
>
> Reports on the behaviour of these children suggest that nursery school attendance is not followed by better than average emotional adjustment or less delinquency in later life.

But it goes on:

> The conclusion to be drawn depends, however, on the original selection of the children and it may well be that a group who were highly vulnerable at entry have been given substantial help.

We shall not, of course be able to prove or disprove this, but it seems a sensible assumption.

Two other points seem relevant. Could the decline in initial advantage for these children be the result of years of contact with schools whose basic attitudes and outlook differed so markedly from those of children of this kind as to put them, in the end, at a disadvantage? If so the importance of all teachers understanding the backgrounds of the children they teach is underlined once again.

The second point is related to this. If it is true that the basically middle-class orientation of the average school puts working-class children at a disadvantage, one remedy might be, as just suggested, deeper understanding of these children's problems and a shift of emphasis in primary and secondary schools towards methods and attitudes less likely to handicap them. But another might well be to use nursery education less as an attempt to introduce under-privileged children to the standards of the better off, and more as a way of preparing them linguistically and in habits of thought for the learning situation in the infant school. If nursery education is to assist the schools to make a reality of equal educational opportunity then it should work purposefully to that end.

Bereiter and Engelmann, in their arresting book *Teaching Disadvantaged Children in the Preschool,* have argued convincingly that pre-school provision which progresses at the normal rate is no real use in helping disadvantaged children catch up. They show that language deficiencies for these children are not deficiences in vocabulary and grammar as such, but failure to master certain uses of language.

> Language for the disadvantaged child seems to be an aspect of social behaviour which is not of vital importance. The disadvantaged child masters a language that is adequate for maintaining social relationships and for meeting his social and material needs, but he does not learn how to use language for obtaining and transmitting information, for monitoring his own behavior, and for carrying on verbal reasoning. In short, he fails to master the cognitive uses of language, which are the uses that are of primary importance in school.

They suggest therefore that pre-school education for these children should have specific academic goals, describe the results of a successful experiment with this technique and present a most thorough and detailed programme.

Nursery education is not cheap, and pressure from the statutory sectors of the service makes any widespread extension unlikely in the immediate future. Substantial increase at present can only come about through the Urban Programme for socially-deprived areas, which implies concentration on the needs of the disadvantaged in order to try to give them something nearer an equal chance when they start primary school. If then we are to make this provision we must be sure it is effective.

One practical point might be mentioned, in relation to expense and making best use of scarce resources. Part-time provision is one obvious way in which the advantages of nursery education can be spread more widely. Many people dislike this and point out how much more can be done with the children in a full-time course.

Yet can it? It is doubtful if young children are ready for a full day's activities, particularly of the purposeful kind we have advocated: one result is that they may spend part of the day in sleep. This is an expensive way of giving children a rest. There are cases where children would not otherwise get any, but this is an aspect of day-time care rather than pre-school education. If children attend the nursery on a part-time basis, rest and supervision can if necessary be given separately without the attention of qualified teachers.

In this context we must consider other pre-school provision such as day nurseries run by Health Departments. Here priority for admission is given according to parental need rather than that of the child, and education is not normally attempted. Full-time care may be offered as a social service, say, because a widowed mother needs to go out to work to support a child. Of course the child may have other handicaps as well as having no father, and may be in need of pre-school education. Closer links with nursery schools, even if joint administration is impossible, could increase the possibilities of part-time education for these children. High standards are usually set in these day nurseries, and from parents' point of view they have the advantage of being open for longer periods in the year than the school holidays. They too are expensive, however, and scarce.

Standards in privately run nurseries are naturally variable and, as an educational counterbalance to environmental handicap, clearly limited. The same is true of pre-school play groups, a voluntary movement now trying to gain stronger national support. At present legal responsibility for assisting them rests with Health Departments, though many of their organizers see the need for an educational orientation if they are to be more than mere child-minding exercises. Some education authorities give advice on methods of using play constructively as an aid to preparation for school; others allow free or low-rental use of premises and provide equipment: although of doubtful legality, it has been done as a modest gesture of support.

Against their undoubted if limited value and relatively low cost, there is the disadvantage that, being voluntary, they tend to flourish in better areas amongst higher income-groups. Recent experiments in educational priority areas have shown that groups can be started there with advantage not only to the children but to their mothers, in giving them experience of participation in useful community activity. Older pupils in secondary schools can also both benefit and give a useful service by assisting in such ventures.

## Summary

We have tried in this chapter and the previous two to give a brief picture of some of the present methods of detecting and treating the problems of disadvantaged children, some of the difficulties faced by the specialist services and by the schools, and, inevitably, some of their shortcomings. Any picture of this kind is bound to be inadequate. Apart from questions of space and the need, in description, to consider separately things that are really facets of a many-sided whole, the situation is changing rapidly. In any event, in a system of local government and of education such as ours, it is impossible to generalize.

There can be no definitive description. Our aim has been rather to focus on some of the more important aspects of an evolving pattern as a basis for the rest of the book in which we shall look, increasingly, to the future.

# The team approach

## six

Changing attitudes, developing knowledge, growing awareness of the complexity of the problem—all these mean that the challenge presented by inequality of educational opportunity will have to be met in future by a response that is flexible yet well organized. It is by now a commonplace to suggest that future advance will depend in large measure on how successfully co-operation can be developed amongst the various agencies concerned with social work, and between these agencies and the schools. We need to venture beyond the platitude to try to see what it entails in practice.

## Who does what

The first essential is that all those involved should be clear about their own roles and their relationship with other agencies. This is the basis of any successful team-work. It presents formidable problems. Even to describe the inter-play of the various services is a difficult task. The diagram on page 102 presents in a simplified form some of the agencies with whom a school may be concerned.

The school is at the centre of the circle. This may mean that it is the focal point of attention, as Kellmer Pringle suggested that it should be. But the phrase implies a degree of deliberate, co-ordinated intent on the part of the outside agencies that bears no relation to reality. And the corollary is that from the teacher's point of view he may seem to be so surrounded by possibilities as to feel hemmed in by them.

This it bad enough in itself, and made very much worse by a number of things: (i) handicaps do not fall neatly into these compartments; (ii) all the services indicated may not exist, or may have different names or even functions; (iii) there may be (indeed

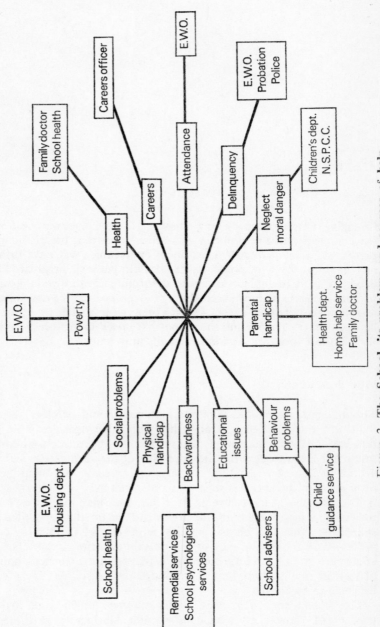

Figure 3. **The School, its problems and sources of help**

there are) other agencies; (iv) the functions of the agencies overlap; (v) solutions frequently cannot be found between a school and one agency—other agencies and other people may wish to be involved; (vi) there is no agreement about how far schools should deal with problems themselves: practice varies between schools and between different disciplines; (vii) the quality of services and of schools varies tremendously.

These problems will not be solved by drawing diagrams, but it is not unusual for schools to know little of what services are available and who deals with what, so that perhaps even a simple chart would help. If one were produced for the schools in their areas by the local education authorities it could be shaped according to their own particular pattern of services.

This might also be useful for the social work agencies who, astonishingly, are sometimes only vaguely aware of each other's functions or even existence. It would certainly be valuable for educational administrators who, unless they have particular experience in special education or related fields (which is rare), tend to have very sketchy ideas about what goes on in their own authorities in what may be regarded as peripheral matters.

However, the diagram would need to be rather more complicated to convey anything of the relationships of the various services. Each of the agencies on the perimeter of the circle that surrounds the school is in turn the centre of a circle of activity of its own. These circles overlap each other like the activities they represent, and they overlap the school's own circle. The diagram should in fact look something like this:

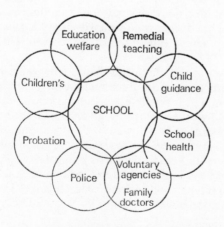

Figure 4. **Overlapping areas of concern**

In fact each of the circles tends to overlap with a considerable number of the others and to move in and out of the school's ambit. Even more important, the circles are more like the tips of tentacles than self-activating units. They are the extremities of a number of different, but again inter-related, administrative headquarters. The picture—again much over simplified, is something like that on page 105. The freedom of movement of these tentacles is normally restricted and the natural tendency of those at the tip is to refer problems that they cannot easily settle themselves back to the point of anchorage. From there, it need not be emphasized, movement is not so easy.

As a simple example, consider a child in trouble because of absence from school, a problem which could not be handled by an Education Welfare Officer on his own. Yet even though the Education Welfare Officer wished to co-operate only with the child care officer in his area there might well come a point at which he might feel that his delegated authority did not extend to doing this alone. For instance if there were any question of bringing a child before the juvenile court, or his parents before the magistrates, the Education Welfare Officer would need to refer the matter back to his headquarters, who in turn might need to report to a committee.

Of course co-operative arrangements are made, but they usually depend on the administrators at base rather than the field workers. There may well be five or six possible agencies involved in any one case, and if each one is dependent on co-operation at headquarters the possible difficulties can be imagined. Time may be crucial, and co-operation between bureaucratic organizations is likely to be slower than that in the field because the legal and administrative framework of organizations is essentially static. Inter-departmental information and decisions depend on communications travelling up lines of command, across to opposite numbers in other departments and down again, and this takes time even if it does not fail at some stage.

What is needed in the kind of problem with which we are mainly concerned is something more dynamic, an inter-play of ideas, support, information and if possible active decision making in the field. For this the field-worker has to be given freedom to act and make decisions: if he cannot be allowed to do this alone (and there may be good reason for that) he has to be allowed to co-operate with his opposite numbers and reach decisions collectively, on the principle that if all the experts in the field agree no one back at base is likely to be able to make better decisions. Once this freedom is given the wide variety of approaches begins to look more like an opportunity than a hazard.

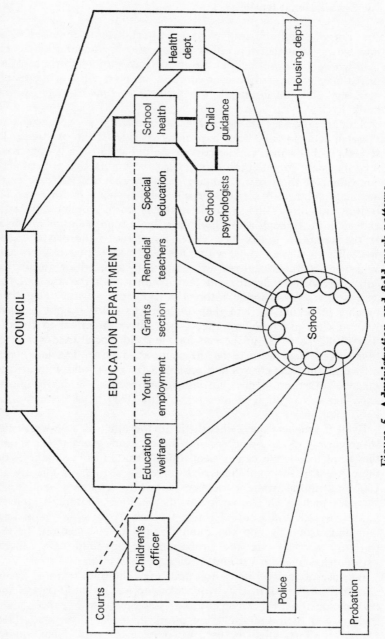

Figure 5. **Administration and field work patterns**

### Inter-professional tensions

But not only administrative compartmentalism is involved. The narrowness of angle from which approaches are sometimes made by field-workers themselves and the restrictions they impose on themselves may in the end be even more inimical to constructive teamworking. This unfortunately is a theme that runs throughout this book.

Similar processes of development in relation to specialism to those in schools have been happening outside. If the counsellor in schools is the trained counterpart of the old-style socially-conscious schoolmaster, so the professional case-worker is the present day equivalent of the early voluntary social worker before there were any national health services or council housing. Growing specialization in many of the social services has led to a demand for specialists in the difficult art of looking at human problems as a whole. In the nature of things there is tension between the two kinds of specialist, as there may be within a school between counsellors and subject teachers. Sometimes direct action by a health or housing or education welfare department may conflict with the aims of the case-worker: for example, a threat of legal action against neglectful parents in failing to send their children to school might perhaps have adverse psychological effects—say, drive the father to drink—that would be worse in the end for the child. Social case-work can thus to outsiders seem to be the same as inaction. Teachers, concerned about their classes and schools as a whole, and with a wide range of other problems than individual cases of hardship, inevitably tend to align themselves with the outsiders in this confrontation.

Even if teachers are sympathetic to the aims of case-work, the sheer variety of case-workers and the necessarily circumspect way they tend to operate can present difficulties. On the voluntary side there are the National Society for the Prevention of Cruelty to Children, moral welfare workers from the churches, children's societies such as Dr Barnardo's or the National Children's Homes, family service units, the Family Welfare Association, Marriage Guidance Councils and the Family Planning Association. In the statutory services are the probation officer, child care officer, psychiatric social worker and medical social worker.

Because of their proliferation and fragmentation, learning about what they do and how they work takes up a substantial part of the time of social work training courses. How then can we expect headmasters and their staffs to know about them, let alone study how their own efforts might be used to complement rather than conflict with them? The problem would be difficult enough if all these people regularly kept in touch with the schools concerned. But they do not. From the headmaster's study there may seem to be nothing happening. If in these circumstances a school blunders into a delicate case-work situation it can scarcely be blamed. Is it the duty of a school to enquire who else may be involved with a pupil before acting in what may be a crisis? Is there not some obligation on the social workers to make their activities known to the schools?

It would be wrong to generalize. There may be occasions when there is no need to keep a school informed, and even times when it may be better not to do so. Sometimes a child's problem may be entirely outside the school, which may be the only place where relationships are normal, and in these circumstances a social worker's report might well bring self-consciousness into the school's attitude towards the child. Confidentiality is also important. But there does seem to be a tendency to regard the school as a source of information rather than a repository of it. A child guidance psychiatrist, for instance, may grow very angry about a school's failure to detect or report problems early enough, but be remarkably thoughtless about informing the school of the progress he is making with a child-client, and remarkably slow to see the connection between his failure and that of the school. Regardless of any detailed information that could be passed on, merely knowing that a child or his family are in touch with a casework agency may help a teacher to give a better education to some child through understanding more about his background.

Quite apart from casework it can sometimes seem, ironically, that the schools that care most can encounter the most hostile reaction from other agencies. This tends to arise when schools step beyond the bounds of what their social worker colleagues think is proper. This may be the result of social workers underestimating the potential contribution that teachers can make, but it can also stem from misguided enthusiasm by the school.

Home visiting is perhaps the biggest danger point. There is a very old story about certain homes being visited so often and by so many people that the key is left under the mat for the social workers to let themselves in without causing the householder to keep getting out of bed. But there are other hazards. If a school concerned about poor attendance decides to round up its absentees by knocking on the doors of their houses, the intention may be very praiseworthy and the object of the exercise apparently very simple. But unless the operation is done skilfully and in full co-operation with the Education Welfare Officer it may do more harm than good. If the need is for a simple round-up then it should not be necessary to take the teacher from his school to do it. If not, then expertise and full knowledge of the circumstances are needed. Then again absence may be the result of antipathy towards the school or a particular teacher, and another teacher may not be the best person to discover that.

The implication that teachers should concentrate their attention first of all on the school does not mean that they should take a narrow view of their obligations. A first aim could be to welcome into the school anyone who can help it to flourish, for example social workers and the parents of children with difficulties. At least some of the possible misunderstandings with social workers might be avoided by visits to the school; and at least some of the parents might come if made to feel welcome. There remains the hard core problem, on the one hand of parents who do not co-operate, on the other of social workers who will not or cannot. As a last resort the school staff must surely be free to act if no one else will.

A school that seeks to act in some matter that is normally the responsibility of an outside agency will be wise to see that its own house is in order first. If records are incomplete or there is failure to detect or report some symptom, or insensitive treatment of a disadvantaged child, the school is scarcely in a position to embark on a wider role. In any event it should be sure that it translates its concern into the most effective form of help for the child.

To emphasize as a first goal for the school the exacting but limited aim of detecting obstacles to equality of opportunity in education is not to try to confine the amount or quality of its social concern, but merely to suggest an appropriate way for a school to to express it; and one that may make working relationships with the agencies easier. The school is often in the best position to detect these obstacles, and sometimes it will be only sensible to overcome them without outside help. On other occasions it may be foolish to do so: for example, where there is fatigue or hunger in a child, it will usually be best to refer the matter to the E.W.O. He will then find out what he can: when he reports back he may have already referred the problem elsewhere for remedial action relating to the social problem, but there is then an important responsibility for the school in adjusting its teaching and pastoral services to compensate for the social lack through extra attention at school.

Similarly a learning difficulty may sometimes be influenced by emotional handicap. A teacher sensitive to this possibility will be wise to enlist the aid of the psychological service. If the psychologist can visit the school he can not only help the child but help the teacher to help the child: if treatment is given in a clinic, full exchange of information can achieve nearly the same result. The psychologist himself may wish to refer certain aspects of the problem to a psychiatrist, to the school doctor, a general practitioner or the E.W.O.: if the school is told what is happening then the teacher can perform a more useful function than, say, forsaking his classroom for a home visit, by adapting his approach at school to meet the child's need.

## Specialization

Co-operation between social agencies outside the schools suffers from the same—or even greater—lack of clarity over roles, and the same sterile inter-professional tensions. Dr Jessie Parfit (seconded by the I.L.E.A. to the National Bureau for Co-operation in Child Care, to investigate the possibilities of an information service in child care and welfare) advocates in an interesting article (*Concern,* Summer 1969) co-operation starting at the grass roots of professional work. She suggests that professionals should 'begin by doing everything in our power to communicate with the other professionals in our area who are concerned with children'. That such an elementary thing should have to be suggested is a sad commentary on what tends to happen. Self-esteem, excess of caution, pride in one's own craftsmanship and sheer thoughtlessness can all play their part. Not all the motives are discreditable—very often they include a perverted kind of conscientiousness—and they are motives shared by most of us. Yet their effect is one of the biggest obstacles to progress.

Dr Parfit says: 'The easiest way to strengthen co-operation is to improve our knowledge of each other's services and to appreciate the fact that light which is shed on one problem from many different angles helps towards a clearer understanding of what that problem is in depth.' Why then does it not happen more often in practice? Do the professionals not know that what Dr Parfit says is true? Almost all of them undoubtedly do. Are they always thwarted by the bureaucracy? Of course not: there are usually opportunities for co-operation of some kind for those who wish to take them. Dr Parfit gives five examples, partly fact and partly fiction, in which professionals put out feelers and made progress. A paediatrician involved in planning a new children's hospital visited children's homes, met the Medical Officer of Health and Children's Officer, play leaders, teachers, house parents and so on. A children's officer called in representatives of other departments, schools, youth clubs, voluntary agencies, churches, police, probation officers, and others to make a survey of all known facilities: this grew into an inter-disciplinary committee. A Child Guidance Clinic held discussions with medical, education and children's officers to plan a joint short-term stay assessment centre. An education officer planned his nursery provision in consultation with the Medical Officer of Health, Children's Officer and voluntary organizations to make best use of the facilities. A Medical Officer of Health arranged weekly conferences with educational psychologists, probation officer, police, housing officer, welfare officer, youth employment officer and so on.

Things can be done in just this way and there must be this spirit of co-operation if any scheme is to succeed. But it is not enough, particularly in big cities. If every professional suddenly became co-operation-minded the atmosphere would certainly be better, but the confusion might be very little less. This spirit is the basis for effective co-operation rather than the co-operation itself. The arrangements need planning and administrative cohesion if they are not eventually to fail through inanition or neglect.

Is the alternative amalgamation of departments or services? This is certainly some people's solution. But we know how hard it is for administrations to merge themselves into each other so that this is unlikely to be more than partly effective. In any event, within individual departments the tensions between branches can be just as great as those between departments. An approach more likely to succeed is one in which separate administrations agree to free their own field-workers to work and take decisions together as a team. Whatever the precise arrangements certain things seem essential.

First, they must be planned, not haphazard. They may be improvised but they should not be casual. Second, they must have administrative backing: they must be organized, not just allowed to happen by default. Third, they must hinge on full sharing of information, used in the way suggested by Dr Parfit to analyse the problem as a whole. Fourth, everyone involved must be clear about his own role and that of the other participants: claiming that new schemes obscure this issue is one of the oldest devices of those who do not want to change, but if the uncertainty is genuine the results will be disastrous. Fifth, the spirit must be willing. One difficult member can, if he wishes, wreck the most imaginative scheme. In practice this means that it is better for a team approach that the group should be small and co-operative than large and contentious.

## Local education authority schemes

This last point is a hint that schemes concerned mainly with educational handicap may be better if they attempt at first to do no more than weld together the services within education. If this is interpreted as including school health and child guidance it may be a big enough job in itself. A tightly knit group like this may also help in another respect—that of providing fairly clear-cut objectives. Even within education the scope is wide enough to give opportunities for failure through woolly-mindedness: if this scope is extended so that in the end it amounts to something as broad as doing good to others it becomes a recipe for disaster. The schemes we describe differ in their objectives, but are similar in aiming at reasonably specific targets.

## London

The first example is the *School Care Committee* pattern in the Inner London Education Authority. This scheme had its roots in the voluntary action committees set up at the turn of the century to cater for the many children who, by reason of poverty, malnutrition or poor health, were unable to take advantage of the education which was provided for them. The School Care Committee made use of voluntary work with helpers in each primary and secondary and special school in the Authority's area. These workers were recruited, trained, and guided by professional social workers called School Care Organizers, and they worked from local offices within the Authority's administrative divisions. Their work was planned by committees' representatives from heads of schools, organizers, and education committee members, as well as the social workers.

The objectives of the scheme are clear and far reaching and reflect the aims of the original voluntary committees.

> It is the duty of the School Care Committee, in constant contact with the Heads of Schools, to ensure that all children obtain full benefit from the education for which they are best suited by their aptitude and ability; to ascertain the needs of their families and in co-operation with all available statutory and voluntary services, endeavour to prevent or alleviate any physical, or mental stress within the family.
>
> (Craft, Raynor and Cohen, 1967.)

The emphasis upon co-operation of schools and ancillary social services again reflects the early pioneering work of the voluntary committees which were responsible for ensuring that medical recommendations were understood. Medical inspections helped the doctors to learn in more detail about particular family backgrounds from the voluntary workers. This aspect of their work was continued by the Care Committee, though the emphasis changed over the years from persuading parents of the value of routine medical care such as eyes, teeth or immunization to the modern need to interpret the work of the Child Guidance Clinic and the nature of psychiatric treatment.

Follow-up work with young school leavers in need of supportive work led to the development of the Young People's Advisory Service. Begun in 1957 in North Kensington, this aimed to establish a friendly relationship with young people in their final year of schooling. With a starting point in vocational preparation, the scheme encouraged the youngster to talk in a frank way of any problems and fears, hopes for the future. Again, workers in this scheme were voluntary, recruited from amongst married people with maturity and sensitivity to the needs of young people and perhaps experience in home visiting.

In 1964, the Authority decided to intensify outside assistance. They began in Lambeth with techniques that have since been extended to other areas of the city. Significantly the emphasis was placed on help at the infant stage: it included weekly visits to schools by voluntary care workers, assistance by secondary school pupils and the provision of an extra half-time helper in the reception class.

The main aim was to establish individual relationship between a child and an older person and the scheme was successful in resolving tensions leading to anti-social behaviour in school, in building up friendly contact with parents, and in freeing teachers from ancillary tasks, so that they could give more time to the children.

In 1965 the authority commissioned the Social Research Unit of the Department of Sociology, Bedford College, to undertake an independent enquiry into the welfare services for school children and to suggest improvements. The ensuing report considered that there was a need for better co-ordination and integration of the various parts of the education welfare service and a need for greater interchange of information between all the people involved with the education and welfare of children in inner London. They recommended a unified education welfare service with full recognition of the need for training of staff, both paid and voluntary.

On the basis of the recommendations of the Social Research Unit a new unified education welfare service was planned to operate from October 1970 in which combined area teams of educational welfare officers and voluntary workers (associated with the school care committees described above) became responsible for social work in groups of primary and secondary schools. The Schools Sub-Committee described the task of the new service as: '. . . not only to identify and assist children in social distress but to help foster close relationships between all parents and their children's school'.

The welfare teams are intended to keep in touch with parents of pre-school children, advising about pre-school activities, about school places, and about welfare to which they are entitled. Parents are encouraged to co-operate with schools and to ensure that their children make full use of the school health services. The teams, concerned also with behaviour difficulties, make recommendations for special treatment. They investigate irregular attendance and advise on appropriate action and are of course closely concerned with liaison with other welfare services.

In recommending the establishment of this unified service, the Schools Sub-Committee noted that school health service workers were excluded because of their important links with and membership of other medical services, and school psychologists were excluded because of their relationship with psychiatric teams. This exclusion illustrates the practical difficulties of securing effective organized co-operation amongst all the specialists. In view of the close link between many educational, welfare, health, and psychological problems it seems unfortunate that these practical difficulties could not be surmounted.

### Glasgow

In a somewhat different scheme pioneered by the Glasgow Education Committee, qualified social workers are attached to the staff of schools with direct responsibility to the head for social work. This service developed from a recognition of the need for more concentrated help for schools where juvenile delinquency was a very real problem, and an understanding of the importance of intensive parental contact in this situation. The concept of using social workers in this way was developed in the 1940s but was not finally adopted until 1957.

The social workers, who must hold a recognized professional case-work qualification, lead a team of welfare assistants, formerly school attendance officers, who have been seconded to a special modified course of social work training. They assist the School Welfare Officer by undertaking work related to clothing, lateness, neglect, etc., and also assist in case-work with individual families.

The scheme is administered by the Authority's School Attendance Department, and the aims, which differ somewhat from those of the Inner London Education Authority Scheme, reflect this orientation.

> To make contact with pupils with whom the officer is dealing and by various means direct them, the pupils, into interesting and profitable ways of spending their leisure time. It is not intended that the officer should concentrate wholly on the delinquent or potential delinquent or truant, but on those

conditions which will effect a reduction in the incidence of juvenile delinquency and truancy (Craft, Raynor and Cohen, 1967).

These aims also emphasize the concern with high delinquency areas, and envisage work mainly in the crisis situation.

The truant or child with behaviour difficulty referred to the School Welfare Officer sets in train a series of visits. The Officer visits the home and attempts to establish a working relationship with the child and his family. Some families, often with multiple handicaps, may require prolonged supportive case-work; others may require only one or two visits, and the difficulties can be attended to by the Welfare Assistant.

As the Officer is working with delinquent children and with 'problem families' every effort is made to work in co-operation with the statutory services which may also have occasion to be working with the same family. The close co-operation which has been established has enabled the Welfare Officer and the social worker to be constantly alert to the child 'at risk'. An example of a formalization of this co-operation is the Social Enquiry which is undertaken by the Welfare Officer for all pupils brought before the courts for truancy, or failure in attendance. The Social Enquiry makes recommendations based on the intimate knowledge of the Welfare Officer of the needs of the particular child.

Equally important is the relationship which exists between the Welfare Officer and the school staff. The invaluable knowledge of the home background of particular pupils can be interpreted to the class teacher and may help to explain some of the emotional factors influencing behaviour and poor attendance of the child. The issue of confidentiality could arise, but the relationship of mutual trust and respect which is built up between the teacher and the Welfare Officer ensures that the information is used in such a way as to give the child every opportunity to benefit from the school system.

## Oldham

In smaller areas there is room for a less tightly structured approach. In Oldham, which has had a comprehensive school organization in its development plan for many years, these schools are the focal point of a system of care committees, which normally operate through a school house organization. The early meetings were restricted to the senior members of staff and the Education Welfare Officers, but later representatives of the Children's Department, the Probation and School Health Services joined the group. In one school the group also included a local clergyman. The purpose was to pool information so that the families of children at the school could be helped.

Apart from this the Chief Education Welfare Officer has a weekly meeting with child guidance staff and medical officers from the Health Department; in addition he represents the Education Department at monthly meetings of the Town Co-ordinating Committee on which every social agency is represented. In this arrangement the Education Welfare Officer clearly shows himself capable of carrying out duties much more responsible than is often suggested: he is an important common factor in the co-ordinating arrangements at every level and his knowledge of family backgrounds is made available at key points in the services.

### Southampton

An interesting development began in Southampton in 1964. About that time there was an increase in juvenile crime in the central area of the town; there was also a feeling that parents were taking less interest in their children's schooling. It was decided to bring together teachers and social workers to see what could be done. It was accepted that teachers and social workers might not see eye to eye on particular issues, but clearly by pooling their information a course of action might be possible in the interests of both home and school.

An informal meeting was held between a group of teachers at two schools, one secondary, one primary, and an educational psychologist, a psychiatric social worker, the senior social caseworker, the Chief Education Welfare Officer and one of his colleagues. There was no set plan: the aim was to give an opportunity for the teachers to express ideas or complaints. These particular cases began to be discussed and from time time other social workers—child care officer, probation officer, family case-worker and youth leader—joined the group. The same family seen from different points of view was said to be an 'eye-opener to all parties'. This was felt to be the starting point for further progress.

Class teachers were involved from the beginning: the crux of the situation was thought to be communication between them and the social worker. Lack of knowledge was the chief obstacle, and even during the early meetings the teachers tended to become confused as to who did what. Eventually each specialist explained his own function, and the Chief Education Welfare Officer explained something of the relationship between all these overlapping agencies with the aid of a diagram used as a guide for referral by the Education Welfare Officer. The teachers accepted that the overlap was not necessarily a bad thing, provided there was co-operation: as to the complexity it was suggested that greater use of the Education Welfare Officer could help them to link up with the various agencies, and that he should be regarded as a member of the school.

After meeting monthly at first, the group settled on termly meetings at the secondary school. The aims were '(i) to get to know each other and (ii) to try and find some way of helping those children who were suffering from severe social handicap, and particularly to do all we could to prevent them being brought before the Magistrates' Court' (Luckhurst, 1969). After a year the first aim was thought to have been very satisfactorily achieved. The staff of the school learned a good deal about the various social services and which they could go to for help. Knowledge of each other's jobs helped to reduce duplication of effort.

At that stage however, little progress seemed to have been made with the second aim. Individual cases were considered and referred to members of the group for action but the processes of interview and diagnosis were lengthy and the existing case loads of the social workers were heavy. Parental co-operation was sought and usually, but not always, given. This was found to be a key factor in many aspects of the problem, for instance in arranging for preventive help by Probation Officers before an offence had been committed. Family visiting was increased and a useful working relationship with the Child Guidance Clinic was established.

A year later it was still not possible to make extravagant claims for the scheme, but it was felt that fewer cases needed to be discussed because of the scheme's efforts. Co-operative working between meetings also represented an advance, but the time lag in dealing with behaviour problems through initial referral to Child Guidance was still a problem. The overriding need was to give treatment as early as possible and the group realized that they had to make 'every effort to catch them young'.

*Liverpool*

We shall deal in rather more detail with the concept of the social education team developed in Liverpool. This is largely because, in the nature of things, we have more knowledge of this than other ventures. It is possible, for such is the haphazard nature of our education system in matters of research and innovation, that there are similar schemes operating elsewhere, though our enquiries suggest otherwise. In any event, it can at least be claimed that this is an interesting venture with features not seen in other schemes.

Characteristically, its beginnings owed more to pragmatism than research.

The Education Department felt the need for a new kind of specialist officer, one concerned with the detection and possible redress of social and environmental handicaps: this led to an examination of the orientation of the work of existing staff, notably the Education Welfare Officers. At the same time there was an urgent need to implement long-standing plans for the creation of a school psychological service to parallel the existing Child Guidance Service.

Discussions between Health and Education Departments on this second point produced different views about whether any new staff should owe first allegiance to Education or to Health services. In practice, as we have suggested earlier, any psychologists would have to work closely both with teachers and with doctors and specialists, and would have to be prepared to deal with children's problems that might be either 'educational' or 'health' in origin. Indeed, expressed in this way, the limitations of an approach to staffing on departmental lines were exposed. There followed a fuller analysis of the work of all officers serving the Education Committee who offered guidance to children and to schools. This, in turn, led to deeper study of the objectives of these services in schools and outside.

The process started from simple observation of the child in school. This showed for instance that:

1. social, physical and psychological factors influence the educational process, and mishaps in education may stem from causes outside the school;
2. one mishap may be a symptom of another, e.g. poor attendance or something more serious;
3. children with one handicap may well have others (e.g. those with emotional problems may find learning difficult).

The conclusion, equally elementary, was that it would be wise to consider the child as a whole and not as a possible manifestation of some particular handicap.

It seemed also in Liverpool that one type of handicap tended to crop up most in certain environments that also produced a greater incidence of other handicaps. Thus, one of the worst districts for serious attendance problems was also the area from which most pupils in e.s.n. and other special schools originated, and one in which there were many behaviour problems. It was a district with poorer school buildings than elsewhere and with many staffing difficulties. The same district was high on the priority list of the children's and housing departments and the police. The conclusion was that children's handicaps should be

A.E.C.—I

considered in the context of their environment and notably the family.

What of the resources available in the district? First, there were teachers in the schools, struggling to teach children but baulked by absences, misbehaviour, inability to respond, and so on. There were Education Welfare Officers who were called in to deal with cases of poor attendance, working within a system of reference back ultimately to a committee considering whether to prosecute or not. There were doctors and nurses in the School Health Service concerned mainly with health problems but having all manner of information about children and their families as a result of their work, information that was either unused or used too late. There were psychologists and psychiatrists, social workers, and remedial teachers, trying to diagnose and treat behaviour and learning problems. Their paths crossed those of children's officers, probation officers, the police juvenile liaison officers and housing department officials, not to mention various voluntary agencies.

Each had a specialism and therefore a tendency to look at a child from that angle. Each worked within an administrative framework that encouraged him to reject cases falling outside his own ambit and to refer bigger problems back to his own headquarters rather than across to colleagues working in the field. At best this seemed a recipe for inertia, for children falling between six or seven stools, perhaps being regarded as cases fitting (or not fitting) a particular professional and administrative outlook. Although everyone working in the field did his best to work with others, there was no machinery of co-ordination.

The Education Committee decided first to re-organize their services in this area. They brought together specialists, pooling their resources; first, to share information; second, to look at problems together and decide which specialism—or combination of several—might be the best approach; and third, to clarify objectives, to reinforce one specialism by another and to evolve a common philosophy. The result was a social education team with a specific brief: to try to get at trouble at its source and then to take early concerted action.

The team includes a doctor, a senior nurse, a psychologist and related social worker, and a group of Education Welfare Officers. It is led by an educational guidance officer whose job is to co-ordinate the team's activities and also to pay special attention to social factors that inhibit educational progress.

This basic team, from Education Department and School Health Service staff, began by meeting once a week to discuss certain children from families thought to be in need of special investigation, to decide on a line of approach and if necessary to call in other agencies. Then the Children's Officer, Probation Officer, Chief Welfare Officer, Director of Housing and Chief Constable were invited to send representatives to join in the work. They began meeting once a month with the team and, of course, helping between meetings. At the very minimum, then, a link was established between statutory departments and a simple channel of communication was set up for schools in the area. Instead of having a choice between a multiplicity of agencies they knew they could turn to the team.

The meetings were at first concerned mainly with individual problems. The scope gradually widened towards a more general effort to build up a common philosophy and method of approach, so that individual members of the team and the schools they serve could begin to handle problems at source and thus enlarge the sphere of the team's influence.

The first stage is linking home and school. The Education Welfare Officers' function within the team is to foster a good and close relationship with parents and to try to create an atmosphere in the home in which parents are prepared to talk about their difficulties. This is an invaluable first step which has helped to solve problems that might otherwise have seemed intractable. The officers' connection with the education service is never a disadvantage and often a great help in striking up a relationship. The E.W.O.s and the Educational Guidance Officer have the job of bridging any gaps between home and school. They convey information from one to the other and keep close contacts with heads and, very important, individual class teachers.

The psychologist advises on the approach to behaviour or learning problems and forms a link with the remedial teaching service. (The remedial service, although not part of the team, is seen as an essential complement working within the schools in areas of greatest need.) Copies of social and psychological reports are sent to schools so that the staff can be kept informed of what is being done, and so that they can themselves use the advice and information in their own approach to these children and others with similar problems.

The School Medical Officer has made an invaluable contribution. Apart from medical advice, the information she can contribute from a much wider range than strictly medical problems has broadened the base of discussions. She has also set up a useful link between the team and general practitioners in the area. Again this has helped to avoid duplication of effort among those dealing with known problems. The nurse acts as liaison between the team, the home, and the school in matters concerning general health and cleanliness, and she can often advise on special needs. But her visits to homes, like those of the Education Welfare Officer, are valuable not only for the specific purpose of the visit but for the incidental knowledge they bring back and the relationship they help to build up with the family.

For six months the Social Education Team operated in fourteen schools: during this period they made some 400 visits to homes. These were some of the schools and homes with the biggest problems. Nevertheless, whilst the small-scale pilot experiment was under way, the pattern was of small-scale intensive cultivation. To be a practical proposition, the experiment had to be shown to work over a wider area, spreading the resources more thinly.

It should be pointed out that the concentration of resources was not unduly great even in the early stages. Most of the officers concerned were part-time in that they continued with other duties when not engaged in team-work. However, the Educational Guidance Officer himself was full-time: also the team had its own remedial teacher, and three Education Welfare Officers, available for specialist duties in the light of emerging needs throughout the City, were seconded to the team. So for more significant success the resources had to cover a wider area. And, just as important, the team itself had to grapple with the somewhat different approach required when larger numbers, both of children and of staff, were involved.

Thus, when the team's task was enlarged to take in forty-seven schools, the whole establishment of Education Welfare Officers for the area (a total of eleven) were asked to work with the Educational Guidance Officer and his colleagues. Again, instead of an individual remedial teacher, a team of four, under its own leader, was set up as a partner to the Social Education Team. This not only made it necessary for the team to spread its philosophy over a larger number of staff, but required also more formal arrangements for consultation between E.W.O.s and remedial teachers and their colleagues. Since easy consultation is one of the keys to success in this approach, this is a crucial problem: much depends on the senior Education Welfare Officer in the area and much on the educational psychologist member of the team, through whom the remedial teaching team now works. Success, particularly long-term success, is difficult to measure. But the Education Committee are so confident of the value of the method that they first set up a second team in another area, and then five covering the whole city in which all the social, psychological and medical services within education operate on a similar, though not necessarily identical basis.

In part, the scheme represents a movement away from clinics and into schools and homes; in part, a movement away from decision making at headquarters towards action in the field. It tries to replace the complex and fragmentary traditional method of operation of the personal services by a simple co-operative approach, one that seeks to look at children in the round rather than in the context of their family situation. At the same time it has strongly reinforced available evidence that many apparently 'educational' problems can only be solved by regard to more deep-seated emotional and environmental factors.

## Characteristics of the schemes

Any fair assessment of progress must have regard to the past rather than an unattained ideal. By these standards substantial headway is already being made through team efforts in various parts of the country. Naturally, they have their limitations. Deep-rooted and complex problems that surround inequalities in educational opportunity must look for their solution beyond the re-deployment of professionals, however skilful and imaginative this may be. The orientation of these schemes is inevitably towards individual cases that have reached crisis or near-crisis level. Emphasis on the problems of primary school children adds the dimension of preventive work. But the basic causes of the crises, and thus the inequalities, are likely to be eradicated only by pro-found changes in society itself. In our kind of society only so much can be done by legislation. The greater part must be brought about by changed attitudes within the community.

The sponsors of the schemes are, of course, not unaware of this need. In Liverpool, for instance, the Educational Guidance Officers have co-operated from the outset with voluntary bodies as well as statutory. This is essential if the danger is to be avoided of seeking to modify family life in order to make it fit in with the preconceived notions of acceptable social behaviour of the Establishment. They have also sought to involve parents at every stage. But inevitably the emphasis is on the circumstances sur-rounding individual cases. The climate in which these problems of individuals arise is profoundly affected by the attitudes of the community in which they live. The education of this 'community' to enable them to come to grips with the forces (which must sometimes seem overwhelming) that hinder them from collectively creating a better environment is a problem in another dimension.

Within the realm of the possible, then, the schemes emphasize several crucial issues.

There is the important link between home and school; recogni-tion of the need to extend help into the family; acceptance of poor school attendance as an indicator of deeper trouble and realization that court action is not an effective means of tackling the worst problems; concern to involve school teachers with outside specialists for mutual support in helping children; attempts to co-ordinate the efforts of different professonal workers and to link with voluntary agencies.

Though working primarily in crisis situations, they seek to extend their aid to all children and to work in a preventive and supportive role where possible. Apart from the difficulties of the techniques required the transition from crisis cases to preventive work is made infinitely more difficult by the sheer weight of outstanding cases of deprivation and handicap. The need to concentrate on existing backlog is also another factor tending to force continued attention to children at the secondary school stage: crisis situations are, of course, at their most spectacular amongst older children. Any new scheme has to contend at once with the difficult practical question of whether to neglect problems of older children with whom the specialist services may have been concerned for many years in favour of attempting to institute remedial action at the incipient stages of difficulties. There is no doubt in which direction the logic points, but it is a hard decision.

Administratively, sometimes schemes of this type involve officers responsible to the authority working on, not just with, the staffs of schools. This raises the difficult question of the extent to which they can become fully integrated members of the school staff. Are they able, easily, to identify with the school, rather than a social work agency? Do they experience difficulty in communicating information about home circumstances to their colleaguees in the schools? In the Glasgow Scheme the training of the social workers tries to help them 'acquire some knowledge of the organisation of schools, recognise that there is a hierarchy and accept that there is authority. Identification with the school is necessary if one is to function as a school social worker.' Clearly, it is essential for success of any scheme that an attached social worker should be accepted by the teachers as a colleague, and this may naturally be more difficult for someone without teaching experience. Teachers may, for instance, consider certain case-workers as unappreciative of the problems of those who have to teach large classes and care for all the children at once. This is the converse of the situation in which experienced teachers with little or no social work training may be expected to achieve successful relationships with social work agencies outside the school.

Some authorities have avoided much of this difficulty by concentrating on using existing resources. Thus the Southampton and

Liverpool ventures aim at close involvement of teachers with specialist services that have long worked in the schools. They provide co-ordinating machinery as a framework for co-operation. The Southampton scheme emphasizes an important problem in tackling educational handicap, the role of the teacher. It sees the teachers as an invaluable early warning device: 'In welfare terms, the class teacher is a field worker and this has been an essential recognition.' Participation of the class teacher in group meetings allows and encourages a sense of involvement in the welfare process which may be lacking with the class teacher who communicates formally through the Head of the School or some other third party.

The Liverpool Social Education Team aiming at a much wider area does not seek to involve the teacher as an auxiliary social worker overtly. Instead it tries to demonstrate how the solutions to problems that directly affect the teacher may be made easier by the knowledge and expertise brought by the outside agencies who come to the help of children in difficulties. Thus the psychologist, in helping to overcome the child's reading problems by relating them to psychological or environmental factors, may also help the teacher to look at these influences in an organized way. A similar approach with school attendance problems may simultaneously enlarge the teachers' horizon and give them easy access to a team of co-operating specialist workers.

In the next chapter we shall consider wider issues arising from the concept of the team approach, issues which require attention at national as well as local level. Co-ordination of the social services, for instance, has for several years been seen as in urgent need of attention, not only as a means of giving a better, less confusing, service to the public but also as a means of ensuring a more economic use of specialist resources. But two points can fairly be made about the team idea as exemplified by the Social Education Team, both of which point to the need for the continuation and development of ventures of this kind, whatever administrative structures are proposed for the future.

First, co-operation between teachers and professional social workers, on a properly thought out and mutually acceptable philosophical basis, is essential if the social services are to play an effective part in helping to counteract environmental handicaps that affect children's schooling, and if education is to play its part in counteracting social deprivation. Second, questions of efficient and economical working need to be examined at operational level, not just in the disposition of administrative structures. It is significant, for instance, that management consultants called in by the Liverpool City Council were impressed by the idea of the

Social Education Team and not only supported the Education Committee's plan for coverage of the whole city, but recommended that similar teams of social and welfare workers should be set up by a new Personal Health and Social Services Department of the Corporation.

Within the context of inequalities in educational opportunity, the significance of the Social Education Team idea could perhaps be even greater. The education service has been increasingly forced by circumstances towards preoccupation with institutions rather than individuals and, as we have seen, within the institutions the difficulty of achieving a personal approach to personal problems has been intensified by the inevitable changes of recent years, with bigger units and more specialization. Remedial and guidance services within the schools and outside them will have an increasingly important part to play and the institutionalizing tendency will grow. The Social Education Team concept has tried to personalize the education service in its contacts with the handicapped and at the same time to use scarce resources to best **advantage**.

# Partllership and planning

## seven

Teams are not merely a preliminary to planned co-ordinated services, but a way of achieving something more. Co-operation, based on common understanding and partnership, is of greater value than co-ordination, which seeks to secure links through administrative machinery. Clearly co-operation can be impaired by poor supporting administration: we have been at pains to point out that goodwill and specialist knowledge will not achieve co-operation in themselves. They need to be well organized. On the other hand it is possible to expect too much from co-ordination, and even to regard it as an end in itself.

The intricate patterns of administration created by the piece-meal accumulation of a multiplicity of tasks by the various agencies over the years cries out for co-ordination. Administrators have a weakness in common with the rest of mankind: they are suspicious and fearful of change, particularly as they get older. Since responsibility tends to increase with age, the top men are often the least willing to change. Like other people they tend to like best what is familiar and to be unable to step outside their own situation and examine themselves critically. Since the social services have grown up bit by bit in response to *ad hoc* needs, the result is a tendency to adhere out of habit to ways of doing things that are no longer appropriate. There are also straight-forward operational weaknesses—inadequate consultation, *ad hoc* rather than organized co-operative effort, and failure to pool information, resulting in many visits by different people to the same family.

Can we assume that it is because too many departments are involved? Unfortunately these problems arise within individual departments as well as between them, simply because of competition for recognition, status, and material rewards, and the unconstructive tensions that arise between various specialists each trying to solve (or tending to reject) a problem by looking at it from a narrow angle.

However, we must look deeper if we are to come to grips with what are ultimately the most serious problems surrounding the way we manage the social services. We must concentrate attention first not on the implementation of policy, but on the policy-making itself. It is not surprising that the uncertainties surrounding the difficult business of reaching agreement about standards and values in a democracy should be reflected in the policy-making committee rooms of the country. No one is really certain what the objectives of particular services should be, and the uncertainty rubs off on administrators and field-workers alike.

The dilemma of the schools in knowing how far they should go in the direction of social work has its parallel in the uncertainties of the policy-makers. Knowledge of the various services can help, and willingness to co-operate can take us further, but there is a deeper need, one that can only be met by the politicians and senior administrators responsible for the social services. They have to determine the objectives of the various branches. After that, and only after that, they can begin to create satisfactory administrative machinery.

## Co-ordination of the social services

Two documents published in the 1960's illustrate the problem: the report of the Central Advisory Council for Education (England) *Children and their Primary Schools* (Plowden, 1967) and the report of the Committee on Local Authority and Allied Personal Social Services (Seebohm, 1968).

We have already referred extensively to Plowden, as anyone must who writes today about any aspect of the education of young children: it is a model of the broadly based reports presenting a consensus of enlightened thought that have become a feature of policymaking in education. Here our concern is with one relatively small but admirably treated part of the report—that which deals with the links between schools and the social services.

Plowden begins by considering the child and its needs, then looks at school children in relation to their environment including their parents, develops a philosophy for an organized approach to their problems (through, for instance, the education priority area concept and the notion of the community school) and only then turns to matters of organization. It says:

There has to date been no official report covering all the
services we have discussed. But the Younghusband, Ingleby
and Kilbrandon Committees—although starting from
different, and restricted terms of reference—reached similar
general conclusions about the need for an integration of the
social services. What are the implications of this for the
schools? Many American school districts employ school social
workers with a general training in social work and a
minimum of specialisation. They work in a group of schools
and are responsible to the principal, and ultimately to the
Superintendent of Schools, but they can call on the help of
specialist social workers in other fields. Most of our evidence,
however, has led in a different direction, making a strong
base for a broader integration of the personal social
services.

We think the following arguments carry great weight:
(a) workers in a variety of services are increasingly finding
they are concerned with similar families having similar needs;
(b) the atomisation of social services leads to contradictory
policies and to situations in which 'everybody's business
becomes nobody's business'; (c) continuity of care is difficult
under present arrangements; (d) a more unified structure
would provide better opportunities for appraising needs and
planning how to meet them; (e) it would also accord with the
present tendency of social work to treat people as members of
families and local groups rather than to deal with specific
individuals or separate needs isolated from their social
context; (f) it would make it possible to create viable teams
to operate in areas of special need. Although such teams
should cover carefully selected areas they could be physically
located in many different places, for instance in clinics, in
the local offices of welfare and children's departments, or
medical group practices. Since all children spend several
hours a day in school for most of the year, and since it is
relatively easy for parents to visit schools, there is much to
be said for choosing the schools as a base for social work units
responsible for helping families facing many kinds of
difficulties. For social work units that were also concerned
with old people, single people or the mentally disordered,
other bases would be needed.

The idea Plowden puts forward emerges logically from a
coherent and consistently argued attitude towards the education
of children. It accepts the importance of a family approach as a
philosophy not just as a matter of administrative convenience. And

it contains two important points—that all children are at school for an appreciable part of their lives (which emphasizes the value of the school as a possible base for social work with children), and that services concerned with other community problems would need a different organization (because, by implication, they would have a different philosophy).

The Seebohm Report in comparison seems to start at the wrong end. Its terms of reference are admittedly more limited: 'to review the organisation and responsibilities of the local authority personal social services in England and Wales and to consider what changes are desirable to secure an efficient service'. Yet it is surely not incompatible with such a brief to begin by considering what the services ought to be doing and why, before plunging into organizational matters.

In the event the method chosen is to begin with the organization of the services, their history, current activities and practical problems, and to recommend a new structure without reference to underlying purposes. It recommends a new local authority social services department including:

(a) Children's Department functions
(b) Health Department functions such as home help, mental health, social work services and day nurseries
(c) Welfare Services under the National Assistance Act 1948
(d) Certain Housing Department functions, and
(e) Education Welfare and Child Guidance services.

It considers the organization of the proposed new department in some detail and urges speedy implementation, specifying in particular, curiously, that this should not wait until after local government reorganization.

Comparison of these proposals with those of Plowden is therefore difficult, since the arguments in the two reports are for the most part at different levels. Against Plowden's thoughtful exposition of the rationale of integrated services for children, Seebohm says little about the ethos that would inspire and bring together such a miscellaneous collection. Is concern with the welfare of families a sufficiently strong and sufficiently tangible bond?

Even at a more practical level, Seebohm is disappointing in its analysis of the functions that would need to be performed by the specialists, either separately or collectively, in the proposed pattern of working. For instance, its discussion of Education Welfare Officers is not only limited in scale, but seems to lack perception of the inter-action between social problems and children's educational handicaps, and to fail to see that links between home and school are a means, not an end in themselves.

There is even less discussion of child guidance services and of their central role in the educational process.

Lady Plowden herself in an article in 'Social Work'. although finding 'much to be welcomed in the Seebohm Report' finds this a weakness:

> The Report of the Central Advisory Council for Education, 'Children and their Primary Schools' recognised the interest of schools in social work which arises from the need to identify and help families with difficulties leading to poor performance and behaviour of their children in school. To undertake this, positively, social work amounting to family casework is needed, supported by specialist services equipped to deal with the more serious physical, environmental and psychological problems. This is in line with the Seebohm thinking, but it is difficult to find in Seebohm exactly how this specialist support would be used. In some cases the wisdom of the absorption of specialist facilities into the social service department may be doubted. For instance, para. 703 urges the need for an overall assessment of the psychiatric services, which are already under considerable strain, but believes that they, including of course child guidance, should be removed from the school health service to the social service department. Is it right that this should be done before the assessment? Might it concentrate these valuable and scarce resources too much in the social service department, with possible deprivation of both the hospitals and the schools?
>
> (Plowden, 1968.)

From the point of view of educational handicap another of Lady Plowden's criticisms seems justified:

> There seems to be some lack of appreciation in the report of the wider meaning of education. The outstanding characteristic of English schools, as compared with many of those elsewhere, has been their broad interpretation of education. Contributory factors to this have been the early age of compulsory education, the high quality of the few maintained nursery schools, and the tradition of boarding schools. Primary school teachers have recognised the contribution of play and informal learning to education; secondary teachers have made a parallel contribution by their organisation of out-of-school activities. The youth service has been supported from educational resources. Increasingly there is no hard and fast line between what happens in or out of school-time. *(ibid.)*

In consequence,

> The same lack of appreciation of the relationship between
> education and out-of-school activities comes in the
> Seebohm suggestion that area teams of social workers should
> play a major part in the development of community schools.
> This is a misunderstanding of what is needed. This is not
> a social but an educational task. These extended schools
> require the skills and concern of the entire community, and
> an opportunity for these to be made available for learning
> in all kinds of ways to people of all ages. It is sculptors,
> carpenters, engineers and dramatists who are needed in these
> community schools, rather than social workers. It is true
> that if community schools become focal points in the
> community, they will often provide good bases for social
> workers, but the social worker should depend on the school
> and not the other way round.
>
> *(ibid.)*

Again this seems to stem directly from Seebohm's starting-point
—in organization. Such references to philosophy and purposes as
there are inevitably suffer from the impression they give of coming
in piece-meal rather than as the foundations for thinking about
organization. One of the best features of the report is that it
specifically makes the connection between crisis-oriented social
work and preventive work with the community. Yet the implications of the idea are not fully pursued. The Report of the Youth
Service Development Council (1969) commenting on Seebohm,
says:

> As far as it is known, this is the first government report to
> envisage community development as a normal and proper
> function of all local authorities, and this is most welcome.
> However there are only a few references to the Youth
> Service in the main body of the Report which does not
> include the service in the list of services with which it is
> concerned. The implication is that the new social service
> departments would assume responsibility for community
> development in their area, without taking over all the work
> of this kind that may be going on. Since we see youth work
> as part of community development, and since the Report, if
> implemented, would affect the situation in which the Youth
> Service operates, further discussion about the relation
> between the Youth Service and the social service department
> is required as early as possible. Our concern is that in these
> discussions and in the consequent action taken, the
> particular needs of young people are given proper attention,

and the contribution of the educator to community
development is made.

It would be wrong to suggest as a result of this comparison, that
the ideas of Plowden and Seebohm are incompatible. On the
contrary, the very preoccupation of Seebohm with organizational
questions strongly emphasizes that it can only properly be regarded
as complementary to the concepts and aspirations of Plowden. It
seems equally obvious that any decisions regarding new patterns
of organization ought to be made to fit the philosophies of reports
like Plowden rather than the other way round. The notion of the
school-based area team, for instance, could and should be an
important means of co-ordinating social services in practice, whatever the administrative arrangements that support them. Indeed,
experience suggests that, quite apart from their specific value to
the education service, the kind of team approaches discussed in
the previous chapter may be more likely to bring about full
co-operation with other agencies than, in itself, a social service
department, simply because of their sense of inner organic convic-
tion and because of their recognition of the different but complementary specialisms of other professionals.

Thus the Liverpool Social Education Team's philosophical
link is with Plowden rather than Seebohm (though it was conceived
before either of the reports were published). The differences from
Seebohm are clear. One is the Social Education scheme's perception of a fundamental connection between educational and social
and psychological problems. This is important not only for itself
but for its bearing on the role teachers are to be called on to
play in any social service organization. Teachers are after all
basically concerned with teaching. The word has wide implications
which bring many teachers' objectives close to those of some
social workers: nevertheless, the Liverpool scheme enlists the
'social worker' help of teachers at the critical point—the learning
process—and so is able to get this support by the paradoxical but
logical way of offering help with the teachers' own main concern.

Another difference is the acceptance in this approach that social
workers' involvement in the private affairs of families may be
more successful and more justifiable if it has a specific purpose,
and one lacking overtones of moral superiority. This has implications not only for philosophy but for future planning and organization. It points in the direction of closer team-working within the
education service, with the Youth Employment Service and Youth
and Community development. Ultimately perhaps it points towards
friendly, familiar local places and people to whom anyone can
turn for help with any educational or related problem. This

contrasts with Seebohm's ethos of general welfare and an appropriate administrative structure.

Yet the differences have not prevented the teams from making a practical contribution to co-operation amongst field-workers and administrators in the social services generally. Perhaps they may also underline the importance of starting from objectives, not situations. There are obvious advantages in grouping together closely related services under the same sympathetic management, but we must be sure that the services in question are closely enough related to have a reason for existence outside the specialist field in which they originate, otherwise administration becomes an end in itself.

In this context the proposals of the Local Authority Social Services Act, 1970, though still open to the criticism of grouping elements of 'social work' according to administrative convenience rather than clear principles, at least leave the way open for the education service to develop on its own complementary lines. The new social services departments are to include:

> services for the elderly, handicapped and homeless,
> services for children,
> family case-work and social work with the sick and mentally disordered,
> day centres, clubs, adult training centres and workshops,
> day care of children under five, day nurseries and child-minding,
> care of unsupported mothers, including residential care,
> residential accommodation for those who cannot live at home but do not need continuing medical supervision,
> home helps.

Education welfare, however, remains outside, and the future of 'child guidance' is to be considered further. It is to be hoped that careful study of the Summerfield Report (referred to on page 44) will be included in this consideration.

Perhaps the greatest value of the Seebohm Report is in its emphasis on the need for training and professional standards in many jobs hitherto thought of as needing only intuition and goodwill. The danger is that this important and long overdue emphasis will be confused, in the creation of a general social services department, with a crude aim of reducing specialism in favour of general social workers. A general social services department will itself have to contend with the tendency of all large organizations to sub-divide into specialisms; and health, education and housing will still need their own social workers unless they are to become insensitive and institutionalized.

Whether social services departments are a good idea or not, they affect only part of the picture. The uneasy division of health services between hospital boards, executive councils, and local councils is a major source of difficulty. Probation service and police have different patterns of control. Within education, teacher training is divided in responsibility between universities, the churches, the D.E.S. and the L.E.A.s. Local government needs reorganization. The Report of the Royal Commission on Local Government, the Green Paper on the Health Service, the new legislation for children in trouble, and the possibility of a new Education Act are just some of the things that have to be considered as a background to the creation of social service departments.

Whatever plans are finally made for all these, one crucial issue will remain: the relationship between central government and the various national, regional and local agencies. At local level co-operation can only be partial as long as national policy is issued through separate departments. And the connection between government policy and local control needs to be clarified. Although separate central departments each interpret their own policies, government aid is in the form of general (rate support) grant to local councils for them to distribute according to their idea of of local priorities. This is an unexceptionable principle, but there is a need for something beyond the basic financial system that will both stimulate local government along the lines of national policy and draw together the threads of policy to make a coherent whole.

There is an obvious need for this in education and other social services. A recent development gives hope of a possible solution. The Urban Programme, started in 1969, provides a seventy-five per cent capital grant and, for at least some years, a similar amount on revenue expenditure, for certain kinds of project—for example nursery schools and community development ventures. This seems to be a way in which the central government can influence policy and yet leave reasonable discretion to local councils. The Government, in this, offers the local authority grants towards the kind of project likely to remove social disadvantages whether sponsored by education, children's or other departments. Apart from the advantages to the Government, the necessary consideration of priorities in compiling the programme encourages local authorities to think about their social problems as a whole, and their different departments to work together on them.

Another advantage of the Urban Programme is that although the central government agencies give guidance on the type of project eligible for grant, and indeed approve specific projects, the control is less detailed than in, say, the normal education building programme. This means that only broad objectives are set

A.E.C—K

nationally; the onus of analysing local need in detail is that of the local authority. The nearer the ground, the more specific the analysis can usefully be.

Again the Urban Programme allows approaches from different disciplines: it does not assume that because some of the activities in social work of, say, Health and Education Committees overlap, the objectives of these services as a whole are the same and must therefore share an identical approach in the area of overlap. The aim is to ensure that all departments turn their attention to the same focal point.

### An environment for co-operation

The value of the Urban Programme approach may well outlast that of temporary and partial organizational changes. Philosophy is more important than administrative structures. Furthermore, there is often much more seriously amiss with an administration than the shape of its organization. Traditional administrative machinery is often entirely unsuited to running the social services adequately. Education departments may tend, for instance, to be preoccupied with institutional management, with physical provision, and so to neglect the individuals for whom the schools are being built. All departments tend to be too hierarchically rigid, too concerned with not creating precedents, too afraid to take risks.

These features of administration are often assumed to be innate, reprehensible qualities characteristic of people who become bureaucrats. It is an interesting speculation whether only those with tendencies towards caution, status-consciousness, and so on become administrators, or whether they start out like the rest of the world but are forced into these attitudes by the job they have to do. No doubt it is a mixture of the two, but it is worth asking whether in this they are so different from other people. The essence of the situation is that they have been given responsibility for a task, they may gain credit from doing it well, and they may be blamed for failure. When any of us have such responsibilities we are likely to adopt similar attitudes to avoid the consequences of failure.

By no means all administrators are negative, but even the most adventurous must often seem to their field-work colleagues to say 'no' more often than they say 'yes'. This may have unfortunate repercussions for the field-work, but worse, perhaps, is its influence on the thought processes of the administrator in considering policy. Because he must always have in mind the practicalities, the realities of financial resources, and so on, he may tend to form opinions as a result of rationalization rather than reasoning. What we call administrative convenience has deeper implications than simply looking for what is easiest.

The further away, either in rank, physical distance or under-standing, from the specialist function of the field-worker, the greater this tendency is likely to be. Thus it is a bigger hazard for Directors of Education than for their assistants, and bigger still for the kinds of overlords nowadays being proposed for local government generally. We can take as an example something which in itself is a practical problem in the way of co-operation between social services—the different areas covered by different specialists.

We may find, for example, in a large city that the School Attendance and Welfare, School Health, Child Care Services, the Planning Department, Health Department, Remedial Teaching ser-vices, and many more, all have sub-divisions of their area. Some may have eight, some six, some five. Inevitably their boundaries overlap in a most complicated way. The E.W.O. who wants to consult a child care officer may have a choice of three in his area: a teacher may have to approach four or five different local head-quarters for these services. It would clearly be an advantage to have close correspondence between the areas, so that, for instance, information would be more easily pooled.

Yet the exercise of bringing about the improvement may not be just a question of knocking heads together or standardizing on a pattern devised from above. The existing areas may be merely the result of history, and there may be a need for change: but the basis on which the area was established needs careful thought. One branch may have as a criterion the number of schools, another the number of people, a third the likely number of cases of hardship from a particular district. To have the right criteria for the unit of working is more important than to have an area completely co-terminous with that of colleagues who really need to use other criteria.

An investigation into the possibilities of rationalizing areas may, of course, throw up genuine possibilities of helpful change, but the biggest value is likely to come from a critical examination of what the basis of each department's area sub-division is. If it is just habit it can be changed: if something more, then the contact between field-workers can be achieved in other ways; they can often for instance share an office, even if the exact boundaries of their territories do not coincide.

The implication of all this is that administrators, specialists and field-workers in their own departments need to come closer together just as much as the field-workers from separate disciplines. The barriers are largely those of language. There are perhaps two main sources of trouble: language as an aspect of procedure, and language as an aspect of expertise; or, if you like, gobbledygook and jargon.

What many practitioners in the field dislike is the foreign language dialogue they seem to have to conduct with anyone at headquarters. The words, terms, concepts of the world of committee resolutions and estimates are foreign: very few teachers other than heads have any clear idea of what actually goes on in an education office, for instance. Unfamiliarity is part of the trouble, but something apparently built into the role seems to impel the use of stately cadences in most administrators. Again history plays its part; once the rules are made no one feels bold enough to suggest that they be altered. Young men come in, eager for change, but have no authority to make it (and no responsibility, if it should be a bad change). By the time they have authority they may have grown used to the system; or else they may bring in their earlier theories, dated by ten or fifteen years.

Consider these letters:

1.  Dear Sir,
    There will be a meeting of remedial teachers at 2.30 p.m. on Monday, February 4th, in the main committee room for the purpose of considering possible designs for new primary school record cards. I should be grateful if you could arrange to be present.

    Yours faithfully,

2.  Dear George,
    Are you free on Monday, the 4th, at 2.30, to come in and talk about the new record cards? I have asked Harry and Fred to join us in the main committee room. Look forward to seeing you.

    Yours,
    Stan.

Most people would perhaps get a warmer glow from the second than the first. Clearly there are occasions when the second would be inappropriate or impossible, but there are many more when such a letter could be sent, but something more like the first is sent instead: and there are plenty of possibilities in between.

It is not merely the words themselves that are important, but what they represent. It may be argued that the second letter would be inappropriate for the kind of meeting envisaged in the first. This may be so, but it may equally be that the kind of language used in the first letter will help or determine the nature of the meeting—one might guess, rather stiff and formal and not very lively. In the whole business of administration there are innumerable examples of situations and procedures where it is difficult to know how far language is being used, as it should be, as proper clothing for the occasion, and how far it is dressing itself up so much that it makes all occasions formal.

Communication, not concealment, is the true function of language in public service and, if the procedures and situations themselves require a specialized style, there is no reason why explanations cannot be offered to let those on the outside in on the secret.

In the social services there is another opportunity for estrangement by the use of language. Specialists are inclined to use words that their lay colleagues find incomprehensible: administrators yearn for good plain English (or its administrative equivalent) and the specialists are appalled at this Philistine attitude. They point out, rightly, that delicate or precise shades of meaning are involved.

But it is not quite so straightforward as that. Words in ordinary use with a reasonably well understood meaning may suddenly acquire a specialist one: the specialists take it over and resent others trying to use it in the ordinary way. 'Community' and 'development' are two such words. Most reasonably educated people would feel competent to put them together and use them to describe a certain kind of activity. Yet 'community development' to its exponents has an esoteric meaning, one that can be distinguished for instance from 'community organization'.

Administrators who have themselves been specialists may have an initial advantage, but after a lapse of twenty years perhaps their understanding may be dimmed, or, worse, the concept behind the words may have changed. Just as one's language patterns can freeze in the positions of earlier days, so can the ideas the language tries to convey. Different styles of language may represent different modes of thought.

Perhaps the biggest danger for the administrator is that, separated by years of concentration on theory or broad principle from the latest working practice, he may have reached a position in which his judgments are rarely questioned as they should be. He himself may be in the grip of unconscious rationalization, and his specialist colleagues may not be close enough to him, in rank or in working contact, to compel him to think through his ideas to a truly logical conclusion.

Part of the administrator's business of creating an environment for effective specialist activity is creating machinery in which he himself is confronted by the latest thinking from the specialists and obliged to take it into account. This confrontation will contain something of value for the specialists, too, in the closer contact with the realities—of resources, committee policy and so on—that the administrator has to face. This may seem merely an elaborate way of suggesting that the two sides should meet. In fact rather more than that is involved, but even the physical fact of meeting would be an advance on what tends to happen.

What we have tried to suggest is not that all is well administratively, but that to place the emphasis in future reform on organization is to take too narrow a view. We should begin our changes elsewhere, at the point of contact. We have pointed to some of the difficulties with which any organization will have to contend, the built-in hazards, such as conflicting specialisms, and the limitations imposed by confused patterns outside their control as well as by inadequate finance.

We have tried to distinguish, too, between levels of administrative activity. The level concerned simply with smooth operational working can be improved, but this is not the most vital area of concern. At the senior level the policy makers have responsibilities that can profoundly affect the success of the operation. Developments like the Urban Programme suggest ways in which these responsibilities might be shared amongst the various partners.

For central government the main tasks will be to settle broad policy, to give appropriate financial incentives so that it can be implemented without restrictive regulation, and to simplify and clarify the national picture in social work. For the other partners, regional and local, statutory and voluntary, the need is to narrow down and refine their objectives in the light of national policy and local need, and thereafter to create a system capable of achieving them.

Social administrators have to create an environment in which field-workers in all services can co-operate fully and effectively. Before they can begin this job they have to clarify the objectives of the service in which they themselves work. To do this for the relevant branches of educational administration is not only the best contribution the education officer can make for the sake of his own colleagues in the field, teachers, school doctors, nurses, psychologists, E.W.O.s. It is also the best service he can render all who work in the other agencies.

# Education in social work

## eight

In considering the role of the local education authority in social work, the starting-point is the essentially practical one that in any co-operative enterprise it is better if each partner puts his own house in order before spreading himself abroad. So far as education is concerned, this is far from being a narrowing parochial exercise, for in probing deeper into the educational needs of children one must inevitably learn a good deal about their physical, emotional and social handicaps and the multiplicity of skills and services required to detect and counteract them. No one is likely to conclude that this is a simple business to be tackled by one service alone or by several in isolation. It is a matter for partnership, and clarity about the objectives of education is essential before educationists can co-operate with their partners.

There must clearly be some limitation: the aim is not simply doing good generally. One distinction between education and other social work seemed to emerge in the first chapter of this book in considering the ethics and practicalities of intervention into a family's affairs: the justification was that a child has rights quite distinct from those of its parents.

But to suggest as a limitation for education as social work that its orientation is towards the child does not take us very far. Other services are also concerned solely with children. We may come nearer to a helpful distinction by suggesting as a main purpose for education in social work that, in trying to provide appropriate education for each individual, the service must also ensure that particular individuals are not prevented from taking advantage of what is offered.

This, too, spills over into foreign territory. Should the education service offer maintenance grants to parents so that they can afford to keep their children warm and well fed? In practice we cannot distinguish this objective from the general one of ensuring that no family starves. Should the education service provide special grants to enable poor parents to keep their children on at school after the statutory leaving age? In practice it does, but it is arguable that this, too, is a general welfare matter. Certainly there is no inexorable logic in insisting that these grants should be administered by the education service: it is a matter of convenience. What seems clear, however, is that it is the business of the education service to be sure that someone gives grants of this kind: if no one does, then education cannot carry out its duty to all its pupils.

Here perhaps we have the beginnings of a tenable theory. Within the range of its general objectives and the resources available it is proper for the education service to ensure that certain activities are carried out in relation to children: whether they are carried out direct or by agents is a matter of convenience and common sense. The guide-line might well be the degree of relevance to the main educational process, teaching.

If we apply the test to the work of the Education Welfare Officer, for example, we may agree that of his present duties his work in linking home and school and his functions in relation to attendance are essentially educational. His job as a provider of information on pupils' residence and movement (on which education authorities base their calculations about building needs and their charges to other education authorities for out-county pupils) is so closely bound up with the authority's work that if the E.W.O. did not do it someone else within the education service would have to. But his function as provider of application forms and guide as to their completion in relation to grants for clothing, footwear, and free meals is merely a matter of convenience.

It is interesting that the activities most relevant to the education process are the very ones used by some people to argue that the E.W.O. should cease to be part of the education service. Their grounds—that this kind of activity is often an essential part of wider family needs—are valid ones. On the other hand it is a legitimate source of anxiety for education authorities that the specific function of School Attendance and Welfare branches in the crucial question of absence from school, and the reasons for it, should not be lost in any general welfare service. Can another agency do this job as well as the Education Welfare Officer?

The issue is clouded by the assumption sometimes made that E.W.O.s ought to be equipped to carry out social casework. Most educationists would think that if the problem is of this dimension then it should be handed on to a professional case-worker outside education. This entails the E.W.O. knowing enough about these matters to know when to leave off—hence the need for training—

but the aim, which seems to have little to do with casework, is to find out all he can about the causes of absence or other social problems impinging on the child's school life and to try to associate the parents with the school in doing something about them. This will almost certainly involve a visit to the home, but the object is to establish lines of communication and perhaps create a climate in which the child's problems can be discussed with the school (preferably by the parent direct but, if not, by the E.W.O. and the teacher concerned).

How well could this be done by someone outside the education service? Who else would care as much whether a child attended school or not and what the reasons for his absence were than a combination of people dedicated to the cause of education? Who else would get to know as much about it? In the more neutral sphere of census work the element of caring is less important: in matters concerning children and their educational needs it is vital. Would the same result be achieved through teamwork between the school and agencies outside education? In Chapter 6 we have seen how well purposeful combination can work. But it has to be purposeful. Educational, emotional, and environmental factors interact; using the teacher not as an auxiliary social worker but through his actual teaching can bring about the strongest links. None of this can happen unless those involved are united in common objectives, something more compelling, because more real, than a general concern for one's fellow-men.

The test, then, is a philosophical one, tempered when it comes to details by pragmatism. Education must insist on having its own resources to tackle work essential to meet its objectives, both in providing education, and detecting and treating the handicaps of children who need it. Conversely, those in education should not enlarge this concept into a generalized concern for children—still less their families. Here again pragmatism must settle the details of the points at which those in education refer problems to those outside.

In suggesting this approach we do not have in mind demarcation lines, which are impossible as well as undesirable. We are concerned chiefly to ensure that fundamentals are not forgotten in superficial talk about unifying services.

An approach from different angles, provided it is not parochial, is not the unmitigated horror it is sometimes made out to be. At least it ensures that the essential purposes of important services such as housing, health, education are not forgotten; overlap is better than underlap.

And overlap is not the same as duplication. Duplication occurs when the same thing is done by different people; overlap is the result of different people trying to do somewhat different things. Provided it is not too substantial this can have as many advantages as disadvantages. It is in any event inevitable that people will approach human problems in different ways. What we have to ensure is that in making this approach they combine rather than compete with those tackling the problem from other directions.

## Planning by objectives

To agree on broad general lines is not enough. One of the points made in the opening chapter was the need to analyse the causes of educational handicap carefully and reinterpret them regularly if we are to achieve progress in making a reality of educational opportunity. The objectives an education authority sets itself must be the result of similar analysis and regular re-appraisal.

The elected members of the education committee have responsibility for establishing these objectives, but of course they are unlikely to be able, or to want, to do this alone. The education officer's responsibility is to see that committees have the information they need to make an informed decision. In this context information does not mean an undifferentiated mass of figures or reports, but rather a process by which the issues the committee have to decide can be weighed and selected. To make these decisions satisfactorily committees must first consider and carefully decide what exactly they wish to achieve.

So the education officer's responsibility might properly begin with an ordered appraisal of possible objectives. Before presenting them to the committee he will need to clarify his own ideas. This would seem an excellent opportunity for him to work out draft objectives together with the various specialists, for example those engaged in education welfare, school health, and the psychological services.

It may be helpful to begin, as suggested in the first chapter, from a proposal to eliminate a negative factor, rather than, at this stage, to aim at a positive goal. What categories of children are we concerned with, and what needs or lacks have they? Our clientele consists of all children whom some impediment prevents from taking full advantage of the normal education offered in primary and secondary schools. Next, what action do we have to take to adjust the situation? We have to identify and make special provision for these children, either alone or in association with others, and, if we are prudent, to take preventive action. Thus our basic objective might be (a) to identify the particular needs of all children who are, or may be, prevented from taking full advantage of primary or secondary education without special arrangements and (b) to make those special arrangements.

The next stage is to present this general objective in such a form and in such detail as to clarify the issues that have to be faced and the best methods of dealing with them. This can be tackled equally pragmatically by asking what kind of factors are likely to be identified as handicaps. Let us say:

| *Process* | *Factors* |
|---|---|
| | Health |
| Identification | Emotional and behaviour |
| | Intellectual |
| | Social |

We shall need to return later to the question of identification, and also the very important problem of multiple or inter-acting handicaps, but first we need to break down these factors in more detail. This might give a picture something like this:

| *Factors* | *Elements* |
|---|---|
| 1. Health | 1.1. Blind |
| | 1.2. Partially-sighted |
| | 1.3. Deaf |
| | 1.4. Partially-deaf |
| | 1.5. Delicate or invalid |
| | 1.6. Epileptic |
| | 1.7. Physically handicapped |
| | 1.8. Speech defective |
| | 1.9. Dental |
| 2. Emotional and behaviour | 2.1. Psychiatric |
| | 2.2. Disturbed or undeveloped |
| | 2.3. Socially maladjusted |
| | 2.4. Delinquent |
| 3. Intellectual | 3.1. Organic: mental disorder |
| | 3.2. Organic: special problems e.g. dyslexia |
| | 3.3. Educationally sub-normal |
| | 3.4. Backward |
| 4. Social | 4.1. Family influence |
| | 4.2. Family handicap |
| | 4.3. Neighbourhood |
| | 4.4. Other |

The next stage is to list all the ways in which the authority attempts to deal with the problems. This will include treatment, institutional provision, assistance to voluntary effort, and so on. In the later stages it will also include reference to other agencies outside education. It can be sub-divided to show the nature of the service, e.g. guidance or treatment, day or residential special schooling.

The first draft might then look something like this:

**Factor : Health**

| Elements | Guidance and treatment | Institutional provision | Welfare |
|---|---|---|---|
| 1.1 Blind | | 1.1 Day Special School (D.S.S.) Residential Special School (R.S.S.) | |
| 1.2 Partially sighted | | 1.2 D.S.S.; Special units (S.U.) | School health nurses |
| 1.3 Deaf | 1.3 ⎱ Peripatetic | 1.3 ⎱ D.S.S.; R.S.S.; | |
| 1.4 Partially deaf | 1.4 ⎰ teachers | 1.4 ⎰ S.U. | Education welfare officers |
| 1.5 Delicate and Invalid | 1.5 Home teaching | 1.5 R.S.S.; Hospital School | |
| 1.6 Epileptic | | 1.6 Referral | |
| 1.7 Physically handicapped | 1.7 Peripatetic teachers | 1.7 R.S.S.; D.S.S. | |
| 1.8 Speech defective | 1.8 Speech therapists | | |
| 1.9 Dental | 1.9 Dental clinics Referral | | |

**Factor : Emotional and behaviour**

| | | | |
|---|---|---|---|
| 2.1 Psychiatric | 2.1 Child guidance service | 2.1 D.S.S. R.S.S. | 2.1 Psychiatric social workers |
| 2.2 Disturbed or undeveloped | 2.2 Psychiatrists. Special remedial teacher | 2.2 D.S.S. R.S.S. | 2.2 Psychiatric social workers |
| 2.3 Socially maladjusted | 2.3 As above. Referral to children's dept. | 2.3 D.S.S. R.S.S. | 2.3 Psychiatric social workers Education Welfare Officer |
| 2.4 Delinquent (including attendance) | 2.4 As above: Education Welfare Officer. Referral to Children's Dept., Probation, Police: juvenile liaison; Court action | 2.4 As above | 2.4 As above |

## Factor : Intellectual

| Elements | Guidance and treatment | Institutional provision | Welfare |
|---|---|---|---|
| 3.1 Mental disorder | 3.1 Referral to specialists | 3.1 Junior Training Centre | |
| 3.2 Special problems | 3.2 School health, Child guidance specialists | 3.2 Special units | |
| 3.3 E.S.N. | 3.3 School psychological service | 3.3 D.S.S. R.S.S. S.U. | School nurses |
| 3.4 Backward | 3.4 School psychological service. Remedial teaching teams. Individual Remedial teachers | 3.4 S.U.; School department | |

## Factor : Social

| | | | |
|---|---|---|---|
| 4.1 Family influence | 4.1 Guidance officers | 4.1 Nursery education. Boarding school | 4.1 Education Welfare Officers. Teacher-social workers. Referral |
| 4.2 Family handicap | 4.2 Referral | 4.2 Boarding school | 4.2 Education Welfare Officers. Referral. Grants: meals, clothing, maintenance |
| 4.3 Neighbourhood | 4.3 Guidance Officers. Youth and Community officers | 4.3 Youth and Community groups | |
| 4.4 Other | 4.4 Careers Officers. Counsellors in Schools | | |

The resulting rough draft can be refined and reshaped (preferably by representatives of the various branches involved) until it represents a schematic picture of the authority's targets for action, and the action itself. To pursue the exercise further would be outside the scope of this book, but it should extend to setting out in detail

(a) the services being provided—numbers of staff, premises, grants;

(b) their costs;

(c) their performance in quantitative terms—numbers of cases handled, numbers of children on roll and so on.

It will then be possible to establish how much is being spent on what service.

The next stage is more difficult, but crucially important. This is to measure the performance and weigh its success against the cost. It is relatively simple to measure provision and even output, but measuring its effectiveness is another matter. It means referring back to the objectives, to consider the real purpose of the service. Is the object for instance to provide as many special schools as possible, or rather to identify and treat a handicap early enough so that when possible a child can stay in or return to the normal primary or secondary school? Assuming it is the second the number of children in, say, e.s.n. schools and their costs would have to be considered against success in achieving the real purpose. If it were discovered, for example, that there were twice as many children in these special schools than the national and regional average, and that very few ever went back to their own schools, it would be necessary to investigate, to find out why.

In such a difficult matter as this it is not suggested that short-cut simple answers can be found; rather that questions will be raised that need to be thought about and argued in depth. If it emerged that a high proportion of children in the e.s.n. schools were of secondary age, it could be that the processes of detection were too slow, badly organized or under-staffed. If many of those admitted were not so much educationally sub-normal as backward; if environmental factors had tended to influence the performance in ascertainment tests of many children, it might be that earlier detection and therapeutic measures such as nursery classes or remedial teaching at the primary stage would reduce the numbers. It would then be a matter for debate whether to divert resources from special education to early detection and preventive services. The exercise is useful not only in assessing the effectiveness of services and in justifying expenditure but also in re-examining objectives. We might for instance return to our draft objectives and begin to inject a more positive note into them. At this stage it might be on these lines:

'To enable children with any form of handicapping condition or circumstance to take advantage of appropriate educational provision in the schools.'

## Action programmes

The next phase is to plan the way this objective is to be carried out. Our schematic objectives will indicate general lines but we need to go further in order to clarify the roles and relationships of those involved. At this point we must return to the all-important process of identification. If this is taken to include detection, screening and diagnosis a rough chart of the process might look something like that on page 148. (There is bound to be some overlapping of function, but the main role of the participants can be indicated. In this, in order to emphasize that children may have more than one handicap and that prime causes inter-act on each other, we abandon the division into health, intellectual, emotional and social factors.)

A rough chart of this kind already gives a clue to the services (guidance and treatment, institutions and welfare) that need to be provided for children of particular ages. The aim is to collect information from all sources about children who may be at risk educationally because of what is known about their families or about them as babies. This information can be analysed by the school health and education welfare services, and priorities drawn up in advance relating to admission to nursery schools and classes. The nursery schools would not only attempt to compensate for adverse environmental or other factors but assist in a further screening process together with school health and child guidance services. Careful records would be kept in infant schools of these and other suspect children, and special attention given to them during routine medical inspections. This with the help of specialist remedial teachers' visits should enable the great majority of known or suspected cases to be referred (to school health, child guidance or remedial teaching service, depending on the apparent main cause of difficulty) towards the end of the infant school course.

Children likely to be in most difficulty in the ordinary school situation would be encouraged to go to special neighbourhood schools or units at local primary schools. In any case remedial and diagnostic attention would be given to them so that at the age of eleven or thereabouts decisions could be taken about whether a school for e.s.n. children was indicated or whether they could embark on a full secondary school course.

Secondary schools would, of course, need to develop remedial and guidance services more than at present, and after-school arrangements—such as special evening institute classes—would be needed. These would not only fill a gap (in most authorities) in the early years after school leaving and give practical help in dealing with form filling and similar problems, but also provide an

| Identification Processes | Source of Handicap | Infancy | Nursery Years | 5 to 8 | 8 to 11 | 11+ |
|---|---|---|---|---|---|---|
| Detection | Learning difficulties | Health Department Health visitors Education Welfare Officers Children's Department Probation Police | Nursery schools and classes Health Department nurseries Other departments Voluntary agencies General practitioners Education Welfare Officers | Infant school records School health inspections School Nurses' visits to school Education Welfare Officers Other departments, etc. | As earlier stages | As earlier stages |
| Screening | | School health doctors (family case-histories) Guidance Officers (social factors) | Nurseries Selective medical inspections Child guidance service Education guidance officer | Schools Remedial teachers Child guidance service Education guidance officer | As earlier stages Neighbourhood remedial schools or units | As earlier stages |
| Diagnosis | | | | School health Child guidance Referral to — specialists — other departments — neighbourhood special schools or units | All services working with specialists in neighbourhood remedial schools or units Referral to special school or secondary school | |

opportunity for follow-up work by the services who have dealt with these children and their families during their school lives.

This is a simple—and much simplified—example of a possible approach to one aspect of the problems faced by education authorities in planning provision for children with special needs. Assuming for the moment that planning for these children could be followed through in isolation, the next stage is to revise the objectives statement, re-allocating costs and planning re-deployment of resources over a period of years. (In practice all the objectives of the whole service will need to be tackled in this way.)

This is the point at which sound economics and the educational requirements of the situation must be brought together. Fortunately they appear to coincide at many points: it is sensible to spend more on prevention and less on cure; and it is desirable to operate jointly as many services as possible, not only for economy but to take fully into account the effects of the interplay of different handicaps on individual children. For example it is clear that the process of identification should be regarded as a joint enterprise, an information and advisory service available to all the separate specialisms.

## Organization

It is only now, after thorough exploration of objectives and a review of resources and their possible re-deployment, that we can effectively consider the right kind of organization. The organization should, of course, be shaped to carry out the agreed objectives. This makes it difficult and undesirable to generalize about organization. Furthermore there are usually several different ways of achieving the same thing, and existing local circumstances may make one approach more promising than others.

We shall make certain assumptions. First is the existence of sufficient resources to require organization. This is largely, though not entirely, a matter of size, and in taking as a model a reasonably sized unit we are to some extent anticipating the effects of the recommendations of the Royal Commission on Local Government, whilst at the same time accepting that in smaller units the very limitations of the problem may make simpler methods possible.

The second assumption we have to make is of a particular kind of overall organization, one in which for example there is a separate school health service and in which the youth employment service is run by the local education authority, not the Department of Employment and Productivity. This is not to suggest that this is necessarily the best arrangement (although we

A.E.C.—L

do in fact think that it is) but merely to try, in choosing an arbitrary arrangement as an example, not to complicate the issue too much. It will be understood that there are just about as many variations in patterns of control as there are L.E.A.s, and since at this point it is the method that matters, not the pattern itself, there would be no purpose in exploring these variations. For the same reason the possible effects of reorganization of health services are not taken into account; whether the education authority actually administers a school health service or not does not affect the issue; the closest possible links between the services within education and those outside it will be needed, and co-operation will need to be organized by the relevant education branch.

The third assumption is of a county borough rather than a county organization. The reasons for this are mainly those outlined above, but implicit in the choice also is the belief that it is in the big towns and cities that the greatest inequalities and handicaps are to be found.

The organization shown in the diagram on page 151 is far from typical. In many education offices Special Services includes things like school meals as well as school health and attendance matters. Here administrative convenience, grouping together the miscellaneous activities outside the main stream, may be the basis. Sometimes special schools may be included, perhaps through association of the names—special schools, special services. It is rare for related activities like identification, guidance, and special education in all its forms to be grouped coherently under a leader with freedom to deploy resources according to changing needs within a context of regularly reviewed policy.

This would be a good start. But no family-tree organization can be more than a start. It can only be a fairly crude indicator of basic responsibility, too static to be helpful as a guide to patterns of working. For this we might begin with a somewhat different diagram (see p. 152).

This again is no more than a start, but from it the analysis of functions by the various field-workers can begin, preferably from the key link between class teachers in the schools and the various specialists. If team co-operation is to be the basis of their activities the basic organization will be no more than framework within which the complex processes of consultation and co-operation can happen. In a framework like this with all or most of the related services in education working together there is every opportunity for the essential purposes of an education committee to be carried out relatively smoothly, for changes to be made as necessary, and for the effectiveness of the service to be, to some extent at least, measured and assessed.

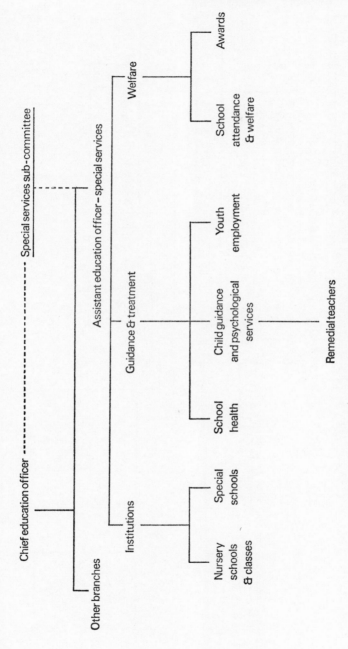

**Figure 6. Educational special services: possible administration**

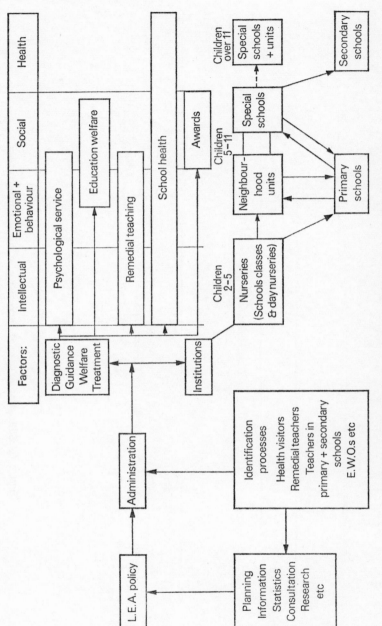

Figure 7. **Educational special services: from policy to action**

That this kind of organization infrequently exists is in part due to the fragmentary and *ad hoc* origin of most of the services involved. In part it is the result of neglect, perhaps because work of this kind has been regarded as an after-the-event charitable gesture to the unfortunate rather than a preventive service designed to detect and put right trouble at the earliest possible moment in the interests not only of the individual but also of the nation. In part it often arises, however, from undoubtedly worthy but in the end unhelpful sentiment. This above all, it is said, is a personal service needing personal and individual consideration at every stage. From this has grown a ludicrous and dangerous myth that seems to require everyone engaged in this work to become an amateur social caseworker, with the ultimate in organization represented as a case conference.

Committees and administrators need to clarify their roles just as much as the specialist field-workers. Their task is not to indulge in Solomon-like judgments in individual cases, but to establish policies based on clear objectives and on such facts as are available and then to produce an organization that will enable and encourage the specialists to co-operate in applying their talents to the problems. This particular myth is part of a more general one which seems to suggest that, because large and complex organizations tend to be impersonal, to be really effective top people in them should forget about organization and planning and concentrate on the personal touch. In fact a large organization can only be effective (which is its first job) and also humane if its administration is of the highest quality. This depends on how its exponents collect and use information just as much as on how kind their hearts are. In the social services the first obligation upon an administrator is to achieve every possible ounce of value for the limited amount of money that is likely to come his way. He will not manage to do that unless he values efficiency and clarity of purpose just as much as good intentions.

# Research and innovation

## nine

The process of clarifying objectives, if it is to be done properly, is an exacting and complicated one. The more information relevant to the purpose that can be gathered the better the end product is likely to be. Much of this information may be factual, but in education, information of another kind is needed. The attempt must be made to settle, in as much detail as possible, the needs that are to be met by the service. Impression and partial understanding of needs can be a disastrous basis for a programme aimed at reducing inequalities of opportunity.

The logical way to approach acquisition of knowledge of this kind is through research. Yet the impact of research on this aspect of the education service is slight: not surprising, perhaps, since the personal and social elements in education are the most neglected part of a service in which research is pitifully inadequate generally. British education spends a microscopic amount on research: it had reached some £2½ million out of £2,000 million total annual expenditure by the late 1960s. Even this represented a dramatic increase largely owing to the growth of spending on curriculum development. Richard Bourne took up this point in *The Guardian*:

Not only is the present sum small, but the dispensers are many and ill-co-ordinated. In 1968 the Department of Education distributed £367,000 for 40 research projects. The Schools Council spends about £125 million on curriculum research and development. The National Foundation for Educational Research—which has just completed its big 'streaming' project and is still heavily involved in its comprehensive schools project —is a powerful agency. The Social Science Research Council —although it gave only 25 studentships in education out

of a total of over 1,000 in the current year—regards itself as responsible for this area.
In addition there are the independent foundations—where would we be without Nuffield maths?—and the *ad hoc* efforts of university departments, colleges of education, and the more ambitious local authorities. (Bourne, 1969)

When research projects are undertaken whether by universities, by official, semi-official and independent foundations, and by individual scholars, the national attitude to them, the lack of an organized purposeful approach, suggests that no one really intends the results to be put into practice. Mr Bourne goes on to suggest that the trouble is a 'lack of direction from the top'. Tempting though this conclusion may be it is not quite so simple as that: we are face to face with one of the implications of democracy. Anything from 'the top' would have to be inspirational, not dictatorial. This is partly because in our society the value judgments on which basic educational issues depend are, quite properly, not regarded as matters that can be settled by research and dispensed by the central government. Hence the traditional independence of schools in devising curricula and the governmental freedom of local education authorities.

We are proud of these freedoms, and rightly so, for they more than anything preserve the essentially democratic structure of the education service. Yet their existence means that any research findings from a higher level, whether they are on basic issues or not, have to be implemented by persuasion and infiltration rather than by edict. Educational policy in Britain relies heavily on the reports of such bodies as the national advisory councils.

The now accepted pattern in which governments ask broadly based advisory councils to report on major matters reflects the suspicion with which any directly sponsored governmental research would probably be received (by political opponents, local councils, and teachers). The corollary is that governments reserve the right to accept as much as they want of any report, and indeed to choose the subjects on which they wish to be given advice. Advisory councils do not necessarily use organized research to help them reach their conclusions. Even if they did, in the unlikely event of complete acceptance of an entire report by a government, there would be overwhelming difficulties in seeing that the findings were put into practice by the local education authorities.

One of the ways in which the central government was traditionally able to secure that at least a substantial part of its policy in education was carried out in spite of local freedom was through finance. Since 1958, however, there have been no specific grants

for education. Government subsidy goes to the local council according to a general formula and the council has a considerable measure of freedom to distribute this money throughout all the services
according to its own priorities, which may well not coincide with
those of the government. In these circumstances control by the
Department of Education and Science where it exists at all tends
to be negative.

## Local authorities and research

The L.E.A.s are in a much better position to make policy changes:
theirs is the legal responsibility; they maintain the schools and
colleges; their financial relationship with these institutions gives
them all the power they need. In contrast the Department of
Education and Science, particularly since the disappearance of
specific financial arrangements for education, has been preoccupied
with control rather than innovation; and at the other end of the
scale, individual teachers and individual schools are too isolated,
too dependent on L.E.A. resources and perhaps too close to the
problem to make other than small and occasional changes.

It is an unfortunate irony, then, that the L.E.A.s, who are in the
best position to undertake innovation, have in fact commissioned
so little research. Of course they, like the central government, must
settle their major policy questions by democratic means. Yet there
are plenty of other issues on which hard information could and
should replace impression. One reason why this does not happen
is lack of resources: with over 160 authorities ranging in size from
a few thousand to several million, the pattern is likely to be uneven.
Even the large authorities, however, tend not to use research as a
basis for action. This suggests another reason—a basic lack of
sympathy between administrators and researchers.

Sometimes the activities of university research workers may seem
to local education officers and teachers as akin to fiddling while
Rome burns; sometimes the researchers may seem less concerned
with practical implications than they should be. Sometimes the
prospect of change that their activities suggest may be seen as a
threat to the serene and untroubled lives of well entrenched bureaucrats. Sometimes it is the other way round: the researchers with
their passion for objectivity and information try to put a spoke in
the wheel of the quick and easy changes that local politicians and
administrators seem to them to prefer.

Michael Young (1965) puts it this way:

> Innovators and researchers are not natural bedfellows;
> innovators often distrust measurement, so much of importance

is always left out of it. There are two supreme tests of an educational regime. The first (since the child is more than just a potential adult) is how a child is faring now. The second is how he turns out 20 or 40 years later, and over such a period no research can trace a sure connection.

This is the classical attitude of educational administrators and their committees.

We must all accept that the most important issues cannot be measured, because they depend on value judgments. But it is surely better to base these judgments on as much hard information as we can muster. A great deal can be quantified and measured. Statistics may be suspect, but they can surely at the very least help to test what might otherwise be no more than assumptions. A superficial impression of an area, for instance, may persist: it may be the result of no more than a brief visit on a wet day, one or two incidents heavily publicized in the press, or just plain gossip. Description may not be the highest level of scientific research but it is better than nothing.

In the social sciences description may sometimes be almost as far as research can take us. Very little on which firm prediction can be based usually emerges where human affairs are concerned. The complexity of society makes it extremely difficult to isolate specific factors that can be regarded as causes or that can be measured, and the rapidity of social change produces backlash, chain reactions and other equally unpredictable effects.

These limitations apply, whatever method is chosen. Surveys on social questions, where they are factual, leave out important human elements; where they are not, they rely on opinion which may well not be true opinion. Nor can surveys establish incontrovertible cause-and-effect relationships. Experiment, though more valuable potentially, can only be partial because of the impossibility of securing laboratory conditions for measuring the effects on human beings. We cannot—or should not—contemplate using people as guinea pigs.

Consequently a most circumspect approach is required. In a scientific experiment a certain action is taken to see what effect it has. Where people are concerned the experiment should not be completely open-ended, i.e. whether the outcome will be beneficial or harmful should not be in doubt; the measurement should be of degrees of benefit. This implies that the experiment should never be undertaken solely as an experiment. And this in turn implies that what the subject of the experiment is required to do should not be so different from what he would normally be doing as to run the risk of harm. It goes without saying in our society that the subject's participation should be entirely voluntary.

This pattern was followed in Liverpool when, as part of a curriculum research enquiry into problems of raising the school leaving age, it was decided to run an experimental course for non-academic young people in a development centre so that action programmes could be worked out from this experience for possible use in schools. Great care was taken in selection so that no one was chosen who was in a school where the opportunities were not unquestionably less than those on the experimental course. Whatever the outcome of the experiment, it seemed certain—and so it turned out—that the chances of the students would be greater. The experiment was confined to discovering which of the methods of improvement tried worked best.

This principle lies behind the phenomenon of 'action research' on social questions currently being sponsored nationally. The first and best known is that on education priority areas, already given our national mark of acceptance, reduction to the initials 'e.p.a'. In four areas of social need the government made an amount of money available for project directors and researchers in association with local education authorities to try in a small number of schools to raise educational standards, support teachers, and encourage links between home and school and school and community.

Thus within the schools, projects may be carried out designed to help the urban child by their relevance to his own environment; pre-school play-groups may be started, and other ways of involving parents tried. The intention here is not to discover whether extra educational benefits can compensate for poor home environment: this, enunciated by the Plowden report, is assumed to be the case. The action research tries out a number of different ways of giving this compensatory education and tries to discover which are the most effective and the most practical. The pattern clearly illustrates how the philosophy is drawn from a consensus of those considered best qualified to judge, and research is used as a means of evaluating techniques of implementation.

More recently an experimental scheme originated in the Home Office for a number of similar areas (Liverpool has both an e.p.a. and a Home Office project). This is designed to test the not very controversial proposition that the 'vertical' organization of social services to meet particular needs is unhelpful to people with multiple problems. The experiment proposes an inter-service team in places where there are concentrations of severely deprived families to adopt a co-ordinated approach: the aim is to help people to use the social services constructively and to try to make a better way of life for themselves or at least their children. The experiment is in techniques rather than into fundamental questions: the philosophy is implicit; it arises from a consensus of opinion amongst certain of the leaders of society.

In all these projects the real justification will be that, whatever happens, greater attention will have been paid, more resources will have been given, to areas of social need. In terms of evaluation nothing may be learned that we do not know already, though if we accept that the 'research' factor is to be applied to the techniques, not the philosophy, we could conceivably learn a good deal.

As it is, lack of precision in thinking about what is to be attempted, about objectives, may lead to disappointment at the outcome. Many people who care deeply about social problems enthusiastically see in this new approach the prospect of organized, scientific advance. Yet when, as sometimes happens, a variety of schemes, statutory and voluntary, are launched in one area, major problems can arise. First, co-ordination: it is not very sensible to replace overlapping traditional services by a cluster of projects that not only overlap the traditional services but each other. Second, evaluation: it is difficult enough to measure the effects of innovation in a society without introducing several different innovations at the same time. What has influenced what may be hard to disentangle.

Part of the difficulty may be overcome by simple administrative prudence and common sense, but the danger will be lessened if the purpose of the research is subject to proper limitation. Beyond this the important thing, if authorities are to obtain maximum value from these projects, is that they should know why they are doing them. It seems logical to suggest that the basic objective should be to discover principles and practices that can be applied successfully to other schools, other areas.

This has important implications. The first is that no 'research' should depend on providing resources on a scale so lavish that they would be impractical elsewhere. The second is that it is not sufficient merely to apply identical schemes to all other areas without stopping to consider whether they are wholly applicable. The aim should be to distil the essence of the scheme and then adapt it to the needs of the next area or the next problem. It was in this spirit that a modest enquiry into educational need in a district of Liverpool was begun in 1969.

## An example

In describing this enquiry we are not suggesting that it has produced, or can produce, any earth-shattering conclusions. Indeed its methods and terms of reference, in line with those we have just advocated, deliberately limited the exercise so as to avoid any temptation to try to prove things which are not susceptible to proof. It is described briefly here merely as an example of a modest, but useful, effort well within the range of local education authorities.

The enquiry began from the concept of the social education team described in chapter six. This idea was initially developed in one area of the city as a means of using available resources for the underprivileged more effectively. The early results encouraged the authority to extend the teams to other areas, but there was a need for careful enquiry before an identical pattern was imposed throughout the city.

The education committee therefore asked for research to be undertaken, and a team was set up from senior members of social science and sociology departments of colleges of education in the Liverpool Institute of Education. The team itself was an innovation in bringing together college staffs in a co-operative venture directed towards throwing light on a known problem: they and the students were able to take part in a venture that was not a training exercise nor a quest for information for its own sake, but something an education authority really wanted to know. The gap between innovators and researchers described by Michael Young was thus narrowed a little, a point illustrated by the fact that the exercise and the presentation of its findings were co-ordinated as a joint effort by the present authors.

The starting point was thus how best to apply the social education team idea to a new area. The first area chosen for the pilot project was typical of the inner ring twilight zone of large cities. The second was set up in an area with similar slum clearance problems and multi-block developments, but the next area proposed for the team-working was an area of multi-unit housing development on the edge of the city boundary. The physical conditions in this district were manifestly different from the other two, though the general feeling amongst the education committee members and administrators was that the social problems were no less. However, the physical difference emphasized that no one area is exactly like another, so that problems which on the surface appear the same, might in fact require different remedies.

The area was known as a 'problem area', otherwise it would not have been suggested as a district for early extension of the social education team idea, but the researchers were anxious to try to define exactly what was meant by 'problem area'. Occasionally an area is so defined on very flimsy evidence, such as one or two adverse reports in newspapers, or isolated 'statistics' which suggest instability. Once such a label has been attached, it can be very difficult for a community to live it down: it may even be easier to live up to the reputation. Sometimes, too, minority actions become the target for publicity and a whole neighbourhood is condemned as a result. And of course though areas change over the years, sometimes earlier reputations cling.

The first task then was to try to build up a picture of the community as seen by the residents themselves and those who worked in the area, who were concerned with the community in a professional capacity. Limitations of time, personnel, and research funds precluded full scale research such as that undertaken by the Lynds in 'Middletown' but it was possible to undertake a limited survey of the community which would not only provide factual information, opinion and recommendations, but which could also ensure (a) that the community was aware that the local authority was concerned to invite opinion and co-operation, and (b) that the professional workers most concerned with implementation of any policy decisions which might be made, could feel that they had had a fair opportunity to contribute their point of view.

This starting-point exemplifies an important principle that we have stressed in this book. Too often social policy is based on abstract philosophy or, less grandly, hunch. The limit of enquiry may be survey of opinion amongst professional people. When the process has gone further, sometimes the actual residents of the area have seemed to be thought of as mere research fodder. We discussed in some detail in the first chapter the limitations we believe attach to the right to intervene, the right to change a way of life chosen by another person. Whatever else this right includes, it does not, in our view, entitle potential reformers to make blanket assumptions.

For example, a common belief about working class attitudes assumes non-participation and lack of interest of parents in educational processes. This persists in spite of recent evidence that many so called are not in fact apathetic or uninterested but rather inarticulate and hesitant about the educational progress of their children when faced with existing means of communication. It seemed, therefore, not only logical, but a matter of simple justice to attempt to sample opinion of parents before initiating any scheme of welfare in the area.

## (a) Parental survey

The parental survey was by interview of a random sample of householders. The interviews were sub-divided into two sections, which differed in that certain questions were slanted towards either educational provision or housing and social amenities. The questionnaire was designed so that first questions elicited an immediate off-the-cuff response from the interviewees giving their opinion of the area in which they live in general terms, and then on more specific issues such as work, teenagers, old age, and so on. At that point, different questions were given to the two sub-samples.

For the first group the questions were concerned with specifically educational matters such as what was done to care for pre-school children, the parents' view of school discipline, curriculum, buildings, etc., and finally such things as the person or institution parents would turn to if they had any query or problem about the education of their children, and whether a visit had ever been made to the school.

The second group were asked about their major leisure pursuits and their opinion of the adequacy of leisure provision in the area, including interests, actual or potential, in evening classes and youth and community activities. They were also asked about shopping facilities, and as the areas of the survey included many re-housed families from the centre of the city, questions were asked about the distance to work, and to visit friends and relatives as well as doctors and dentists.

## (b) *Survey of professional workers*

A wide variety of voluntary (as well as statutory) welfare agencies were working in the area. Before initiating any reforms designed to secure more effective communication between the agencies (where children of school age were concerned), it was important that the personnel of the agencies working in the area should have the opportunity to state their opinions of the needs of the area, and give their own views as to the most effective use of resources to ensure the maximum welfare of the child and his family. This was a matter of common sense as well as fairness to those concerned.

Since the enquiry was undertaken for the Liverpool Education Committee the main emphasis of the research was upon education and how well it uses its special position in relation to inequalities of opportunity, so that information from heads and class teachers was essential. Whatever measures might be adopted the teachers would need to play a central part.

The first problem was discovering what social work was going on in the area. In the case of the schools it was easy to identify the individual teachers concerned and it was, of course, easy to identify the educational welfare and school health staff and only slightly less difficult with other corporation services. For the rest, letters were sent to the main agencies asking if they had clients in the area. Co-operation was, of course, sought from the headquarters of all agencies and permission asked to interview relevant officers dealing with clients in the area of the enquiry.

Questions were designed to identify clients in the survey schools and to elicit information about the extent to which there was communication with the school about these children. Other questions concerned the social worker's opinion on the adequacy of provision for children with various handicaps, and an attempt to identify the number of families where physical, mental or social well-being of the children was at risk. A most important section concerned the amount and extent of communication between the different agencies working in the neighbourhood.

Finally they were asked the same general questions about the area as the parents, to try to make it possible to compare the opinions of those who lived in the area and those who worked in the area in a professional capacity.

### (c) *Factual survey*

This last point leads to another important aim of this enquiry, to try to compare the opinions of those consulted with the facts so far as they could be ascertained. For example, that parents may be satisfied with standards is of little value if the actual achievement of the children is low compared with others in the city.

It was decided, therefore, to take this opportunity to undertake a more thorough testing programme of children in the primary schools in the survey area than is normally possible. This section of the enquiry was undertaken by an educational psychologist from a college of education in co-operation with the school psychological service. The tests included: (ability) a National Foundation for Educational Research non-verbal group test; (attainment in reading) a National Foundation for Educational Research sentence completion group test with individual reading tests to all children with a low score. In addition, class teachers were asked to fill in Bristol Social Adjustment guides for a 1 in 2 sample of their class. They were also given the opportunity to refer any child considered 'Difficult' or 'At Risk' (not in the sample group) for a similar assessment and later follow-up.

These tests were aimed at providing a survey of academic scores of children in the area using standardized tests, with screening out of those children who scored badly for further diagnostic and individual testing, and a survey of behavioural standard with more detailed discussion of individual children's problems. As well as help to individual children, the findings were used to compare ability and attainment with the average.

In the same way efforts were made to relate social standards generally to the rest of the city. The local authority already had in its possession considerable statistical material relating to housing, welfare, and education as a part of the normal returns from its officers. In addition, the City Planning Department had undertaken a more extensive survey which covered the range of housing and welfare, and, as part of a scrutiny of the education service initiated by a Corporation Management survey, the education department had produced a graduated assessment of the different districts of the city according to social need as measured by six criteria developed from those suggested by the Plowden report (incomplete families, large families, overcrowding, all children ascertained as educationally sub-normal or maladjusted, children on free school meals, and absenteeism).

The relevant figures for the survey area could thus be compared with others and with the whole city, as well as with any national figures that were available.

### (d) Cross-reference

As well as using figures to off-set assumptions and distortions, the research team also used cross-reference. For example, parents' claims to visit schools regularly were compared with Heads' assessments of the situation: one social worker's comment on inadequate co-operation from others was looked at in the light of the others' statement of his position.

One important part of the exercise was a review of one of the existing social education teams' work, and in this a major factor was a comparison of the aims and successes of team members, as they saw them, compared with the estimate by others of what they were doing and how well. The intention was, of course, to try to isolate particular points of conflict or difficulty in working so as to avoid repetition if possible in the new area. To see ourselves as others see us is one of the most difficult but most valuable things we can try to do. The survey hopes to make a small contribution towards this for the harassed full-time workers who have no time or scope for doing so for themselves.

The recommendations and findings are currently being considered by the sub-committee sponsoring the enquiry and are thus not ready for wider circulation. However, the findings themselves are at this point less important than the illustration of a possible method of approach with limited means towards a modest objective. It has been quoted simply to demonstrate that it can be done by any L.E.A. and that it can be useful.

The attainment of the first of these objectives is easy to demonstrate, and the second can, perhaps, be shown by a small example. Before the survey there was little knowledge even of what services were working in the area: this is now known and can be publicized in the schools and other agencies. Further, there was only the dimmest impression of the extent of communication between the services; whereas now the facts are known, not only in general but specifically who communicates with whom and who plays little part in collective effort.

This should be useful in implementing any new co-operative scheme in two ways. At a negative but practical level, in the past it has been difficult to counteract, except by promising hypothetical future benefits from a new system, the arguments of those, resistant to change, who claim that good co-operation already exists. With knowledge, the precise gaps in existing arrangements can if necessary be pointed out. More positively, the participation in the enquiry of those working in the area has not only informed them in advance of possible changes, but given them a chance to comment. Any scheme introduced in this way is likely to seem different from something out of the blue and imposed from on high.

This chapter has tried to show that research within its proper limitations can be valuable and that local education authorities, who are in the best position to undertake innovation, could and should use research more and should harness it to their service. The value of research is likely to be somewhere between the estimates of those who write off the idea as obscurantist or irrelevant in human affairs and those who, stupefied by the scale of the problem, clamour for more research as though it were a St Bernard dog bringing the brandy. Above all we have emphasized the need for hard information whenever possible, to try to get beyond impression, assumption, and prejudice as the basis for policy.

# Lines of advance

## ten

The emphasis of this book has been on action, but informed action. We have tried to explore some of the possibilities of collecting and using information about needs, determining what can and should be done to meet them, and deploying available resources to best advantage in a concerted attack on inequality of opportunity. Anyone who has worked for long in this most complex branch of education and the related social services will know that this attack cannot be organized in the logical, neat and tidy order that theoretically is ideal. Needs and objectives change, measurement of performance and progress is often all but impossible, and new discoveries are made that question the previous basis of working. Thus the provision of a service and the evaluation of its effectiveness have to go hand in hand: the philosophy is existentialist. We cannot always separate standards from techniques.

Yet this is not to say that techniques of intervention should be regarded as ideals in themselves. Unfortunately this tends to happen: links between home and school, for instance, may be regarded as ends not means. The superficial generalizations of educational theorists on these matters have their administrative counterparts in techniques that seem to exist largely for the benefit of the operators, in smooth machinery that is satisfying to control and to use. The result is that much of our activity is based on platitudes, both the intellectual kind and their administrative equivalents.

There is nothing wrong with platitudes. They often express accepted truths. And clichés are so widely used because they conveniently state familiar beliefs or ideas. Unfortunately their very familiarity means that they are too often accepted without proper understanding of, or thought about, their implications. And in matters affecting children's opportunities, however well intentioned our motives and aims, there are enormous possibilities of error through sheer vagueness; just as, however delicate and subtle the process of enquiry, it can be wasted if the method of implementation is insensitive or self-regarding.

This final chapter, in looking to the future, will try to get beneath the surface of some of the clichés of social work in education. There is a broad measure of agreement, at least amongst those who care, about what the most profitable lines of approach are likely to be. They tend to be expressed in slogans, which have their value, but which beyond a certain point can be ineffectual or even positively misleading. Perhaps analysis and reinterpretation can give them greater and more lasting value. That will, at least, be our aim in drawing together the threads of earlier chapters.

## Links between home and school

It is a step in the right direction to perceive that good relations between home and school are desirable and that improvement of this relationship can be the first stage in helping children who are educationally disadvantaged. But as a universal panacea it has its limitations on both philosophical and practical grounds.

Although education can be a potent force for social reform, history suggests that its direct use for this purpose is fraught with hazards. It is a requirement of democracy that the national education system should aim to equip individual children to take their own decisions on social questions rather than to implant particular attitudes in them or in the community generally. If this is accepted the school will see itself as concerned first and foremost with the education of the child, not as an agency to cure all social ills.

In this context the need for a good working relationship with parents is based upon the importance of parental support and encouragement of the educational progress of a child, and the starting-point of the link with parents is, therefore, education, not social welfare. We have suggested that, properly understood, this is in no way restrictive, but can be a source of strength in building up a helpful relationship with parents and fruitful co-operation with colleagues in other social services.

For many children, parental support is lacking because the parents themselves are by our standards inadequate: they may have mental, physical, or personality defects. The desire to put those right may well be strong, but quite apart from the moral issues of intervention the school is ill equipped to act as social caseworker: any support for the parents should be undertaken by those qualified to give it. The Plowden philosophy of compensatory education makes more sense as a role for the school than does that of general social work with families. The disadvantaged child is likely to need extra support from within the school, and with proper liaison between the school and any agencies working with the family this can be education's most effective contribution to a crisis situation, a contribution in keeping with its long-term role of fitting the child to become a better parent when its own turn comes.

This still leaves tremendous scope for home-school liaison within a truly educational context. But it means, for instance, that the suggestion of teachers visiting homes may be regarded more critically if it is accepted that home visiting (as an invasion of privacy) should be limited, that it requires skill as well as tact and a clear idea of what is being attempted and why. The first question is whether the visit is necessary. The school nurse and the Education Welfare Officer may already have considerable knowledge of some children or easy access to knowledge. Initial enquiries about children's home background can therefore be directed to them and only if nothing is known need the question arise of the school making contact with the parents. Even then there is the possibility of inviting the parents to the school. Only if they do not come, or do not acknowledge the invitation, need the question of a home visit arise.

When visits are made, either by the school direct or by the Education Welfare Officer, a number of practical points have to be considered. Home visiting is a skilled role, not to be undertaken lightly. The visitor may have to face any one of a variety of receptions from complete apathy to hostile aggression. It needs skill also to communicate a school's concern for the child to parents who may have little interest in or who completely reject the value of education and the values of the school. Skill is needed to determine the extent to which parental attitudes are based upon apathy or indifference or anxiety. If we add to these points the fact that other agencies may well be in touch with the very families with whom schools seek closer contact, the argument for restricting home visits to those skilled in social case-work becomes clearer.

Such a policy is extremist, and unlikely to work in practice: apart from this there are straightforward matters of specific concern to the schools where failing other means of contact, a home visit can be the best procedure. This suggests not that there should be no visits by the school but that they should be exceptional, carefully planned, and limited in their ambitions. This last point is important in itself. It needs great skill and experience to know how far the problems revealed by the visit can be handled by the school alone, or by the E.W.O., and how far they may indicate more deep-seated problems which require specialist investigation.

Ideally the school will know (either directly, or through the E.W.O.) which families are on the books of social work agencies. If this is not known, some investigation is essential before any visiting takes place: the most well-meaning school visit could destroy a very delicate casework relationship. On the other hand it is sometimes a matter of opinion whether the delicate casework relationship is of more importance than the specific needs of a child. The two are not necessarily opposed, but in order to achieve both objectives it is essential that school and case-workers should work together. If there is a problem impinging upon a child's education, then there should be a link between home and school, an exchange of information and confidence between parent and teacher. If in order to avoid excessive intrusion or overlapping of functions this is not to be achieved by direct contact, then there is a clear obligation on social workers and others who are in contact with the home to strengthen the link.

To be effective, therefore, the notion of links between home and school needs to be interpreted with care and implemented with caution and skill. If it is, then it can be the spearhead of an organized attack on inequality of opportunity. It emphasizes that the individual child in difficulty has to be considered as a whole, as a person not a specimen: seeing him in the context of his family can help to make this clear. Beyond this, where it takes the form of parental involvement in school activities, it may make an effective and democratic contribution to the long-term solution of those deep-seated problems that, we have argued, can only be achieved through changes in the attitudes of the community. It would be wrong to suggest that excessive enthusiasm by schools for home visiting is usual. The other extreme is unfortunately rather more common. Not all teachers are falling over themselves to mingle with parents. Witness for example this comment in the *Times Educational Supplement* of 15 August 1969:

> Everyone now pays lip service to the idea of involving parents in their children's education. But it is plain that, for many teachers, parental involvement is something that must not be allowed to get out of hand. It might, like the 'Frankenstein monster' conjured up by the members of the National Association of Head Teachers, turn and rend them.
> Last week we reported the case of an Essex Headmistress who encouraged neighbourhood mothers to come and help in her school. One of their jobs was to listen to the children

reading. A group of local primary teachers complained that this amounted to the use of unqualified labour and the result was that the Head got a sharp rap over the knuckles from the National Union of Teachers. Today, we carry some stormy parental reaction to this event.

The union claims that its action was dictated quite simply by its 'No unqualified teachers' policy. It appears to have forgotten another bit of policy that it formulated in March. On parental involvement, a special statement read:

'The Head and his colleagues should retain overall control and responsibility whatever kind of organisation is set up'. And decisions on how to involve parents, the statement adds, should be also left to the Head and his assistants.

The N.U.T. manages to appear in one of its more ridiculous poses whenever home and school relations come to the fore. As the new team become established at Hamilton House, the aim should be to chuck this kind of demarcation dispute and take a more positive line about children and parents.

The *T.E.S.* is, we may agree, a little hard on the teachers: parents helping to teach reading is not necessarily the best basis for good parent-teacher relations; nor is it very promising as a means of equalizing opportunity. The project quoted is perhaps a practical example of joint concern for the child, but if ever an aspect of education needed to be handled professionally it is the teaching of reading. Indeed the inadequate amount of research on this fundamental subject and the scant amount of skilled attention it receives as an aspect of the training of teachers are matters of national concern. And bringing in the neighbourhood mothers to help may —assuming each mother helps her own child—accentuate the differences between the 'haves' and the 'have-nots'. (If each mother is not helping her own child the relationship betwen parent and teacher is in danger of failing to focus on what they have in common—concern for an individual child.)

Yet the episode reminds us of the ambivalent attitude of many teachers towards parents, a situation that is unlikely to be resolved by pretending that the ambivalence does not exist or by failing to accept the basis of teachers' anxieties. Professional responsibility should include freedom from unnecessary interference: in satisfactory home-and-school liaison each partner understands and accepts the role of the other.

**School and community**

Description of this kind of home-school relationship is often enshrined in what is fast becoming another cliché, the community school. As on many similar issues there is a tendency for opposing factions to line up in favour of, or against, generalized notions without much analysis of what is involved. The debate about this question is handicapped by the almost infinite range of connotations of the phrase 'community school'.

There is a basic initial difficulty about what is meant by 'community'. Planners will argue happily for hours about it. A bigger problem, though, is the scope of the idea as a whole. If it relates to placing the physical resources of the school at the disposal of the people in the district, there is no problem, apart from the practical ones. But if there is an implication of raising community standards, then fundamental questions arise: for example, who in a democracy is entitled to more than one vote in deciding what those standards are. Planning the participation of other people in a project that is ostensibly for their benefit is an operation of some delicacy. Good intentions are not enough: where they lead is well known.

The dangers exist for education committee members and administrators as well as heads of schools, perhaps more so since they operate at some distance from day-to-day realities. This distance can give breadth of vision but it may mean loss of immediate and sensitive response to emerging needs. Before he begins to contemplate projects like community schools the education officer needs to look at the way he does his own job, the way he runs his office. What efforts does he make to be accessible —to the public, to his own staff? What is the atmosphere like? Does he care about the style of letter he and his staff write? Does he take the trouble to explain his decisions?

There is little glamour in humanizing an office so that it serves the public rather than confronts them with a series of hurdles to be surmounted, but it badly needs doing. Perhaps this is some way off the concept of a folk palace of culture and rest, but in the end the attitude of the administrator may be his best contribution to linking home and school. Unless the attitude is right, unless it permeates the whole of the service, then things like the community school may become mere rhetorical flourishes or, worse, experiments. Experiments are for mice, not human beings.

Nor is there much glamour in looking at traditional and ortho-dox provision to be sure that a consistent policy is being pursued: but it is not unknown for an authority to pursue, simultaneously, imaginative community-centred policies in one branch and insensitive ones in another. They may, for instance, seek to develop strong home and school links in areas of social deprivation, but have a policy on adult education of economic fees for recreational evening institute classes, which means that they tend to be available only for those who can afford to pay.

The first stage in a significant approach towards the community school is to make what exists more accessible, shaping it to meet people's needs. We may justifiably grumble about the apparently inevitable pattern in hospitals where patients have to be woken up at the crack of dawn and scrubbed and tidied up to fit the convenience of the medical profession. How different is the education service? For example, how far does the conventional pattern of starting school on a given date, full-time or nothing (and leaving school in the same way for that matter), fit the need of the individual child?

Teachers have an obligation in this, too. How serious are most schools about encouraging the young to handle their own affairs? Is there not rather more talk in most secondary schools about democracy than opportunities to practise it? How many high-minded lessons about the virtues of co-operation are actually put into practice by schools? Could not, and should not, the long, slow process towards involving the community begin with the child, not its parents?

Educationists are sometimes strangely reluctant to think of children as people. They tend to think mainly in terms of preparing children for something else, rarely of their needs at the time. The developing history of the education service suggests that we have consistently and sadly underestimated the potential of children, and that this is at least in part the result of failing to consider them as individuals, distinct from their backgrounds, with legitimate needs of their own. Perhaps the clash between co-operative ideals and competitive reality in many schools stems from this. If we think of education as preparing children to become adults who will take their places in society as it is, then we would fail in our duty if we did anything else than fit them for a competitive struggle. They need a mouse race at school to fit them for the rat race. But if we accept children as people already, with needs and attitudes, and we gear their education to developing what is there now, might they not have a better chance of shaping their own society?

Of course, parents too need to be given real opportunity to share in making responsible decisions on behalf of their children. Unfortunately the question of parental involvement tends to run aground in discussions about whether parents should be represented on governing and managing bodies, about the role of parent/

teacher associations, about open evenings, and so on. These are all useful activities but they do little to open up the real problems of our kind of democracy. There is, first of all, the deep and growing division between the professional and the amateur emphasized by the kind of situation described in the extract from the *Times Educational Supplement* on page 169. In a complex society like ours this is overlain by the tensions between different kinds of professional experts to which we have frequently referred. The professionals have an obligation to sort themselves out before speculating on the problems of the community. And, again, although there are more democratic safeguards built into the education service than anywhere else, the result, sadly, is sometimes a welter of committees, an elaborate web that makes people affected by the service feel cut off from the real sources of power.

So long as there are assumed to be formal institutional bodies responsible for all decisions, any talk of involving the people themselves is bound to be superficial. Supposing some way is found of choosing a representative parent to serve on the school managers, this achieves little if the managers' meeting is itself a charade, a democratic interlude in the otherwise untroubled lives of the professionals. Community involvement to be meaningful must follow critical examination of the very basis of the education service and of local government as a whole.

First, the role of elected committee members themselves needs to be strengthened by closer involvement in policy making. Second, the professionals must give themselves a new look (by, for instance, questioning the traditional hierarchical ladder-structure of power in which the people nearest the public are the most junior, and therefore have the least experience and the least power). They must be ready to co-operate with their fellows. Third, the field-worker needs to be freed from bureaucratic constraints and established as part of a co-operating, responsible team. These are points to which we must return later in considering ways in which team-work can be extended to government itself. But in these matters and throughout the whole question of community schools the most important question is that of objectives—what are we trying to achieve?

This can sometimes seem to be little more than to have people participating, being in on the action for its own sake. This approach seems doomed to failure, to death through sterility. Participation— in any sphere—has to be *about* something, if it is to be meaningful. Furthermore the notion of indiscriminate participation can represent, quite unintentionally, an essentially patronizing attitude to working class members of the community. They are required to be active and vocal in order to demonstrate their entitlement to be considered good citizens. This is not unlike a type of attitude to certain young people in youth clubs. They may just want to sit down and talk but tend to be urged into constructive and creative activities by their elders, who seem to expect the young to be different animals entirely from themselves.

Adopting an overt and generalized policy of community involvement may also (unwittingly perhaps) seek to impose neat and tidy do-gooding patterns of the most superficial kind on ways and habits of life that the professionals only dimly understand. Of course the professionals should accept the importance of trying to discover the real needs of the people concerned in community involvement; and clearly it is a step forward when this happens. Some education authorities have experimented, for instance, with the appointment of officers especially for this purpose; but just how successful this method alone can be is uncertain. There is no foolproof method yet of discovering anyone's *true* needs, and the gap between our assumptions and the knowledge and interests of some of those we seek to serve, may be too great to avoid the dangers of making this an artificial exercise, achieving in the main little more than emotional satisfaction for the professionals.

Another, perhaps more promising, approach for the education service is to narrow the range of (and apparently reduce the level of ambition in) community involvement. This method does not begin with the discovery of 'needs' that impinge directly on broad social questions but with involvement over more neutral, less ambitious things, things that really do meet a need, even if an apparently less profound one. Thus the involvement of parents in the community school might start, at a very humble level, with a keep-fit class organized by the parents themselves. Association of this kind might later on bring contacts with community workers that would give them a clue to real needs—people are noticeably more likely to reveal their true feelings in this way than when asked about them in cold blood.

If the notion of purposeful involvement is applied to parents' participation in matters that concern their children, could not for instance the schools make special efforts to brief parents about the implications of choice of subjects for their children, and do their best to help them play a part in sharing decisions like these? Apart from its intrinsic value, this sort of parental involvement seems more likely to create good relationships between teacher and parent (since it involves the parent *as* a parent, not as an amateur teacher or representative of the community) than the extremes of bringing parents into the classroom or simply wanting them to be involved for its own sake. It seems more promising also than considering parents as temporary managers. Working together on a matter of common interest is perhaps more likely to be fruitful than serving together on a committee with vaguely defined objectives and little influence.

From limited beginnings wider, stronger opportunities can grow, and the opportunity to launch a full scale community school project will not be lost by 'caring' education authorities. On a sound basis of existing good relationships with parents it is an exciting possibility. Perhaps the start of such a venture may be a vacant school building or one that is seriously under-used, a fairly frequent phenomenon in the centres of some of our cities. A particular example of this is beginning to flourish in a four-decker former all-through school in a down-town area of Liverpool. A dwindling population and much re-development has left it standing, solid if unbeautiful, amongst flattened sites awaiting transformation into car parks or other adjuncts to the surrounding University complex; its other neighbours are a shiny new comprehensive school and a very modern hospital. The school's iron railings now enclose a small primary school.

Under the Urban Programme this is to become a community project. The ground floor will have a new nursery class adjoining a room in which mothers can sit and talk. There they may do their own (or the school's) sewing or simply put their feet up, perhaps persuading their husbands to help in transforming bit by bit the outside of the building into adventure playground, raised garden, pram park, paddling pool and what you will. Next door will be a reading and quiet room for all users of the building, but perhaps particularly the retired and elderly of the district who might find pleasure in being in a building that houses little children. The rest of the ground floor, at present a traditional iron-pegged cloakroom and two open classrooms, will be made into a refectory area : the kitchen will serve not only midday meals, for children and adults, but refreshments all day and in the evenings.

The second floor will be the school itself (classrooms, workrooms, and library) where the emphasis will be on an approach involving parents and linking school work with the environment, perhaps also serving a wider neighbourhood by offering short remedial programmes for backward or severely disadvantaged children. The floor above will be a curriculum development centre for educational priority area schools, where action programmes will be distilled from the work of the school below and put out as practical suggestions to other schools in similar areas.

The top floor (hall, stage, and large practical rooms) will be used jointly by the school, the development centre and the community generally. There will be a community warden whose job will be to work in the community and encourage them to use the project's facilities either as organizations or individuals. Parents of children in trouble or at risk will, it is hoped, meet education welfare officers, social workers and teachers quite informally in this environment and perhaps build up a better relationship than traditional methods allow.

Another venture in Liverpool is in a new housing estate where the comprehensive school is planned to serve the whole community. Not only the physical facilities, which will be used as a community centre, including traditional youth and adult activities, but the staffing of the school will reflect this purpose. A deputy head will have responsibility for community work as well as practical care in the school. Apart from the academic staff there will be three house-masters with responsibility for the welfare of the pupils: each will have a remedial teacher/counsellor in his house. Two other col-leagues will teach part-time by day and undertake youth or adult work in the evening. This may become a family school, in fact.

How well these facilities will be used is unknown. Implicit in the arguments of many exponents of the community school is the idea of the community, eager and responsive, bursting to make constructive contributions to progress, but kept out by the inflexible and unwelcoming system. Of course, this is in part true, but how big a part is more conjectural. Taken at its face value, the view seems to have at least some of the elements of a romantic myth.

We have to acknowledge frankly that there are some members of the community who care nothing about the social system or whether they are involved in it. There are others who do care—or say they do—but who prefer not to be involved, who would rather be free to grumble about 'them'. And there are still others whose attitudes and aspirations we know very little about. Perhaps they scarcely know what they want; certainly they do not express their thoughts.

Any policy must recognize individual needs, not regard 'the community' as a homogeneous mass. The wider use of physical amenities is one thing. Participation, where it is practical, in the process of government is another. But if we consider the needs of the less articulate our priorities may be different. Perhaps the first need is to make easier and less daunting the kind of con-frontation with authority that most people have during their lives—at the time of the allocation of places in secondary schools, for instance—and that so many of them find quite overpowering. It might help if confrontations like this could take place, not in chromium-plated, ocean-going liner style civic buildings or in grim Victorian monstrosities, but in small friendly local places where people could drop in and discuss their problems with sympathetic listeners.

The suggestion concerns more than buildings, because what it implies is a new attitude towards the question of advice and guidance, particularly for those with children suffering from handicaps that come between them and their education. There is at present a world of difference between the situation of those who want advice about, say, university grants and those who need guidance about a backward or maladjusted child. By no means all of this distinction is the result of the attitudes of authority—some of it comes from deep-seated prejudice and superstition in the community itself. But authorities have a prime responsibility to do all they can to eradicate the distinction, and work towards the day when guidance of any kind is regarded on both sides as an uncomplicated, respectable, unemotive right, like national health spectacles.

## Team-work

Stronger links between school and community imply effective working relationships between teachers and other agencies. Earlier chapters have suggested principles on which effective working relationships can be built. Education is concerned with the whole child, and the best practitioners are acutely conscious that the teacher's specialist skills may not be enough to ensure educational progress. This may be hampered by physical, mental, emotional or environmental factors which require expert diagnosis and treatment. Yet the teacher is involved. He may very often be the first person to recognize that something is wrong. The ideal is that the teacher should have enough knowledge to know when to refer the child to the appropriate specialist. This should not be a one-way process, for as long as the child remains in the school the teacher must logically be involved in the continuing process of diagnosis and treatment by outside experts.

This is plain commonsense, but regrettably very often forgotten in the mystiques that surround specialisms. Anyone who has attempted to bring about a simple form of inter-professional consultation will be aware of the difficulties. These do not merely stem from the existence of separate local government departments: they arise within the departments themselves. People, asked to co-operate in this way, tend to claim that they already do it: this can mean anything from actually telephoning other people when a crisis arises to merely knowing the other person's number, but it rarely means more.

Any attempt to combine forces, however simple or however elaborate, has to contend with this difficulty. It is not enough to create structures, or hold meetings, or inculcate team-working. Liaison does not just happen: it has to be organized. It has to be based on clearly understood objectives, on the acceptance of professional and administrative realities and traditions, and on sensible working rules as well as on the good will of the participants. This does not mean that it must be impersonal and formal. Indeed the better organized the system, the more likely it is to create a good atmosphere—personal relationships are not at their best in a shambles.

The basis of satisfactory liaison is a pattern of regular face-to-face meetings amongst those working together on the problems of the same group of children. Telephoning, letter writing and informal meetings of sections of the group may all be valuable additional methods, but without the sustaining influence and discipline of organized full meetings they become merely *ad hoc* and casual.

The most common meeting of this kind is that known as the case-conference: this is certainly better than nothing, but it can often fall short of what is really required. The name itself is unfortunate. 'Case' is a useful form of shorthand but it is unlikely that any of those who come together to confer would like to be thought of as a case. And the horizons of such meetings are often too limited to go beyond making decisions when a crisis situation has already been reached. Consultation about crisis situations for individual children is, of course, important. When a child is referred by a school for treatment by another agency the teacher needs to be involved in the remedial process by giving the right kind of support-ive treatment in the classroom situation. But just as important is the potentiality of these liaison meetings for preventive work. The teacher can sometimes detect strain in a child, a clue which can be followed up by someone who is in normal daily contact with a family. The social worker can point to tension in a family which may affect the child's school work. Ideally, from sharing knowledge and discussion of the different skills required, a common philosophy of concern will arise which, though co-operative, nevertheless recog-nizes that each has a specialist contribution to make.

Much of the value of liaison meetings can be lost if those taking part are not those who have the day-to-day responsibility for tackling the problems being discussed, the field-workers. In the school, the field-worker is the class teacher and if he is to be enabled to accept the implications of his role there is a need for considerable re-thinking by heads of schools and by authorities. This is particularly so at the vital primary school stage. In second-ary schools, size and relative status have led to the creation of senior posts, the holders of which are by now used to being given auth-ority to deal direct with outside agencies. In the smaller, less well staffed, less specialized primary schools, traditional attitudes tend to prevail.

Meetings of field-workers can be the beginning of team work. As

well as being a method of linking specialists in the field, the notion
of team-work has implications for the education service and local
government generally. The team is a natural form of organized
activity for human beings. It is a feature of their play as well as their
work. The reason is, of course, entirely functional: you win more
matches if you play as a team. It is a way of banding together for
strength and in the work situation it seems especially appropriate to
a democracy since it emphasizes inter-dependence.

Now a critical problem for any team is the need to specialize, in
order to grapple with complex opposing problems: under-stated
this can create a disorganized rabble; over-stated it may lead to
over-consciousness of demarcation lines in establishing the roles of
individual members. Over-specialized sophistication is one of the
weaknesses of the highly developed structures that we have set up
to solve our governmental problems. They are particularly restrictive in the social services, where team-working would often be more
appropriate. The characteristics of teams include action directed
towards a particular end and restricted in scope and time, and the
ability to form and dissolve according to need. Our organizations
tend to be permanent, somewhat generalized and operating in an
essentially static situation.

The basic process of decision-making in education and local
government generally is through committees. Classically, committee
meetings are held at stated intervals regardless of the amount of
business; items may go on the agenda regardless not only of their
relative importance but also of their varying nature; and the
decision-making machinery tends to be stereotyped, though the
problems are not. This may mean that whether the question is
philosophical or financial it is the subject of a report from an
officer, and the committee have to make a yes/no decision. Not
surprisingly, this leads to many deferments and much setting up of
sub-committees. In fact, resourceful practice often has to find ways
of working round the theory and trying to inject dynamism into a
static situation.

There is a clear need to explore ways of injecting flexibility into
decision-making, and the team concept seems to offer possibilities.
For instance there are many occasions on which working parties of
officers and elected members are valuable. First of all they represent
a realistic way of involving members in policy making: they come
in on shaping policies as distinct from just pronouncing on them.
Then again they discourage officers from cosily sheltering behind
their role as mere advisers. If these meetings are aimed at specific
problems and the process does not become too formalized we get
the classical team situation in which the officers and the members
collectively accept responsibility for recommendations or plans

emerging from the working party, and they come together in a particular relationship for a particular purpose.

To deal with committees first is not to suggest that they are the chief obstacle to progress. In fact, relatively speaking, committees are aids to flexibility and are an important reason why local government tends to be more flexible than the civil service. Office organization is usually much less susceptible to change.

The traditional local government framework of a hierarchical ladder-structure, immobile and status-conscious, operates even in education departments in spite of the widespread recruitment of senior administrators from teaching, where the common-room notion of *primus inter pares* is well known. The usual assumption is the transmission of instructions from top to bottom and of information and draft solutions from bottom to top, and the usual result is a long straggling chain of command of a highly theoretical kind. Theoretical, because practice cannot live with its implications— such as pieces of paper passing through dozens of hands—so that the official system has to be by-passed. Naturally, practice modifies theory only fitfully and we tend to get the worst of both worlds.

Re-thinking of organization patterns, where it exists, tends merely to replace one static situation by another. Replacing tentacles by shorter lines of communication, ladder-structures by clusters of cells, is an improvement, but it still falls short of what the realities of working require. If we want to apply the team characteristics (action and application of resources to specific problems of administration), a more useful pattern may be one of inter-related cells, but cells that move, that group and re-group according to the job in hand. An acknowledged place in an office hierarchy is necessary as a fixed point of reference, but it is a very inadequate concept to apply to a situation in which a man may find himself playing many different roles in widely differing relationships to his colleagues, every day of his life.

This is a complex question to which only detailed analysis can give satisfactory answers, but two brief points can be made here. One is that most anxieties about relative status within organizations can be resolved by considering the particular context in which the difficulties arise. The other is that project teams, specific groupings to tackle specific jobs, are a valuable way of establishing sensible and unselfconscious working relationships.

Many problems of relationship arise between practitioners of different specialisms within departments and between different departments. If half the energy that goes into struggles over empire went into the job itself we should have more to show for our pains. Local authorities are deeply conscious of this built-in weakness, but most of the proposed solutions seem unlikely to succeed largely because they tend to suggest creating new static institutions for centralizing power. They subordinate specialist field-workers and specialist administrators to general co-ordinating committees and overlords. This may look like progress, but in our increasingly complex world any solution that tries to move away from specialization rather than through it looks backwards not ahead.

We need an alternative solution of a more dynamic kind, one that will translate the specialist's potential into action. To achieve this, the specialist, particularly if he is a field-worker, needs a degree of freedom from his own bureaucracy (this applies whether specialists are employed by different departments or all by the same) and to meet the requirements of a co-ordinated approach he needs the discipline of working with other, different experts. Experience shows that problems of co-operation that may seem insuperable if viewed in terms of handing over administrative responsibility from one department to another may quickly disappear if each separate department delegates authority to its own man on the spot and he in turn works in a team.

Team-working of this kind is, in effect, an operational research exercise in which information and expertise are pooled to permit a problem to be examined from all angles and thus seen (a) as a whole and (b) as potentially responsive to solution by a number of different disciplines. After analysis a particular specialism or combination may seem most likely to be successful: those who undertake specific responsibility then do so secure in the support of colleagues and able to draw on the team's resources of information and skills at any time. This notion is the thread that should run through all attempts to combat inequality by linking specialists. The full rigour of this concept has to be applied at the point of impact—amongst the field-workers—regardless of the administrative framework within which they operate.

## Voluntary effort

There must be a place in the team for others besides the professionals. We have already emphasized the importance of greater involvement of elected representatives, and there could scarcely be better examples of unpaid voluntary effort than most local councillors. It is odd that people do not usually include them when speaking of voluntary work in the social services.

There are perhaps two main reasons for this. One is a historical reason: because of our traditions we are more likely to mean by 'voluntary effort' the work of voluntary agencies like the councils of social service. Another is that, because of the association with the committees of the council and the services they offer, councillors seem to many members of the public—perhaps particularly those with whom the social services are most in contact—to be part of the Establishment. So councillors, like their officers, may not be well placed in all circumstances to help individuals in need (as distinct from promoting policies for society generally), or to help inarticulate sectors of society to express their feelings.

The point can be overstressed. Sometimes those who take this line in the name of democracy may set in train processes that in fact try to by-pass existing democratic machinery (that may be said to be inadequate and insensitive but is in practice too little used to be put to the test). But councillors do have more than one function, and undoubtedly this can limit the extent to which they can act as a bridge between the bureaucracy and people in need.

The same difficulties attach to any official or semi-official body, regardless of whether they are professionals or amateurs. Governors and managers fulfilling statutory obligations, however inappropriate these may be to present-day needs, labour under difficulties if they want to bridge the gap between school and community by voluntary effort. Parent-teacher associations may hover uncertainly between organizing whist drives and an occasional incursion into applying pressure for changes in the school. Even if their role is clear, many parents will feel that this kind of activity is not for them; and these parents are likely to include many with whom the school needs to establish the closest possible links.

These bodies in their present form show in most areas little sign of playing a major part in bringing school and community together. Yet in embryo they offer tremendous possibilities. There are gaps to be filled and there is no point in creating new machinery to do this when it exists already. (Indeed two lots of machinery in the same restricted space can be an embarrassment.) But if it is to do the job properly the existing equipment needs overhaul. So far as governors and managers are concerned, the necessary review of their functions is largely a matter for the authorities, but they themselves could take a lead. Parent-teacher associations have more freedom to adapt themselves to change: perhaps their best contribution would be in concentrating on improved relations between parents and class-teachers.

This re-appraisal could be assisted by such organizations as the Confederation for the Advancement of State Education, who represent more nearly what is usually understood by a voluntary agency. Together with bodies like the Child Poverty Action Group and Shelter, they exemplify, however, an approach by no means in line with the traditional image of voluntary charitable organizations of the past, but one increasingly emerging as the characteristic one of the later twentieth century. Their concern is less with charity than in doing away with the need for charity. Nor is this confined to newly born groups. Thus the General Secretary of the Liverpool Personal Service Society, an organization over fifty years old, in an article on the role of the voluntary social welfare services listed first 'to act as pressure groups uncovering needs and pressing for new services' (Harbert, 1970). This is one argument, then, for voluntary as well as statutory effort in social work.

The pressure-group function is a variant of a more traditional role of the voluntary sector—breaking new ground. Voluntary agencies may, for instance, provide a service where there is a need, but one which society as a whole may not yet be ready to meet as a duty. For example, in family planning the amount of controversy attached to the question of how far the state should go in helping its members—particularly the unmarried—makes it a suitable field for the voluntary effort of those whose convictions persuade them that this is a suitable way of serving the community. The voluntary effort may or may not be accepted by the community as a desirable service in the long run, but even if it is not, the enterprise will at least have had the effect of drawing attention to a problem.

Indeed bigger difficulties for voluntary agencies tend to arise when these pioneering services are accepted as normal and desirable. Nowadays if this happens they tend to become the responsibility of statutory authority. This has been one of the major sources of overlap, confusion, and sometimes bitterness between statutory and voluntary. Hence the new kind of voluntary organization which emphasizes the importance not so much of supplementing as of improving the official provision. For those agencies offering what once were pioneering services the problem is greatest. There is usually little purpose in the voluntary body continuing to provide services for very long after the state has assumed responsibility. They may, of course, fill local gaps; or offer higher standards as a pace-setter. But few voluntary agencies operate without subsidies of some kind, so if the higher standards are apparently only achieved with the aid of substantial grants from the government or local authority this approach raises as many questions as it solves.

When the moment of truth comes, a forward-looking voluntary body is likely to be ready to move on to new ventures; and forward-looking statutory ones should be ready to help them to do this. Much will depend on how broadly based the particular agency is. The highly specialized will find it difficult to transform themselves; and there are dangers in forever seeking new fields to conquer. A more permanent and more valuable role for the voluntary element may be that of helping the citizen to cope with the complexity of modern life.

Few will deny that this is necessary. Indeed a person in difficulties may need help to pick his way through the bureaucratic processes that surround the provision of help, processes that are inevitable in any statutory welfare organizations since public money is involved. In the very nature of things the statutory bodies are unable to perform this job for themselves as Joan Eyden in *Social Policy in Action* (1969) illustrates:

> The growth of personal services within multi-functional authorities can give rise to problems between the authority and the citizens it serves. Thus the local authority may be landlord, enforcer of school attendance, and provider of a casework service to the same family. It can arise that the social worker employed by one department of the authority may be required to give help of a highly personal kind with problems to which the authority itself may be partner.

In tackling this, the voluntary services are not only acquiring a permanent future role for themselves but attempting something that, probably, only they can do satisfactorily. The reinterpretation of the cliché 'voluntary agencies' for the present day has to take into account their value in representing the interests of the community, in giving a constant and tangible reminder that the welfare services exist for the sake of the people. Nor need this function of 'standing alongside the client' apply only to the short-term target of social work, the crisis situation. The voluntary agencies can perform an equally valuable function in the long-term problem of eradicating inequality of opportunity, which must depend for its complete success on changes in the attitude of the community itself. Changes of this kind, where deep-seated prejudices may exist, are likely to take a long time. If the statutory agencies, for example the education service, try to hurry the process along, then the fabric of democracy may be threatened. There is surely a place in these circumstances for the enterprising members of the community to give a hand to their fellow citizens, to set an example, to stimulate discussion of problems. The voluntary agencies are ideally placed to do this.

## A change of heart

In the end, any 'agency', statutory or voluntary, is superficially, a poor substitute for what is really needed. We have suggested an essentially pragmatic approach, beginning with at first, the negative goal of removing inequalities of opportunity, beginning by identifying the targets for reform by careful analysis. It is inevitable that in seeking to introduce order, organization, measurement, precision, into our approach we should concentrate largely on questions of technique. But we have tried to emphasize even more strongly that techniques are of little value unless they are firmly based on principles. Analysis is intended as a way of finding a secure base for these principles, not as a substitute for them. This is particularly important when from our own initial premise—a free, democratic society—the pursuit of principles cannot be an exact science. There is a built-in tension in our society between the desire for equality of opportunity and the desire for freedom. How are we to set any standards in this if individuals are free to reject our ideas? How are we to begin to agree on the basis of these standards?

To say that long-term change must come from the community itself is to take us little further. We are in the realms of attitudes, values and beliefs rather than analysis and reason. We are looking for nothing less than a change of heart. This sounds perhaps like a futuristic vision, but if it is ever to happen it must begin today, making a start in the small ways we have been discussing. When the highly complex technical arguments have all been heard, men are left with decisions of their own to make about what is right and what is wrong. Each man must act in the end according to his own conscience.

In a sense such an attitude may seem to make the prospect of social progress even more slight, by reminding us that the variety of opinion implicit in democracy can fairly easily become unconstructive anarchy. The existence of a society implies discipline amongst its members; and if it is not supplied from above then the members must provide it for themselves. If a democratic society is to continue at all, then either the consciences of the majority must operate in a way that helps rather than hurts their fellow men, or else an enlightened minority must achieve a consensus strong enough to hold its own against the rest.

The hope of social progress in such a society must rest on the belief that conscience is something more than a blinding flash of individual intuition. A decision made according to one's conscience is not a decision made according to criteria that are entirely arbitrary or individualistic: it depends on standards that are an amalgam of all our past experiences and influences as well as our own personality. In other words it depends on nurture as well as nature.

This means that the education system, even in a democracy (where it may seem to follow rather than form public opinion), can make a contribution to social advance by laying foundations for the future. Though we may not all agree about the meaning of inequality of opportunity in education, or what we should do about it, we can find a much broader measure of agreement about eradicating negative tendencies. The consensus of enlightened opinion in the present age takes us at least as far as removing social inequalities as they are discovered and understood. This book has been concerned with ways of discovering, understanding and removing injustices in the education service. If we can achieve this we shall be helping to lay the foundations for a future society, one in which it is possible to envisage an education system in which the chances of all children may one day be truly equal.

# Appendix

Reference was made in Chapter 5 to teacher-social workers and pastoral care departments in both primary and secondary schools. There is at present no general agreement about the value of these innovations or of the form they ought to take. The pattern is largely determined by the individual Heads in consultation with staff, and the two following accounts of practices in a primary school and a large comprehensive school are the personal accounts of the head-teachers concerned. They are not intended as models, but as illustrations of different approaches.

## Social work in a primary school

The role of teacher-social worker was envisaged as having a teaching, an advisory and a cultural aspect. The teacher would not have responsibility for a class, but would be employed in teaching with small groups of six or seven children, who through adverse home conditions, poor attendance, or emotional disturbance at school or at home, were not working at full potential or were showing signs of stress. This work would be basic work in speech, reading and number. Recommendations to join these groups would be made by the class teacher.

In the advisory aspect of the work the teacher-social worker would assist the class teacher, where such help was needed, to diagnose specific difficulties in individual children, and would also provide an opportunity for any child to have a private interview and to receive counsel.

In the cultural role, the teacher-social worker would be responsible for running a club whenever the school was grouped for this kind of activity.

Outside the school, the more experimental and more challenging side of the work was to be done. It was thought that before going out as a school 'ambassador' the new teacher would need some time to become familiar with the ethos of the school—its aims, its problems, its attitudes. After a term or so, the following pattern should emerge and the appointment fulfil these aims: —

(a) to build up home-school relationships with those families who seldom, if ever, visit school, by making visits to their homes. These visits initially would be by appointment, mutually agreeable to parent and teacher, and would concern the child's progress in the teaching group. Most of these visits would be between 9.00 a.m. and 4.00 p.m., but some would have to be in the evening.

(b) to help relationships 'on the Estate' by meeting parents wherever they were likely to congregate—at the Community Association meetings (held at that time in school), at the Church, at the Old People's meetings etc.

(c) to work with all the educational, social and medical agencies likely to be already active with these families. Here the need to make good personal relationships with the officers of the school welfare services, the child guidance and medical services, the child care and probation services, would be of paramount importance.

(d) to inaugurate a system of 'home tuition' in those cases where a continued but justifiable absence from school would not warrant official home tuition, but where the child needs to be kept in contact with his class and its work.

(e) to assist in the transfer of children to secondary schools and to strengthen contact with these schools and to work closely with our own infant school.

I hoped that the teacher appointed would be a mature person, experienced in helping children with learning difficulties, sensitized to the social deprivations of children, with a listening ear, a flexible and non-judgmental attitude, who could gain the respect, not only of parents, but also of the staff of the school. We were fortunate to find such a person and she was appointed to start duty on 1 January 1966.

After three and a half years it is still a difficult exercise to assess the real worth of this appointment. The role has developed very much as originally planned, although one or two unforeseen, but healthy, off-shoots have grown, bearing the imprint of this teacher's own experience and personality.

Currently, she devotes her morning sessions to group teaching, which she will interrupt only for urgent reasons and when she is able to return the children to their own class teachers. Two or three afternoons each week are used for home visiting or meeting parents visiting school, whilst club activities (this term, tropical fish and aquarium maintenance) and music with first year pupils, occupy the rest of her time.

Initial home visits are always planned, but as relationships mature and as her work is now well known, chiefly through the medium of our monthly newsletter to all parents, follow-up or 'emergency' visits are sometimes unannounced.

A most popular and enterprising development has been the Wednesday afternoon Parents' Meeting. This meets in the youth club annexe, adjoining school, and is attended each week by between thirty and forty mothers and their 'under 5' children. This group of parents, most of whom have had home visits from the teacher-social worker, have been encouraged to become a self-help group, supported by school whenever necessary. At this meeting, clothes and footwear, supplied by charitable friends from churches and elsewhere, can be bought at 'Jumble Sale' prices, tea and biscuits are provided, and in the easy chair atmosphere of the youth club lounge, informal talks and discussion are centred around a theme introduced by a visiting speaker. Here, members of staff, the Headmaster, the Headmistress of the infant school, welfare workers, social workers, nurses, probation officers, Citizens' Advice Bureau personnel, marriage guidance counsellors, Gas Board cookery demonstrators, have introduced topics of realistic value to these mothers.

Pre-school children have to accompany their mothers to these meetings, so a play group was set up with the aid of volunteer mums, one with a Child Care training, with help from senior girls from the nearby secondary school for girls and with equipment and materials loaned from school and the infant school. This flourishing group of twenty to thirty children meeting (in a free and relaxed atmosphere) is the first contact they have with school.

Points of contact with most social agencies have strengthened through the years, for whereas in the early days, particularly in the medical field, suspicion and fear of encroachment was not uncommon, worthwhile co-operation and recognition of each other's value is now accepted. The teacher-social worker has fostered these relationships, so that she is a valued colleague on the local Social Services Council, and meets social workers and others at the monthly lunch discussions. Gaps in our social welfare structure are apparent, but when parents seek our help they can usually be directed to an appropriate service. Sometimes, however, parents want little more than a listening ear.

Amongst the staff the main effects of this appointment have been to develop more sensitivity to the needs of the individual child, to see him more distinctly against the confidentiality of his home background, and to encourage each class teacher to meet the parents of each member of the class.

## Social work in a secondary school

Part of the organization I built up in launching this new school— an amalgamation of two modern schools—was a Careers, Remedial and Welfare Department. It is staffed by a Grade 'C' Head of Department, and two Scale III posts, who first of all make themselves known to the feeding junior schools, visit them and see the children working, and discuss them with the Head Teacher and staff concerned.

Before the end of their last year in the juniors they are invited to the school for an afternoon. The Welfare Department and the Senior Mistress talk to them, and our first-year children then conduct them over the school. Apart from this they are invited to the Sports Day, School Concert and school play and many of them take part in the local junior school musical festival which is based at the school. Their new school should not, therefore, be strange to them when they arrive in September and they will know some members of the staff. In addition, there is a 'new parents' evening.

When the new entrants are known, my Welfare staff immediately contact the feeding schools for record cards and other information. Lists of the new children are sent to the Educational Welfare Officer and the school doctor, the health visitor and child care officer with a request for them to tell us the problems of those children on the list known to them. It is vital that we know of problems before they arrive, in particular those attending child guidance clinics, or in contact with remedial teaching or Social Education teams, and medical cases. When this information is collected we have conferences with the departments concerned and the school doctor. Lists are prepared for the staff summarizing information essential to the day-to-day progress of each child. In this way we try to avoid upsetting children and undoing months of hard work.

Children are placed in groups according to their junior school record cards. The children with specialist needs are put into smaller units to make the transition easier. In October the Department tests the entire group to obtain a common assessment. Consequent upon this, those children about whom we are disturbed are referred to the school doctor and the educational psychologist, who then check our findings and advise us accordingly.

Selective medicals are then arranged on the basis of school, home and medical referral. Usually there are about 80 to 90 children, who are examined thoroughly over 12 sessions. Further conferences then occur and decisions are made about particular children.

In December after the school internal examinations, I formulate lists of first-year children who appear to be displaced. The heads of the welfare and academic departments discuss these with me and we decide how best we can help them. The Welfare Department is responsible for allocation of new children to initial groups, and thereafter they can move children on a welfare basis, though all academic movement is the responsibility of Heads of Departments.

Apart from this they deal with all medical matters, accidents, hospital visits, etc. Careers advice cannot be given in isolation and children's problems must be known. There is, therefore, close co-operation with Y.E.O. in 3rd, 4th and 5th years, as far as possible on an individual basis. This also involves the use of parents' evenings and careers conventions, and co-operation with Heads of Departments regarding 3rd year choice of options for 4th year.

There is no separate Remedial Department; all children carry out common courses of work including a foreign language—if they cannot exist in a school society without being labelled how can they survive in the world of work? The problem is to give them confidence and boost their ego, therefore remedial work is individual—the child quietly withdrawn from sets for reading and number. It is also important that our progress and methods should be checked by the educational psychologist and doctor *in the school situation,* not in a clinic.

# References

*Chapter One*

Austin, E., Jr., 'Cultural Deprivation—A Few Questions' in *Education and Social Crisis,* ed. Keach, Fulton and Gardner, New York: John Wiley & Sons, 1967, p. 400.

Jensen, A., 'The Culturally Disadvantaged: Psychological and Educational Aspects', *Educational Research,* Vol. 10, No. 1 (Nov. 1967), p. 19.

Maclure, J. S., *Educational Documents,* Chapman & Hall, 1965, pp. 18; 21; 45; 103; 154; 175; 206.

Plowden Report, *Children and their Primary Schools,* Report of the Central Advisory Council for Education, (England), H.M.S.O., 1967.

Pringle, Kellmer M., 'Comprehensive Assessment Centres' in *British Hospitals Journal and Social Review,* (15 Nov. 1968).

Rodgers, B., *The Battle Against Poverty,* Vol. II, Routledge & Kegan Paul, 1969, pp. 76–9.

Seebohm Report, *Report of the Committee on Local Authority and Allied Personal Social Services,* H.M.S.O., 1968, para. 186.

*Chapter Two*

Bloom, B. S., *Stability and Change in Human Characteristics,* New York: Wiley & Sons, 1964, p. 89. See also Bloom, Davis and Hess, *Compensatory Education for Cultural Deprivation,* New York: Holt, Rinehart & Winston, 1965, for a summary of research findings on the effect of deprivation generally.

Clegg, A., and Megson, B., *Children in Distress,* Penguin Books, 1969, pp. 50–51; 55; 88–89.

Cloward, R. A., and Ohlin, L. E., *Delinquency and Opportunity,* Routledge & Kegan Paul, 1961, p. 86.

Douglas, J. W. B., *The Home and the School*, Macgibbon & Kee, 1964, p. 38.

Goodacre, E., *Teachers and their Pupils' Home Background*, N.F.E.R., 1968, p. 19.

Marburger, C., 'Considerations for Educational Planning', in *Combating Social Problems*, ed. Gold and Scarpitti, New York: Holt, Rinehart and Winston, 1967, p. 77.

Moss, P., *Welfare Rights Project '68*, Merseyside Child Poverty Action Group, 1969, p. 27; obtainable from: 37 Heathfield Road, Liverpool, L15 9 EU.

Plowden Report, *Children and their Primary Schools*, Report of the Central Advisory Council for Education (England), H.M.S.O., 1967, paras. 134; 98; 95–96; 132.

*Preston Family Welfare Survey*, 1965, pp. 43–44; obtainable from the Town Clerk, Preston County Borough.

Pringle, Kellmer M., Butler, N. R., and Davie R., *11,000 Seven Year Olds*, Longmans Green, 1966, pp. 153–4.

Schools Council, Working Paper 27, *Cross'd with adversity*, Evans Methuen Educational, 1970, pp. 25; 44.

Thouless, R. H., *Map of Educational Research*, N.F.E.R., 1969, pp. 305; 304.

Young, M., *Innovation and Research in Education*, Routledge & Kegan Paul, 1965, p. 86.

*Chapter Three*

Clegg, A., and Megson, B., *Children in Distress*, Penguin Books, 1969, p. 176.

Department of Health and Social Security, *National Health Service, The Future Structure of the Health Service*, H.M.S.O., 1970, pp. 10; 11.

Plowden Report, *Children and their Primary Schools*, Report of the Central Advisory Council for Education (England), H.M.S.O., 1967, para. 229.

Report of the Chief Medical Officer, Department of Education and Science, *The Health of the School Child, 1964 and 1966*, H.M.S.O., 1966, p. 7.

Report of the Chief Medical Officer, Department of Education and Science, *The Health of the School Child, 1966–68*, H.M.S.O., 1969, pp. 1; 84.

Summerfield Report, *Psychologists in Education Services*, H.M.S.O., 1968, paras. 5.19–5.21; 6.41.

Taylor, G., and Saunders, J. B., *The New Law of Education*, Butterworth, 1965, p. 143.

Underwood Report, *Report of the Committee on Maladjusted Children*, H.M.S.O., 1955, pp. 144–5; para. 168.

*Chapter Four*

Albemarle Report, *The Youth Service in England and Wales*, H.M.S.O., 1958.

Department of Health and Social Security, *National Health Service, The Future Structure of the Health Service*, H.M.S.O., 1970, pp. 10; 13.

Fairbairn and Milson Report, *Youth and Community Work in the 70s*, Proposals by the Youth Service Development Council, H.M.S.O., 1969, paras. 357–358; 1–2.

Home Office, *The Probation Service in England and Wales*, H.M.S.O., 1964, pp. 4; 10.

Ingleby Report, *Report of the Committee on Children and Young Persons*, H.M.S.O., 1960.

Jameson Report, *An Enquiry into Health Visiting*, H.M.S.O., 1956.

Jeffreys, M., *An Anatomy of the Social Welfare Services*, Michael Joseph, 1965.

Parsloe, P., *The work of the Probation and After-Care Officer*, Routledge & Kegan Paul, 1967, p. 23.

*The Police and Children*, printed at the office of the Chief Constable, Liverpool, 1964, pp. 6–7.

*Chapter Five*

Bereiter, C., and Engelmann, S., *Teaching Disadvantaged Children in the Preschool*, New Jersey: Prentice Hall, 1966, p. 42.

Burgin, T., and Edson, P., *Spring Grove*, Oxford University Press, 1967. See also, The Report of the Chief Medical Officer of the Department of Education and Science, *The Health of the School Child, 1966–68*, H.M.S.O., 1969, pp. 19–20, 33–4.

Daws, P., 'Counselling' in *Educational Research*, Vol. 9, No. 2 (February 1967), p. 84.

Douglas, J. W. B., and Ross, J. M., 'Subsequent Progress of Nursery School Children', in *Educational Research*, Vol. VII (1964), pp. 83–94.

Pringle, Kellmer M., 'Co-operation in Family and Child Care' in *Proceedings of Twentieth Annual Conference of Association of Children's Officers*, 17–19 September 1969, p. 57.

Schools Council, *Counselling in Schools,* Working Paper No. 15, H.M.S.O., 1967, pp. 64–65.

Ulibarri, H., 'Teacher Awareness in Sociocultural Differences in Multicultural Classrooms', in *Education and Social Crisis,* New York: John Wiley, 1967, pp. 142–143.

*Chapter Six*

Craft, M., Raynor, J., and Cohen, L., *Linking Home and School,* Longmans Green, 1967, pp. 157; 168.

Luckhurst, C., 'Experiments in Welfare', in *Trends in Education,* H.M.S.O., January 1969, p. 11.

Parfit, J., 'C.C.C.' in *Concern,* No. 1, National Bureau for Co-operation in Child Care, 1969, p. 20.

*Chapter Seven*

Fairbairn and Milsom Report, *Youth and Community Work in the 70's,* Proposals by the Youth Service Development Council, H.M.S.O., 1969, para. 365.

Plowden B., 'Schools and the Social Service Department', in *Social Work,* vol. 25, No. 4, (October 1968), pp. 33–34; 34; 35.

Plowden Report, *Children and their Primary Schools,* Report of the Central Advisory Council for Education (England), H.M.S.O., 1967, paras. 239–240.

*Chapter Nine*

Bourne, R., *The Guardian,* 5 August, 1969.

Young, M., *Innovation and Research in Education,* Routledge & Kegan Paul, 1965, p. 8.

*Chapter Ten*

Eyden, J., *Social Policy in Action,* Routledge & Kegan Paul, 1969, p. 32.

Harbert, W.B., 'The Role of Voluntary Social Welfare Services', in *Challenge, A Forum on Learning and Living* published by Liverpool Education Committee, January 1970, p. 3.

# Further reading

The following list of books and articles, divided according to subject, may be useful as a guide to further reading.

## Community studies

We have emphasized throughout this book the crucial importance of community attitudes as an influence on children's behaviour and opportunities. This list includes accounts of some of the most important influences on particular groups of children. As far as possible we have listed sociological studies, though personal accounts can also be useful.

BELL, C., *Middle Class Families*, Routledge & Kegan Paul, 1968. Analyses the effects of social and geographical mobility on the structure and function of the extended family and on patterns of social relationships in the neighbourhood.

DESAI, R., *Indian Immigrants in Britain*, Oxford University Press, 1963. Written by an anthropologist, this is a very thorough investigation of a minority group.

FITZHERBERT, K., *West Indian Children in London*, Bell, 1967, Occasional Papers in Social Administration No. 19. A useful introduction to the culture of West Indian groups and the particular needs of their children in this country.

HOOPER, R. (ed.) *Colour in Britain*, B.B.C. Publications, 1965. Though some of the statistics are now out of date, this book, based on a radio series, is still one of the most useful introductory texts on the cultural background of immigrant groups and the implications of the new wave of immigration for the host community.

JACKSON, B., *Working Class Community*, Routledge & Kegan Paul, 1968. Scenes from working class life in Northern England, including leisure and work of young and old. These portraits are used as a basis for analysis of what is known as the working class community.

JACKSON, B., and MARSDEN, D., *Education and the Working Class*, Routledge & Kegan Paul, 1962. An enquiry undertaken in a northern town, which presents a vivid picture of the working class pupil and the way in which the system tended to discriminate against him.

LONDON COUNCIL OF SOCIAL SERVICE, *The Commonwealth Child in Britain*, National Council of Social Service, 1967. A useful and concise introduction to the cultural background of Indian, Pakistani, Cypriot and Jamaican children.

MAYS, J. B., *On the Threshold of Delinquency*, Liverpool University Press, 1959. Relates delinquency in certain neighbourhoods to the total pattern of life in that area and the social tradition which prevails. In a series of pen portraits, describes work in a boys' club in such an area using group work techniques with young delinquents.

NATIONAL COUNCIL FOR SOCIAL SERVICE, *Community Organization, An Introduction*, N.C.S.S., 1962. Describes some community projects as well as outlining the meaning of community organization.

NEWSOM, J. and E., *Infant Care in an Urban Community*, Allen & Unwin, 1963. Analysis of interviews of over 700 mothers of one-year old children. Refers particularly to the difference between socio-economic groups.

ORLANS, H., *Stevenage: A Sociological Study of a New Town*, Routledge and Kegan Paul, 1952. A particularly interesting account in that it shows the communication lines (and gaps) between central government departments and the new local authority.

ROSE, A.M., and C.B., (ed.), *Minority Problems*, New York: Harper Row, 1965. An American book which undertakes a comparative review of types of discrimination and conflict and the position of minority groups. See particularly the section on prejudice.

WILLMOTT, P., *Adolescent Boys of East London*, Routledge & Kegan Paul, 1966. An Institute of Community Studies publication which examines the extent of help given by the education service to young boys in the East End of London.

WILLMOTT, P., *The Evolution of a Community*, Routledge & Kegan Paul, 1963. Examines the transition of communities from old-established districts to new housing estates with particular reference to Dagenham

YOUNG, M., and WILLMOTT, P., *Family and Kinship in East London*. Routledge & Kegan Paul, 1957. An examination of a traditional working class neighbourhood in the East End of London. Though recently criticized as being rather romantic in its approach this is still worthwhile reading as it describes what may be a rapidly disappearing kind of community in the process of current social change.

## The social services

There are very many texts both on the social services as a whole and upon specialized aspects, such as health and child care. In this section we have therefore tried to select up-to-date publications and books which provide interesting comment on those services which have particular relevance to the theme of our book.

BARON G., and TAYLOR, W., *Educational Administration and the Social Sciences*, Athlone Press, 1969. A collection of essays on the application of social science principles to administration in education.

BIRLEY, D. S., *The Education Officer and his World*, Routledge & Kegan Paul, 1970. Analysis of principles and practice in educational administration.

BOSS, P., *Social Policy and the Young Offender*, Routledge & Kegan Paul, 1967. In the 'Library of Social Policy and Administration', a concise and easily read introduction to the treatment of the child offender, giving a historical survey and discussion of the development of current policy.

BRILL, K., *Children Not Cases*, National Children's Home, 1962. This book (which makes a contribution even by its title) considers the principles which should guide the professional social worker in dealing with children, parents and colleagues.

D.E.S., *The Health of the School Child*. A periodical account of the work of the school health services.

FAMILY WELFARE ASSOCIATION, *Guide to the Social Services*, published annually. A most useful reference book to the various social service agencies. It is important of course to consult the current edition.

FORDER, A., (ed.), *Penelope Hall's Social Services of England and Wales*, Routledge & Kegan Paul, 1969. A completely revised edition of a standard work which is still one of the most comprehensive accounts of the social services.

HALE, R., LOVELAND, M. K., and OWEN, G. M., *The Principles and Practice of Health Visiting*, Pergamon Press, 1968. Volume 8 in the 'Westminster Series'. A clear and concise account.

HANCOCK, A., and WILLMOTT, P., *The Social Workers*, British Broadcasting Corporation, 1965. A series of essays arising from a television programme, this is one of the most useful introductory texts on the role of different kinds of social workers.

HOME OFFICE, *The Probation Service in England and Wales*, H.M.S.O., 1964. A brief account of the probation method for the general reader and for potential probation officers.

JEFFREYS, M., *An Anatomy of Social Welfare Services*, Michael Joseph, 1965. A survey of social welfare staff and their clients in Buckinghamshire, which makes interesting comments on the failures in communication and co-operation.

KAHN, J. H., and NURSTEN, J. P., *Unwillingly to School*, Pergamon Press, 1964. A survey of the work of the child guidance team in relation to the problem of truancy and more specifically of school phobia.

LAWSON, J., *Children in Jeopardy*, Education Explorers, 1965. In the series, 'My Life and my Work' this is written by a senior Child Care Officer and presents, in a thoughtful and sometimes humorous way, the day-to-day work of the child care officer.

MACLEAN, I., *Child Guidance and the School*, Methuen, 1966. Designed for students, a clear account of the work of the child guidance clinic with the normal and abnormal child.

MATTHEWS, J. E., *Working with Youth Groups*, University of London Press, 1966. Examines the application of social group work practice to youth work.

NATIONAL COMMITTEE FOR COMMONWEALTH IMMIGRANTS (Now the Community Relations Commission): A series of useful introductory booklets including,
*The Health and Welfare of the School Child*
*The Housing of Commonwealth Immigrants*
*Areas of Special Housing Need.*

NATIONAL COUNCIL OF SOCIAL SERVICES, *Council of Social Service*, N.C.S.S., 1963. Outlines the historical development and organization of the councils.

NATIONAL SOCIETY FOR MENTALLY HANDICAPPED CHILDREN, *Stress in Families with a Mentally Handicapped Child*, 1967. A report of the National Society for Mentally Handicapped Children by a committee set up to examine types of stress, ways in which it might be relieved and facilities available. See particularly part three on integrating services for the mentally sub-normal.

PARFIT, J., (ed.), *The Community's Children*, Longmans Green, 1967. In the 'Studies in Child Development' series, this is a collection of essays on the needs of children who have to be placed in care.

PARSLOE, P., *The Work of the Probation and After-Care Officer*, Routledge & Kegan Paul, 1967. In the series 'Library of Social Work', this is an account of the development of the service, with an analysis of the probation officer's role and some of its conflicts.

PRESTON COUNTY BOROUGH, *Preston Family Welfare Survey*, 1965. A survey directed from the Department of Social Administration, Manchester University; it examines the many inter-related factors which characterize a group of families known to social workers, and the pattern of care provided by the major social services of the Local Authority. (Obtainable from the Town Clerk.)

PRINGLE, KELLMER M., *Caring for Children*, Longmans Green, 1969. Takes as its major theme co-operation both within and between the different services caring for children.

PRINGLE, KELLMER M., BUTLER, N. R. and DAVIE, R., *11,000 Seven-Year-Olds*, Longmans Green, 1966. The first report of the National Child Development Study, a longitudinal study covering the children's abilities, progress, behaviour and adjustment.

RICHMOND, W. K., *Educational Planning; Old and New Perspectives*, Michael Joseph, 1966. A comparative approach which outlines the course of English education since Hadow and describes recent developments in central Europe.

RODGERS, B., *The Battle Against Poverty*, (two volumes), Routledge & Kegan Paul, 1969. Traces the development of social policy from Tudor times to the present day, and critically analyses some current philosophies.

SEEBOHM REPORT, *Local Authority and Allied Personal Social Services,* H.M.S.O., 1968. A review of certain existing services and recommendations for re-organization.

SLACK, K. M., *Social Administration and the Citizen,* Michael Joseph, 1966. Although written for students of social administration, this is a useful guide for laymen. See particularly chapter 11.

SUMMERFIELD REPORT, *Psychologists in Education Services,* H.M.S.O., 1968. A straightforward, well-documented report on the employment and training of psychologists in education with recommendations for their future organization.

TAYLOR, G., and SAUNDER, J. B., *The New Law of Education,* (6th edition with 1969 supplement.), Butterworth, 1969. An invaluable source book on the intricacies of the Education and other relevant Acts.

THORNLEY, J., *Some Voluntary Work in the North West,* 1965. Although confined to S.E. Lancashire and Cheshire, this directory will give the reader a clear idea of the range of voluntary work.

TIMMS, N., *Casework in the Child Care Service,* Butterworth, 1962. Typical case histories are presented together with the 'solutions'. Though intended for child care workers this book will give the general reader a useful insight into the meaning of casework.

WISEMAN, D., *The Welfare of the School Child,* 1969. A pamphlet published by the University of Exeter Institute of Education in the series 'Themes in Education', which gives an account of existing and developing practices concerned with the welfare of children in local authorities and schools.

YOUNGHUSBAND, E., *Social Work and Social Change,* Allen & Unwin, 1964. Examines the evolving role of social work in the social services. Particular attention is paid to the training of caseworkers and the philosophy underlying the casework approach.

YOUNGHUSBAND, E., *Social Work and Social Values,* Allen & Unwin, 1967. Volume III in the series, 'Readings in Social Work'. A collection of essays on topics currently of much concern to social workers. See particularly the chapters on ethics, casework and co-ordination.

## The role of the teacher and the role of the school

As more psychology and sociology are introduced into initial training of teachers, efforts are increasingly made to help teachers to see themselves as parts of a social system within the school and to see the school in relation to the community. Several new basic series designed for use by students in training provide good introductory texts. We have marked them with an asterisk. More advanced reading is also included in this section.

BLYTH, W. A. L., *English Primary Education,* Vol. 1, Routledge & Kegan Paul, 1965. A scholarly work, the first volume of which considers primary schools as social institutions, and relationships among the staff and between staff and pupils.

*EGGLESTON, J. S., The Social Context of the School, Routledge & Kegan Paul, 1967. A good introduction to the role of the school and the teacher, specifically intended for teachers in training.

FORD, J., Social Class and the Comprehensive School, Routledge & Kegan Paul, 1969. Argues that the abolition of the 11+ does not resolve the problems inherent in early selection, and that schools will continue to uphold selection on class lines.

GOODACRE, E. J., Teachers' Attitudes to Pupils' Home Background, Report No. 2, National Foundation for Educational Research, 1968. A valuable enquiry into the basis of teachers' attitudes to pupils and their homes.

HARGREAVES, D. H., Social Relations in the Secondary School, Routledge & Kegan Paul, 1967. This study of fourth-year pupils in a secondary school for boys examines relationships between pupils and teachers and among the pupils themselves. Intensely readable, it emphasizes the importance of peer group in the school setting.

*HOYLE, E., The Role of the Teacher, Routledge & Kegan Paul, 1969. Published in the series the 'Students Library of Education', this book is intended as a text for teachers in training. It contains a particularly good section on teacher-role which can be easily understood by the non-sociologist, whilst at the same time including an account of recent sociological analysis.

KELSALL, R. K. and H. M., The School Teacher in England and the United States, Pergamon Press, 1969. An interesting comparison of the findings of empirical research into teacher role in the United States and England.

KING, R., Values and Involvement in a Grammar School, Routledge & Kegan Paul, 1969. A case study of a boys' grammar school which suggests that the pupil's experience of school is related to his home background, his stream and his age, and that the influence of the school is variable.

MAYS, J. B., Education and the Urban Child, Liverpool University Press, 1962. Discusses the role of the school as initiator of change in a disadvantaged area.

*MORRISON, A., and MCINTYRE, D., Teachers and Teaching, Penguin Books, 1969. Published in the 'Penguin Science of Behaviour' series, this is a most useful examination of current studies of the role of the teacher and the role of the school.

*MUSGRAVE, P., The School as an Organisation, Macmillan, 1969. In the series, 'Basic Books in Education', this text is an easily read introduction to a comparative analysis of the English and Scottish school systems. It includes an examination of the role of the class teacher, that of the headteacher, and of the school as a whole.

*MUSGROVE, F., The Family, Education and Society, Routledge & Kegan Paul, 1966. Examines the twin pressures of home and school on success and achievement, suggesting that these produce the 'joyless personality'.

MUSGROVE, F., and TAYLOR, P. H., Society and the Teacher's Role, Routledge & Kegan Paul, 1969. This book describes research conducted by the authors into teachers' and parents' and pupils' perception of the teacher's role. Some interesting misconceptions are revealed.

\*OESER, O. A., *Teacher, Pupil and Task: Elements of Social Psychology Applied to Education,* Tavistock Publications, 1955. Although an earlier study than many others in this section, this is still an essential piece of reading for anyone with an interest in the practical application of psychology to the classroom situation.

\*SHIPMAN, M. D., *Sociology of the School,* Longmans, 1968. Written by a sociologist with experience of teaching in schools and training teachers, this book is a very clear and practical introduction to the school as a social organization.

TAYLOR, W., (ed.), *Towards a Policy for the Education of Teachers,* Colston Papers No. 20, Butterworth, 1969. This book arises from a symposium held in Bristol in April 1968. The main papers and extracts from discussions are included. Objectives in teacher education are considered together with an examination of the role of the teacher in contemporary society.

WEBB, J., 'The Sociology of the School', *British Journal of Sociology,* 8, iii (1962), pp. 264–272. Considers the difficulties which face teachers in down-town schools where discipline is a problem, and discusses the ensuing pressures on a teacher to conform to certain types of role.

WESTWOOD, L. J., 'The Role of the Teacher', *Educational Research,* vol. 9, ii (1967), pp. 122–134, and Vol. 10, i (1967), pp. 21–38. These two articles examine some of the social and cultural forces external to the school which may influence conceptions of the teacher role. The second article includes a useful review of relevant research.

## Guidance and counselling in schools

The idea of specialist social workers or counsellors in schools is not new, but its development in this country has been slow. There are many American publications on the role of the counsellor in the school, but as these are not directly relevant to our own system, we have tried to indicate mainly British texts.

CRAFT, M., RAYNOR, J., and COHEN, L., (ed.), *Linking Home and School,* Longmans Green, 1967. See particularly chapters 8, 14 and 15.

DAWS, P., *A Good Start in Life,* The Careers Research and Advisory Centre, 1968. A concise appraisal of guidance and counselling in career choice.

GIBSON, A., and DAVIES, B., *The Social Education of the Adolescent,* University of London Press, 1967. Concerns particularly the Youth Service, but reference is also made to the school and the role of the teacher. The general thesis about 'casework approach' is relevant.

MILSOM and FAIRBAIRN REPORT, *Youth and Community Work in the 70s,* H.M.S.O., 1969. See particularly paragraphs 237-286.

ROGERS, C., *Client-Centred Therapy,* Boston: Houghton Mifflin, 1951. A useful guide to counselling techniques.

ROWE, A., 'The Home and the School', *Where*, No. 34 (1967), pp. 16–27. An account by the headteacher of a large northern comprehensive school of the way in which counselling works in his own school.

SCHOOLS COUNCIL, WORKING PAPER NO. 15, *Counselling in Schools,* H.M.S.O., 1962. A record of current developments in counselling in today's schools with a useful section on relevant training courses currently provided in Great Britain.

TYLER, L., *The Work of the Counsellor*, New York: Appleton Century Crofts, 1953. A comprehensive and easily read text which covers the groundwork of counselling in the U.S.A. and suggests some general rules applicable in all situations.

VARIOUS, 'Counselling', *Educational Research*, vol. 9, 2 (1967). A special edition devoted to looking at counselling in schools and including papers by; Daws, P., 'What will the School Counsellor Do?', Raynor, J. M., and Atcherley, R. A., 'Counselling in Schools—Some Considerations', Fuller, J. A., and Juniper, D. F., 'Guidance and Counselling in School Social Work'.

VENESS, T., *School Leavers*, Methuen, 1962. Concerns the aspirations and expectations of school leavers based on an enquiry carried out in a number of English schools.

WRENN, G., *The Counsellor in a Changing World*, Washington: American Personnel and Guidance Association, 1962. A scholarly review of the current trends in counselling.

## Home-school relationships

An increasing number of books and articles on this subject are now appearing, though many of them tend to support much closer co-operation between schools and parents without penetrating too deeply into the implications.

COWEN, N., 'The Place of the Parent', *Trends in Education*, iii (1966) pp. 21–8. A survey of the relationship between parents and teachers over half a century.

CRAFT, M., RAYNOR, J., and COHEN, L., (ed)., *Linking Home and School*, Longmans Green, 1967. A collection of papers presented at a conference on 'Linking Home and School' held at Edge Hill College of Education in 1965, together with contributions from other specialists in this field.

DAVIE, R., 'Local Authority Services for Children', *Concern*, No. 3 (1969). A paper presented at the Annual Conference of the National Bureau for Co-operation in Child Care in November 1969, in which attention is drawn to the need for schools to do more to contact reluctant parents.

D.E.S., Reports on Education, no. 41, *Teachers and Parents*, H.M.S.O., 1967. Suggestions about how informal relationships can be established between schools and parents, and accounts of established practices in different kinds of primary schools including a special school.

GOODACRE, E., (ed.), *Home and School Relationships,* published and obtainable from the Home and School Council, 1968. A useful list of references, with notes; intended for parents, teachers and teachers in training.

GREEN, L., *Parents and Teachers; Partners or Rivals,* Allen & Unwin, 1968. Some useful practical suggestions from the head of a primary school.

PLOWDEN REPORT, *Children and Their Primary Schools,* (Vols. I and II), H.M.S.O., 1967. Chapters 3, 4 and 19 are particularly relevant. Volume II contains invaluable reports of research conducted on behalf of the Plowden committee and some useful tables of statistics.

POLITICAL AND ECONOMIC PLANNING UNIT, *Parents' Views on Education,* 1961. One aspect of a survey carried out by the P.E.P. to ascertain parents' views on the social services. Evidence of social class differences in desire for more information from schools about children's education.

SCHOOLS COUNCIL, Working Paper 27, *Cross'd with adversity,* Evans, Methuen, 1970. Concerned with disadvantaged children at the secondary school stage: chapter VII is on 'Home and School'.

SHARROCK, A., 'Relations Between, Home and School', *Educational Research,* 10, N.F.E.R., (June 1968). pp. 185–196. A review of the research undertaken into home-school relationships pointing out some of the gaps in the information available.

STERN, H. H., *Parent Education, An International Survey,* University of Hull and Unesco Institute of Education, Hamburg, 1960. A comparative review showing insufficiently sound relationships between teachers and parents in a number of countries. Points to the poor relationships arising from a lack of understanding on both sides.

YOUNG, M., 'How can Parent and Teacher Work Together?', *New Society,* 24 Sept. 1964.

YOUNG, M., and MCGEENEY, P., *Learning Begins at Home,* Routledge & Kegan Paul, 1968. Describes an experiment conducted on behalf of the Plowden Committee, which involved parents in the work of the school.

The following three books allow comparison between British and American traditions.

BAILARD, V., and STRANG, R., *Parent-Teacher Conferences,* New York: McGraw-Hill, 1964.

HYMES, J. L. JNR., *Effective Home-School Relationships,* Englewood Cliffs, N.J., 1953.

LANGDON, G., and STOUT, I. W., *Teacher-Parent Interviews,* Prentice-Hall, Englewood Cliffs, N.J., 1954.

## School curriculum

In this section we include a number of recent publications which suggest that a radical re-thinking of curriculum is necessary for work, not only with underprivileged children, but for all children. The major publications in this field are from the Schools Council and local development groups. For reports from these groups, the reader may have to make direct application.

BEREITER, C., and ENGELMANN, S., *Teaching Disadvantaged Children In the Preschool*, New Jersey: Prentice-Hall, 1966. The first section of this compelling and readable book considers the relationship between cultural and language deprivation. The second section considers different kinds of school programmes that can be developed to provide compensatory education to very young children.

BIRLEY, D. S., 'It's Later Than You Think', *Education*, 14 July 1967. Argues the need for early preparation for raising the school-leaving age.

BURGIN, T., and EDSON, P., *Spring Grove*, Published for the Institute of Race Relations by Oxford University Press, 1967. A personal account by the Headteacher and one of his colleagues of a school with over 50% immigrant pupils. Of particular interest to teachers meeting this situation for the first time.

DERRICK, J., *Teaching English to Immigrants*, Longmans Green, 1966. The director of the Schools Council Project has written a concise and useful book for teachers of Immigrant Children.

EYKEN, VAN DER, N., *The Pre-School Years*, Penguin Books, 1967. An account of the educational processes from 1–5 years. Underlines the need for adequate pre-school experience to combat deprivation.

NEWSOM REPORT, *Half Our Future*, H.M.S.O., 1963. An examination of traditional secondary curriculum and school organization in relation to the non-academic child.

SCHOOLS COUNCIL, *English for the Children of Immigrants*, Working Paper No. 13, H.M.S.O., 1967. The Council is sponsoring a project which involves the testing of materials in selected schools. Some of these materials are now available for general distribution.

## Deprivation and education

This final section contains a number of books which span many or all of the previous sections. The emphasis is upon education of underprivileged children. We have included some American texts where we feel the basic issues are relevant to our own educational system.

BLOOM, B. S., DAVIS, A., and HESS, R., *Compensatory Education for Cultural Deprivation*, New York: Holt, Rinehart and Winston, 1965. An important review of information about cultural deprivation, including an annotated bibliography.

CLEGG, A., and MEGSON, B., *Children in Distress*, Penguin Books, 1968. The concern of the authors for children in need is apparent throughout this book which is a highly personal statement of educational priorities.

DOUGLAS, J. W. B., *The Home and The School*, Macgibbon & Kee, 1964. A study of a large sample of children in England and Wales from birth, through primary schooling up to the results of 11+ selection tests. Of particular interest is the light thrown on the relationship of individual attainment not only to socio-economic factors but also to teacher-attitude and expectation.

EVANS, K. M., *Attitudes and Interests in Education*, Routledge & Kegan Paul, 1965. Describes the development of attitudes and interests in children in relation to home, school and society, and to authority.

FRAZER, E., *Home Environment and the School*, University Press, 1959. An enquiry into the extent to which primary school progress of children is related to home background.

GOLD, H., and SCARPITTI, F. R., (ed.), *Combating Social Problems: Techniques of Intervention*, New York: Holt, Rinehart and Winston, 1967. An American text consisting of a series of readings which cover poverty, education, race relations, urban planning, mental health, crime and juvenile delinquency, addiction and professional problem-solving. Whilst the specific references are American, the underlying principles are universal. See particularly chapters 3 and 11.

KEACH, E. T., FULTON, R., and GARDNER, W. E., *Education and Social Crisis*, New York: John Wiley, 1967. Sub-titled 'Perspective on Teaching Disadvantaged Youth'. This is a series of readings including a particularly good chapter by George Kneller on 'Education and Social Values'. See also chapters 47–49.

LAWTON, D., *Social Class, Language and Education*, Routledge & Kegan Paul, 1968. Relates the comparative failure of working class pupils at school to sub-cultural differences in attitude and response to education. Includes a particularly useful review of research in the relationships of language and socio-economic groupings.

PASSOW, A. H., *Education in Depressed Areas*, New York: Teachers' College Press, Columbia University, 1968. Analyses the influences of environmental factors such as housing and a limited range of experience on the learning processes.

# Index